CRUCIBLE OF THE MILLENNIUM

A New York State Study

CRUCIBLE

OF THE

MILLENNIUM

THE BURNED-OVER DISTRICT OF NEW YORK IN THE 1840s

BY MICHAEL BARKUN.

We are living, we are dwelling
In a grand and awful time;
In an age on ages telling,
To be living—is sublime.
Hark! the waking up of nations,
Gog and Magog, to the fray;
Hark, what soundeth, is creation's
Groaning for its latter day.

—Oneida Community hymn—

SYRACUSE UNIVERSITY PRESS

Photographs appearing on pages 74, 76, and 78 are from the Oneida
Community Historical Committee, those on pages 6 and 7 are from
the George Arents Research Library, and those on pages 4, 5, 34, 38,
and 48 are from the Loma Linda University Heritage Room.

The paper used in this publication meets the minimum requirements
of American National Standard for Information Sciences—Permanence
of Paper for Printed Library Materials, ANSI Z39.48-1984. ∞™

Library of Congress Cataloging-in-Publication Data

Barkun, Michael.
Crucible of the millennium.

(A New York State study)
Bibliography: p.
Includes index.
1. Millennialism—New York (State)—History—19th
century. 2. Utopias—History—19th century.
3. Christian communities—New York (State)—History—
19th century. 4. New York (State)—Church history.
I. Title. II. Title: Burned-over district. III. Series.
BR555.N7B37 1986   277.47′081   86-5777
ISBN 0-8156-2371-2
ISBN 0-8156-2378-X (pbk.)

For
DEBBI and MIRIAM

MICHAEL BARKUN is Professor of Political Science at Syracuse University. He is the author of *Disaster and the Millennium* and *Law without Sanctions: Order in Primitive Societies and the World Community,* as well as numerous articles on millenarianism and on international law. He has held fellowships from the National Endowment for the Humanities and from the Ford Foundation. His Ph.D. in Political Science is from Northwestern University.

CONTENTS

ILLUSTRATIONS

ACKNOWLEDGMENTS

I N AN EARLIER WORK, *Disaster and the Millennium*, I attempted to provide some answers to the question of millenarian origins: why do individuals expect this imperfect world suddenly to be transformed into one without pain, suffering, or injustice? I proposed that catastrophic stress played a pivotal role in inducing people to abandon old loyalties in favor of an imminent millennium. I also suggested that disasters were as much a matter of human perception as of measurable damage and, hence, interacted in complex ways with the mental categories a culture provides.

A subsequent Fellowship from the National Endowment for the Humanities permitted me to reflect further on the nature of these complexities. Of all the distinctions that might be made among calamities, one of the most significant appeared to be that between natural disasters and those caused by human actions. The mixed blessings of modernity imply the gradual replacement of the former by the latter. At this early stage of the inquiry, as I sought to understand the nature of these two types of disaster, the comments of a number of people helped me refine the problem; those of J. David Greenstone, Adda B. Bozeman, and Arthur N. Gilbert were particularly useful.

It became evident that the emergence of artificial disasters could not be fully explained or analyzed in the abstract, especially inasmuch as my interest remained the link between collective stress and millenarian movements. With the aim of identifying a historical situation which displayed the concrete details of the process, I examined and discarded a number of possibilities before my attention fell upon the United States in the 1840s—

more specifically the region in which I live, the so-called Burned-over District of upper New York State, for I realized that the very ground on which I stood had been the center of American millennialism, flourishing precisely during the nineteenth-century transition between natural and artificial disasters.

In tracking the millennialism of the 1840s, the rich collection of Burned-over District materials at Syracuse University has been of particular value. The staff of the George Arents Research Library, and especially its Rare Book Curator, Mark Weimer, have been patient and helpful guides to the Oneida Community and Millerite holdings. I am also grateful to Imogen Noyes Stone for granting me permission to work with the Oneida manuscripts collected by her father, George Wallingford Noyes.

For assistance in securing illustrations, I am grateful to Mark Weimer at Syracuse, and to James R. Nix, chairman of the Department of Archives and Special Collections at the Library of Loma Linda University.

A number of individuals generously shared unpublished or prepublication materials with me: Ronald Abler, the late Catherine Covert, Lawrence Foster, Otohiko Okugawa, David Rowe, and the late Ernest Sandeen. I drew particular stimulation from conversations with Robert Fogarty, Lawrence Foster, David Rapoport, and David Rowe.

If there is an "invisible college" of those who study American millennialism, then surely it convened in the Spring of 1984, when Ronald Numbers and Wayne Judd organized a conference in Killington, Vermont, on "Millerism and the Millenarian Mind in 19th-century America." I profited greatly from the intellectual community they fostered. Subsequently, much of the material presented at Killington was included in a volume edited by Ronald Numbers and Jonathan Butler, *The Disappointed,* and I have made use of it in the chapters that follow.

The model with which I conclude was given an informal airing at the 1981 Annual Meeting of the International Society for the Comparative Study of Civilizations in Bloomington, Indiana. The occasion for a systematic reworking of these ideas was presented when Edward Wynne invited me to contribute an essay to his journal, *Character.* In its pages, Robert Fogarty offered an incisive and useful critique of the model, and the incarnation which appears here benefitted a good deal from his comments. The discussion of contemporary fundamentalism and apocalypticism in the final chapter grew out of an article in the Fall 1983 issue of *Soundings,* "Divided Apocalypse: Thinking About the End in Contemporary America," and a paper presented at the 1985 Annual Meeting of the Society for the Scientific Study of Religion, in Savannah, Georgia, "Nuclear War and Millenarian Symbols: Premillennialists Confront the Bomb."

Completion of the manuscript was made possible by release from normal teaching obligations, for which I am grateful to Syracuse University; to its former Vice Chancellor for Academic Affairs, John J. Prucha; and to the Department of Political Science and its former Chairperson, Thomas Patterson. June Dumas and Judy Jablonski typed more versions of the manuscript than I am sure they care to remember, but did so with unfailing good humor. My wife Janet offered the encouragement and support that made the book possible, and our daughters, Debbi and Miriam, can now finally see "Dad's book," about which they have been unceasingly curious. This book is for them.

Syracuse, New York   MB
Spring 1986

CRUCIBLE OF THE MILLENNIUM

INTRODUCTION

I N 1843, the following letter appeared on the front page of the March
15 issue of the *New York Daily Tribune*:

> The millennium of the sacred writers and the golden age of the poets
> have buoyed up the drooping heart in every age and every condition of
> life. The harmony of the material world, its ability to supply our wants,
> and the constant swelling up of the Soul for a purer and better state,
> convince every reflecting mind that a benevolent Creator designed Man
> for Happiness in the present state of existence, in spite of all the teach-
> ings of the Church.
>
> That the Paradise of Eden is to be regained at some period or other,
> there are but few who doubt. By what peculiar means this Heavenly
> boon is to be secured is yet altogether problematical.

The letter was written by John Collins, a Boston abolitionist associated with William Lloyd Garrison. Later that year he left Boston to establish
the Skaneateles Community in central New York, a utopian experiment
based on the teachings of Robert Owen. His letter was not sent to the
Tribune's publisher, Horace Greeley, but rather to a *Tribune* columnist, Albert Brisbane, who had established himself as the principal American ex-
ponent of the French utopian philosopher, Charles Fourier.

The occasion for the letter's publication in Brisbane's column was the
rise of the religious movement known as Millerism. Led by a largely self-

taught Baptist preacher, William Miller, it swept the northeastern United States—and most especially upstate New York—between 1840 and 1844 with predictions of the imminent Second Coming of Christ. Miller at first predicted that the Second Advent would take place some time between March 21, 1843, and March 21, 1844. When that year passed uneventfully, he gave his approval to a revised deadline of October 22, 1844. Collins' letter, dated "Boston, February 20, 1843," was written as millennial expectations neared their peak. Given the state of intercity mail at the time,[1] the letter probably arrived in the first days of March, about the time the *Tribune* on March 2 devoted an entire issue to a furious attack on the Millerite movement. Brisbane included the letter in his March 15 column, with the end of the world less than a week away.

This conjunction of a millenarian preacher, an Owenite utopian, and a Fourierist publicist suggests the richly textured fabric of American religious and social experimentation in the 1840s. Like "The Movement" of the 1960s, which loosely linked civil rights, antiwar activity, and the counterculture, a pre-Civil War network drew together those committed to the perfection of the world. The intricate linkages among social reformers, community builders, and revivalists—roles sometimes combined in the same individual—suggests how difficult and ultimately misleading it may be to categorize the ventures of the 1840s as either religious or secular, for the protagonists do not fall neatly into mutually exclusive compartments.

In retrospect the slow nineteenth-century separation of a secular from a religious vision of the perfect society depended upon the presence of transitional figures, neither fully secular nor conventionally religious. While some like Miller continued traditions of scriptural interpretation little changed since the Middle Ages, others—such as Collins, Brisbane, and John Humphrey Noyes, founder of the Oneida Community—constructed millennia-in-miniature. Their utopian communities grappled with earthly issues of property distribution, sex roles, and work relationships, seeking to wrest from the earth a perfection Miller insisted must be thrust down from heaven.

THE BURNED-OVER DISTRICT

Millenarian and utopian fires burned across much of the northeastern United States, from New England to the Western Reserve of Ohio, but nowhere with greater intensity than in the belt of upper New York State called the Burned-over District. The incendiary metaphor evoked the emotional conflagrations of religious excitement that later led the greatest nineteenth-century revivalist, Charles Grandison Finney, to observe, "I found that region of the country what, in the western phrase, would be called, 'a burnt district.' " Defined by the route of the Erie Canal, the Burned-over District extended from just east of Utica to just west of Buffalo, north to the foothills of the Adirondacks and the shore of Lake Ontario, and south to the tip of the Finger Lakes.[2] But the fires of the District burned with uneven brightness as movements rose and declined, so by the end of the decade of the 1840s Millerism, which had once swept the region, was discredited, while John Humphrey Noyes's Perfectionism was just beginning to marshall its energies.

In 1848, William Miller's family, excommunicated from their local Baptist church, built a small, green-trimmed white clapboard chapel on their farm in Low Hampton, New York, at the eastern edge of the Burned-over District. Set on a country road, it was intended for the personal use of the Millers and their friends in the years that followed what became known as the "Great Disappointment," the failure of the Second Coming of Christ to occur at the time Millerites had predicted. The fields that once surrounded the chapel are now wooded and overgrown, but a path still winds down a hundred feet or so to "Ascension Rock," the smooth stone outcropping on which, tradition has it, the Miller family awaited the Second Coming. In those days, when fields instead of underbrush surrounded the Rock, it commanded a vista across the valley toward the Green Mountains of Vermont. Millerism, whose symbol was once a vast revival tent set up in city after city along the Eastern seaboard, was now reduced to this backcountry redoubt. Virtually the chapel's only ornamentation is the defiant motto painted in an arc across the wall behind the pulpit: "For at the time appointed the End shall be."

In the same year the Miller chapel was built, the members of the Oneida Community began the first Mansion House in the very center of the Burned-over District, on the edge of Oneida Creek. Enlarged in 1849 and 1851, it was dwarfed by a second Mansion House in 1862, which by the final additions of 1877–78 assumed the form of a large quadrangle.[3] The great Victorian edifice, with its 300 rooms and spacious courtyard, its high-ceilinged library and graceful assembly hall, was as powerful a statement of confidence as the Miller chapel was of embattled fortitude.

One can scarcely imagine two more dissimilar structures, yet both represented the same millenarian aspirations and both emerged from similar adversities. Despite their differences, religious millenarianism and utopian experimentation coexisted in space and time, flourishing in the same region at almost the same moment. Each was an unorthodox response to

The Miller family chapel was erected in 1848 adjacent to Miller's home on a country road in upstate New York near the Vermont border. *Courtesy Loma Linda University Heritage Room*

the state of the world, rejecting the imperfections of the status quo in favor of radical transformation. Thus it is tempting to emphasize the similarities and to see them as manifestations of a regional ethos that encouraged radical religious and social experimentation, which contemporaries called "ultraism."[4]

Yet the differences are as striking as the similarities—militancy versus withdrawal, mass movements as against small, insular coteries, the venerable language of religion confronting the embryonic language of secularism. Indeed, the very coexistence of these polarities in the Burned-over District begs the question: If some current of cultural radicalism was indeed running in Upstate New York, why were its forms so strikingly different? Granted a widespread intuition that the world of early nineteenth-century

The interior of the Miller chapel is nearly as austere as the exterior, the
severity broken only by the defiant motto on the wall. The plaque lists
the church's twenty charter members. Miller himself died the year after
the chapel was built. *Courtesy Loma Linda University Heritage Room*

America needed systematic renovation, why were the putative instruments
so extraordinarily diverse, pulling apart both ideologically and organiza-
tionally? Some sought to convert an erring world before it ended, while others tried to create a new world of their own. The religious chiliasts awaited
a millennium-in-macrocosm, while the utopian experimenters tried to construct a millennium-in-microcosm.

These tensions expressed themselves in three problems, connected, respectively, with causation, organizational and intellectual forms, and with
future significance. The causal problems involve questions of common spatial and temporal location, as well as precipitating circumstances. Did chiliasm and utopianism spring from discrete or common causes? If the former,

COMMUNITY-HOUSE AT ONEIDA RESERVE.

This wood cut, made by an Oneida Community member, is probably the earliest existing picture of the Community's building. Seen here from the side, the structure was in fact a combination of three connected buildings. At the right is the four-story first Mansion House, erected in 1848. An L-shaped addition was placed behind (left) in 1849, followed by a long shed in 1851, when the picture was made. Source: *The Circular,* November 30, 1851. *Courtesy George Arents Research Library, Syracuse University*

then their common location in space and time may have been fortuitous. If the latter, then the identification of the causes may have utility far beyond the early nineteenth century. And if there were common causes, what characteristics of Upstate New York turned it, however briefly, into an area in which these factors produced such extraordinary effects? Thus, one important aspect of causation is the potential interaction between demographic characteristics of millenarians and utopians and situational factors in the Burned-over District.

If both Millerism and the utopian communities sprang from common causes, then their radically different forms of organization must be explained. Millenarians and utopians were both transformationalists, committed to the radical restructuring of society. Yet the former moved aggressively to increase the number of believers, while the latter concentrated

Community Buildings, Oneida, N. Y.

By 1862, the Oneida Community had erected the second Mansion House (foreground), and in 1869–70, a large Children's House to the left of the new Mansion House. Part of the original Mansion House appears here at the extreme left; it was torn down shortly after this engraving was made. The building at the rear is the Tontine, built in 1863 to accommodate kitchen, dining room, and workshops. In the late 1870s, a rear wing was built onto the second Mansion House that connected it with the Tontine to form a quadrangle. Source: *Frank Leslie's Illustrated Newspaper,* April 2, 1870. *Courtesy George Arents Research Library, Syracuse University*

upon separation from the world. The former spoke a venerable language of religious argumentation, based upon the exegesis of such Biblical texts as the Book of Revelation. The latter, while often elaborating a theology of their own (as, for example, among the Shakers and at Oneida), paid increasing attention to social and economic issues, and often consciously invoked an early socialist vocabulary. We may expect interaction between beliefs and forms of organization. To what extent, therefore, were the disparate organizational forms simply the social implications of beliefs, millenarian prophecies mandating proselytizing and utopian blueprints requiring withdrawal? Or was the relationship precisely the reverse, in which beliefs bent or were formed to explain and justify social arrangements?

Just as the groups may have formed under common pressures, so their survival as groups may have required the solution of common problems. Advocating the total transformation of society has rarely been a popular position and hence has been difficult to sustain over long periods. Proselytizing and withdrawal are alternative strategies for maintaining commitment to deviant beliefs. Some reinforce group loyalty by converting unbelievers, while others do so by separating from them.

The problems of future significance are just as difficult to resolve, for knowing how things turned out does not imply that the logic of intervening historical development is clear or simple. The millennium which visionaries invoked after the Civil War was increasingly secular rather than religious, preoccupied with bread and butter issues, the redistribution of wealth and redistribution of political power that was assumed to follow wealth. Millenarians drifted into a new world of financial conspiracies and monetary panaceas. Some on the fringes of Populism in the 1890s railed against the "money power," a dark cabal of bankers and manipulators whose alleged designs for domination blocked the way to a perfected America. In the 1930s, Dr. Frances Townsend and his followers claimed that all would be well if only the government would place cash in the hands of elderly Americans, who could then spend the country into prosperity. Utopian colonies after the Civil War attracted decreasing popular attention and numbers of people. Far fewer were founded, and those few passed their brief lives for the most part in rural obscurity. Consequently, the sudden prominence of "communes" in the 1960s and of the "new religious right" in the 1970s and '80s was as dramatic as it was unanticipated.

The chapters that follow consider these problems in the order given: causation, form, and significance. The argument to be presented is that Millerism and the utopian communities arose from common causes. The steadfastly rural character of much of the Burned-over District, together with the New England origins of most of its inhabitants, modified the stresses of the period in ways that produced a special receptivity to millenarian and utopian appeals. The District functioned as a reservoir collecting and discharging individuals in search of beliefs concerning imminent world transformation.

The common origins of millenarian and utopian groups does not, of course, account for their pronounced differences. I shall argue that those dissimilarities resulted from the different strategies used by millenarians and utopians to grapple with a common set of intellectual and organizational tasks, as well as by the differential challenges of urban and rural environments. Both had to explain and make sense out of a troubling and confusing reality, and translate their explanations into social patterns that could command allegiance. For the Millerites that involved pushing out into the world. I shall argue that their decision to seek converts in the cities had at least as much to do with their collapse as did the failure of William Miller's prediction.

The utopian experiments were a way out of the seemingly insurmountable problems posed by trying to organize urban populations. The new utopian communities were means through which millenarian expectations could be expressed and partially satisfied without risking total organizational failure. The utopians' withdrawal was thus the result of a shrewdly intuitive reading of reality, rather than, as has been implied in the innuendos of their detractors, the consequence of moral cowardice or distorted perceptions. The communities functioned as both sanctuaries and laboratories, pushing conceptions of the future into more avowedly secular forms, confronting problems of social and economic change that traditional religious constructs did not address, and preserving nuclei of adherents to fight another day.

Religious chiliasm—the belief in the imminent consummation of human history—developed from the late Middle Ages to the early nineteenth century as a symbolically powerful way of organizing experience. Its special quality lay in its ability to make sense of certain types of troubling events— wars, governmental successions, and natural disasters. Its intellectual failure in the 1840s lay in the fact that these calamities were of declining significance. Rather, Americans were concerned about the transformation of village-oriented, deferential, traditional society in which sentiments of community were taken for granted, to an increasingly city-oriented, competitive, modern society peopled by men-on-the-make. Associated with this broad transformation were more particular dislocations such as the rise of industry in the Northeast, the exhaustion of marginal farmland in New England, the vulnerability of the economy to panic and depression, and the intractable political problem of slavery. To all these, religious millenarianism had little to say, not because its followers failed to perceive the problems or because they failed to feel deeply about them, but rather because the problems did not fit within the literary conventions of traditional millennialism.

Millenarians could not effectively mobilize and maintain commitment outside the rural areas where their initial strength lay. In the cities they were prey to competitive forces, such as the religious denominations that perceived them as rivals and the new mass press that saw their eccentricities as "good copy." Intellectually, Jacksonian and post-Jacksonian economic transformations posed problems to which interpreters of the Book of Revelation had given scant attention. Hence the apprehension of change, the vague feeling of teetering on the edge of calamity, combined with the inability either to do anything about it or even to articulate it very clearly.

Thus the overlap of millenarianism and utopianism in space and time was not coincidental; nor were the two simply slightly different manifestations of the same underlying factors. Both sought to demonstrate that despite stresses and calamities in which the innocent seemed to suffer, the world was still a moral order where the righteous could expect vindication. They also shared a commitment to a reconstructed world free from sin and evil. Millenarianism, much the older tradition, was an ancient way of trying to envision and control the future, for knowledge of God's timetable for the world explained present suffering and promised future salvation. Nonetheless, millenarianism performed its traditional tasks less and less effectively in a world where social and economic dislocations were becoming ever larger and more threatening, and where diverse and worldly urban populations could only with the greatest difficulty be persuaded to put aside their usual ways. The utopians, whose origins were far more recent, displayed greater intellectual flexibility in attempting to understand the new stresses modernity had brought. Abandoning the cities and their organizational problems, the utopians sought a "clean slate," totally new communities in the countryside whose very smallness made every aspect of life controllable.

The millenarians were not totally misguided in seeking the city, for in an urbanizing America fundamental change demanded that city populations be engaged. Yet at the same time utopians shrewdly recognized that the tools to rally such populations effectively were not yet available. Hence the issues connected with the transformation of society were vigorously debated in the 1840s but scarcely settled. It was left to later generations to wrestle anew with the gap between religious and secular visions, and between movements of expansion and withdrawal.

The period under consideration suggests that a cycle of sorts can be traced, from mass religious millenarianism through utopian experimentation to a new mass secular millenarianism in the late nineteenth and twentieth centuries. Another turn of the wheel may now be in progress. The "armed visions" after 1865 burned themselves out in the 1960s, just as religious millenarianism caught terminal fire among the Millerites. The New Left may be considered the Millerism of the twentieth century. The "end of ideology" that Daniel Bell announced in 1963 arrived approximately on schedule and, like its nineteenth-century predecessors, came on an overlapping utopian wave in the form of the countercultural communes. They in their turn have given way to the resurgent fundamentalism of Jerry Falwell, Hal Lindsey, and Pat Robertson.

Finally, some comments are in order about the terminology I employ. Terms commonly used by social scientists, such as "interest group" or "voluntary association" do not lend themselves to groups that believe they possess ultimate truth. In addition, those who have written about such groups have not always agreed on what to call them or about how terms borrowed from theology ought to be applied. J. F. C. Harrison has suggested, for example, that "millenarian" should be used for popular, unlettered religious movements, while "millennialist" should be reserved for more cerebral considerations of the end-time, such as the creation of chronologies to match Biblical prophecies.[5] However useful such a distinction might be in some contexts, it seems out of place here, since the scholarly musings of one generation had a way of emerging in the popular religiosity of another. In any case, the division is not yet supported by the weight of scholarly usage, which has treated the terms synonymously, a practice continued here.

The terminology for utopian experiments has been, if anything, more confusing. In part, the confusion stems from the pejorative connotations of "utopian," with its overtones of impracticality. These negative associations were incurred during the doctrinal wars between Marxian and non-Marxian socialists, in which the former sought, in general successfully, to supplant and stigmatize the latter. Since ideological weapons sit uneasily in scholarly discourse, attempts have been made to find a more neutral term— for example, Arthur Bestor's "communitarian."[6] Unfortunately neither "communitarian," "communal," nor any alternative has come into general academic usage. Since, despite its negative connotations, "utopian" continues to have wide currency, it will be used here, with "communitarian" and "communal" employed as occasional synonyms. "Commune," having come into common usage during the 1960s, will be used in the everyday speech sense of a contemporary group-living experiment. For present purposes, individuals will be considered to participate in a utopian experiment if the following attributes are present: conscious creation of a separate social unit, as evidenced by voluntary measures of withdrawal from the dominant society, and attempts at a relatively high level of group self-sufficiency, combined with a commitment to the realization of some ideal state of social relationships. These criteria may still be met by the many groups whose effective life was very brief but whose desire was for long-term autonomy.

"Utopia" and "millennium" are to one another as microcosm is to macrocosm. What the utopian community hopes to achieve within a small and self-sufficient group, the millenarian movement anticipates on a cosmic scale. In the most general sense, millenarians look to a coming world transformation. Millenarianism is, therefore, the belief that the world is about to experience an overturning, in which all that is imperfect or corrupt will vanish and in its place will stand a new order of things, where human beings will live without sin, evil, or suffering. An achieved millennium is a realized ideal, not on the scale of an insular community that cuts itself off from an imperfect environment, but on a scale so vast that no corner of the world exists any longer in an imperfect form.

Beyond this broad characterization, millenarians have gone their separate ways, arguing about the speed of the transformation, the causes of its occurrence, the fate of those unworthy to enjoy it, and the exact nature of the promised heaven on earth. These competing conceptions of a perfected future have been articulated in the idioms of countless cultures, Western and non-Western; as well as in the voices of differing religious traditions, social philosophies, and political ideologies. Although most of the discussion that follows concerns a few limited manifestations of the impulse to perfection, we shall begin by tracing, however sketchily, the manifold currents that have made up the broader millenarian stream.

1

THE MILLENARIAN STREAM

 THE MILLERITE MOVEMENT seems an exotic growth, set against American religious institutions, yet it grew out of a tradition that substantially predated America itself. Indeed, it is a useful corrective to note that the very phenomenon of millenarian movements—groups driven to such extravagant expectations about the future—possess continuity through time and an extraordinary extension through space such that few regions of the world have lacked examples.

THE MILLENNIUM IN THE WEST

In its most abstract form the concept of a millennial age refers to a future time free from cares, imperfections, and suffering. Within Western religions such a time was first expressed by the prophets of the Hebrew Bible, who, reflecting upon the defeats and exile of their people, envisioned a time of in-gathering under a restored Davidic kingdom. Beginning in the immediately pre-Christian centuries, this theme of restoration was gradually expanded to the dimensions of a cosmic event. God would not merely restore Israel, but would redeem all the righteous of the world. As the event took on the scope of total historic consummation, it became entwined with the Resurrection of the Dead, the Last Judgment, and a panoply of natural calamities accompanying the intervention of God in history.[1] With the exception of the

13

Book of Daniel, these fully apocalyptic visions were not articulated in canonical works, developing instead in a separate Hebrew and Aramaic literature that purported to explicate the hidden eschatological meaning of
prophetic teaching. Although God necessarily was to be the agent of the
transformation, divine will was expressed through and personified by the
Messiah, now more than simply the scion of the Davidic line. The person of
the Messiah would not merely restore Israel to its former glory; he would
inaugurate the period of divine rule preceding the Last Judgment.

Christianity developed in this apocalyptic ambiance, filled with speculations concerning the nature and imminence of Last Things. Christian es-
chatologists, having imbibed Jewish apocalyptic ideas, developed them
within a Christological framework. Christian apocalyptic literature dwelt
upon the promise of a Second Coming and the links between it and the consummation of history. Their central text was the Book of Revelation and its
vision of a time when the righteous "lived and reigned with Christ a thousand years"—the literal millennium, after which only the Resurrection of
the Dead and the Last Judgment would remain.[2]

Both Jewish and Christian views of the end-time continued to develop
in subsequent centuries, within the framework that early apocalyptic writing provided. The ambiguous language and vivid yet imprecise imagery this
literature employed meant that significant questions remained unanswered:
How was one to know how close the day of fulfillment was? Was progress
toward it inevitable, or could it be accelerated by human effort? As the millennial time came closer, did its imminence affect the duties owed by citizens
to the state? These and cognate issues kept millenarian authors occupied
through the Middle Ages and into the early modern period. Submerged during periods of stability, millennialism had a way of thrusting to the surface
during times of disorder and unease, as it did during the mid-seventeenth
century in England.

THE MILLENNIUM IN THE NON-WESTERN WORLD[1]

One of the discoveries Western observers made as they explored and dominated the non-Western world was that Europeans were not the only peoples
attracted to a perfect future. The reports first of travellers, missionaries, and
government officials, later of ethnographers, historians, and journalists,
contained numerous descriptions of ideas and groups in Asia, Africa, the
Americas, and Oceania that in broad outlines resembled the Judaeo-Chris-
tian craving for a consummation of history. At first it appeared that these

were instances in which native peoples had adapted imperfectly understood missionary teachings to their own situations. Faced with incomprehensible and seemingly invulnerable Western forces, it was tempting to believe that transcendent powers would save them and re-establish the comfortable world they had known before conquest. And, indeed, well-documented cases exist of non-Western movements at least partially based upon Christian models, of which the most famous is perhaps the Taiping movement of 1856–61, whose leader, Hung Hsiu-ch'uan, had been profoundly influenced by a chance reading of a missionary's pamphlet.

However, as evidence accumulated it has become clear that these non-Western millennialists have not been living solely upon the ideas of the West. Rather, many chiliasts of the Third World came naturally to their inheritance, drawing upon independently developed salvationist themes. Recoverable oral traditions that pre-date Western contact, as well as closer analysis of the relation of non-Western movements to indigenous popular religion and culture, make clear that while the millennium as a literal thousand-year period may be exclusively Western, the concept of a historic end-time is not.

Native American peoples of both eastern and western America developed large and influential millenarian movements, from the religion of Handsome Lake among the Iroquois to the Ghost Dance among the Plains Indians.[4] Elsewhere in the Western hemisphere, sketchy documentation produces a blurred and incomplete picture, but such movements almost certainly existed among the Indian peoples of what is now Brazil, and quite possibly among Andean tribes as well.[5]

Information concerning Southern Africa is far richer and more complete. Indigenous millenarian movements assumed a major role in the first organized resistance to colonization, and continued to emerge periodically throughout the colonial period, although with the passage of time borrowed Christian motifs became more conspicuous.[6] Northern Africa and the Near East exhibit a quite different millenarian tradition, drawn from the popular Islamic belief that a divinely sanctioned Imam will inaugurate an age of religious purity. While numerous claimants have arisen, the most famous and powerful was undoubtedly the "Mahdi," whose followers controlled much of the Sudan between 1881 and 1898.[7]

Writers prone to identify millenarian impulses exclusively with their Western manifestations occasionally asserted that Asian peoples, who allegedly lacked a linear conception of history, were immune to chiliastic appeals. There is now ample evidence that, at least at the level of popular religion and culture, this is not the case. Popular Buddhism, with its concept of the "Buddha of the future," is merely one example. The Taiping Rebellion, already referred to, is a far more potent one, for this millenarian challenge to the Chinese Empire ranks as the bloodiest civil conflict of the nineteenth-century. Far from constituting merely an adaptation of Christian doctrine, it also drew heavily from the murky but well-established teaching of the Chinese secret societies.[8]

Although the cultural significance of Oceania may come less immediately to mind than that of East Asia, millennial doctrines have exerted extraordinary influence there. Nowhere has this been clearer than in the case of the Melanesian cargo cults. The zeal of anthropologists has given rise to a vast literature, a product of both the wealth of ethnographic data and the tendencies of the movements to proliferate in marginally differentiated, island-specific forms.[9]

In short, one can scarcely identify a region that has not, at one time or another, generated its own version of the millenarian dream. That this has so often occurred against the backdrop of struggles with the West is a product of both the accidents of access to data (Western scholars had to be there to collect it) and the need for some extraordinary stress-event to trigger discontent with the present. In any case, such movements are far too widely dispersed and far too deeply rooted in their respective cultures to be attributed simply to the borrowing of Western religious motifs. Instead, there appears to be some common human propensity to foresake incremental in favor of total change when conditions demand, a matter to which we shall return at a later point.

THE RISE OF SECULAR MILLENNIALISM

This necessarily compressed outline of a rich and complex subject would be incomplete without consideration of the idiom in which chiliastic yearnings have been expressed. The focus to this point has been upon religion as the carrier of millenarian expectations. For many peoples and historical epochs this has indeed been the case, with the redemptive age brought forward through a supernatural intervention into the flow of mundane events. Although human beings might in some cases accelerate the process, the fundamental agent of change was taken to be some divine force.

Beginning in the eighteenth century in the West, however, this exclusively religious conception began to split into separate religious and secular forms. The modern era might, in fact, be viewed in terms of the increasing dominance of secular millenarian visions, in which total transformation was to occur by organized human effort. Millennial potency was attributed to a wide variety of secular forces—the power of reason, so beloved by the *philosophes;* science and technology, with their apparently limitless potential for resolving seemingly intractable problems; concepts of national mission favored by romantic nationalists; the power of race, in the eyes of rightists in the late nineteenth and twentieth centuries; and the Marxist conception of a class struggle unfolding in history.[10]

The ideologies of these movements in fact take on the character of, as it were, secular religions, in which ideas that are not conventionally religious perform religious functions for those who believe in them. They speak to ultimate concerns, seemingly answer the most vexing questions with certainty, hold out hope of future salvation, and demonstrate that an apparently chaotic world is underlain by profound moral order. Thus in an analytic sense secular millenarianism is neither a contradiction in terms nor devoid of religious overtones. Its political and social belief systems differ from religion as it is conventionally known by dispensing with conventional religious language and symbols, while at the same time serving as religion's functional equivalent.

This bifurcation of millennialism into religious and secular variants is of special significance for the period of the 1840s when the competition between them was both intense and still novel. To those for whom the millennium was inconceivable without the exercise of divine power, doctrines of non-religious salvation were heralds of error, while for those more impressed with the potency of human effort, continued confidence in divine intervention resulted only in wasted opportunities for change.

MILLENNIALISM AS A GENERIC PHENOMENON

The differences participants saw between religious and non-religious visions have not always been so apparent to outside observers. Similarly, the cultural gulfs separating Western and non-Western concepts of total transformation seemed far wider to those who first observed them than they have to later scholars. Thus the tendency of recent scholarship has increasingly been to recognize millennialism as a global phenomenon, transcending historical periods as well as cultures, encompassing the traditionally religious as well as the avowedly secular. While respecting the distinctiveness of individual movements, this tendency has also recognized their common substratum.

The identification of commonalities has occurred alongside an awareness that no single discipline holds the key to understanding millennialism. By convention, Western movements have most often fallen under the purview of historians, while non-Western movements have engaged the interests of anthropologists. However, sociologists, political scientists, and psychologists have made equally significant contributions. The interdisciplinary character of the study of millenarian movements received its most significant recognition in the 1960 University of Chicago conference, "Millennial Dreams in Action," among the first scholarly meetings to systematically draw together social scientists from different disciplines and geographical competences for an examination of chiliastic phenomena.[11] In the quarter-century since the Chicago conference, the interdisciplinary character of research on millennialism has become firmly established.[12]

One of the most influential products of the Chicago conference was the definition of "millenarian" proposed by Norman Cohn and subsequently incorporated into the revised edition of his highly influential *Pursuit of the Millennium*[13]:

> any religious movement inspired by the phantasy of a salvation which is to be
>
> a. collective, in the sense that it is to be enjoyed by the faithful as a group;
>
> b. terrestrial, in the sense that it is to be realised on this earth and not in some otherworldly heaven;
>
> c. imminent, in the sense that it is to come both soon and suddenly;
>
> d. total, in the sense that it is utterly to transform life on earth, so that the new dispensation will be no mere improvement on the present but perfection itself;
>
> e. accomplished by agencies which are consciously regarded as supernatural.

Useful though it is Cohn's definition remains excessively narrow in its insistence that a movement be "religious," its assertion that the motivation is a "phantasy," and its identification of the operative powers as "supernatural." Ironically, armed visions of modern political ideologies would have little place in such a definition, despite the fact that Cohn's own initial concern was to trace the millenarian roots of communism and Naziism.[14] Nonetheless, Cohn's definition proved an admirable starting point for the comparative study of Western and non-Western movements, without the necessity for viewing the latter as distorted offspring of the former.

THE MILLENNIUM AND RATIONALITY

One goal has been not simply to describe and classify such movements but also to explain the reasons for their occurrence. When the question of origins is joined, the issue of fantasy versus reality, of subjectivity versus objectivity, becomes critical. A fissure runs through millenarian studies between those who attribute millennialism to a fundamental misapprehension of reality, as against those who view the movements as the product of a particularly acute perception. These antithetical positions are most clearly represented in the work of, respectively, Cohn and Anthony F. C. Wallace.

The vision of the millennium can be considered a fantasy to the extent that predictions of the millennium's imminence have been uniformly invalidated. In addition, movements that have done political and military battle with the authorities have usually been defeated. It thus has seemed persuasive to argue that prophets and followers relied upon an incorrect understanding of the world. Cohn has gone further, insisting upon the psychopathological character of the movements. Where there were people "living in a state of chronic frustration and anxiety," that frustration and anxiety would "suddenly discharge...itself in a frantic urge to smite the ungodly— and by doing so to bring into being...that final Kingdom where the Saints ...were to enjoy ease and riches, security and power for all eternity."[15] This was not the calculated advancement of group interests; it was, rather, expressive behavior designed to exorcise inner demons.

Although Cohn reached this position from an essentially psychoanalytic perspective, scholars with different theoretical baggage drew parallel conclusions. Thus Marxist writers such as E. J. Hobsbawm attribute the chiliasts' failure to their imperfect understanding of the causes of their misery and a flawed grasp of the need for effective organization. Since they do not know how social and political change may be brought about, they utilize methods that can only lead to failure. Their grievances against the established order may be real, but their remedies remain parochial and naive. The Southern European peasants Hobsbawm studied lashed out against adversaries in acts that may have had cathartic value but left them worse off than before.[16]

The work of Anthony F. C. Wallace represents a different orientation. Wallace argues that under conditions of extreme collective stress, communities face the alternatives of dissolution or revitalization. If they persist in traditional modes of thought and behavior, they face loss of group integrity through conquest or absorption, because of their inability to meet new challenges. If they recast their world view and begin to act upon this changed conception of reality, new energies can be tapped and the group's life can be reinvigorated. Millenarian movements serve this function by presenting an alternative set of beliefs and way of life, which promises to cure the ills against which established institutions have proved powerless.[17] Hence millennialists may correctly judge when a society can no longer conduct business as usual. Existing institutions possess an inertial character such that they encourage repetition of old patterns of behavior even in the presence of radical challenges to the status quo. Liberated from such allegiances, millennialists more readily grasp when usual ways of doing things have become dysfunctional.

Wallace's concept of the revitalization process is cross-cultural and cross-historical, yet grew out of anthropological research on the survival dilemmas of non-Western peoples. In tribal settings, where millennialism often engaged the loyalties of most of a group's members, it was tempting to view it as a creative and ultimately healthy response to mortal dangers. In Western societies, larger and more diverse, millennialism has been more apt to pit some members of a society against others. Where non-Western millennialism may be likened to international conflict, with state set against state, Western millennialism often has had the character of civil war. As in much fratricidal warfare, the conflict of millenarians with their fellow citizens has had an unusually bitter edge, to which may be traced perhaps the propensity to view chiliasts as not simply misguided but incapable of rational thought.

The view to be taken here will probably satisfy neither the irrationalists who view millennialism as an aberration nor the rationalists who see it as a sensible and self-interested response. At least some of the millenarians we shall consider drifted into non-falsifiable assertions incapable of being checked against confirming external evidence or, by contrast, into predictions so patently without external foundation that disconfirmation was inevitable. As we shall see, Millerism in particular evoked strong charges of abetting insanity both in its own time and in later years. By the same token, millenarians will also be seen to have grasped, sometimes more clearly than their neighbors, the fragility of American society and the extent to which old truths could no longer be taken for granted. Notwithstanding their worldly failures, they possessed an insight that their more complacent contemporaries lacked.

AMERICAN MILLENARIANISM BEFORE 1800

The millenarian ferment that reached its climax in the Millerite debacle was an intellectually respectable feature of New England Protestantism, which grew from English roots. The English Civil War (1642–46) had been the occasion for millenarian speculation and organization on a grand scale. The millenarian Puritan sects subsequently suffered major political and intellectual defeats. Feared as disturbers of social order and stigmatized as irrational "enthusiasts,"[18] the chiliasts melted away into obscurity after the Restoration. Gone were the Diggers, a fragile community that rejected the institution of private property, and gone too were the Fifth Monarchy Men, whose belief in an imminent reign of Christ on earth led them into a disastrous attempted coup against the government of Cromwell. While groups such as these dissolved in disillusionment and defeat, their attitudes and writings did not in fact vanish. Popular religion in the English countryside and among urban artisans continued to take the promised millennium seriously, long after it had passed out of middle and upper-class fashion.[19] Biblical exegesis with strong millenarian overtones retained its respectability among scriptural scholars. The invitingly ambiguous imagery of the books of Daniel and Revelation provided continued warrant for millenarian scholarship among clerics otherwise cut off from or unsympathetic to the more emotionally gripping popular millenarianism which hung on among the lower orders.

New England, as an outpost populated by Dissenters, was perhaps more than usually receptive in the eighteenth century to survivals from the seventeenth. Cerebral chiliasm, concerned with the unravelling of scriptural puzzles (what were the beasts in Revelation, for example, and which of them had already arrived?), was intensified and modified by the religious revivals of the Great Awakening (1730–45), which encompassed much of colonial America. Its New England phase spread from Northampton, Massachusetts, up the Connecticut River Valley, and reintroduced and partially relegitimated emotional religiosity. At the same time, its major intellectual figure, Jonathan Edwards, gave millenarian thought a characteristically American tone. Millenarianism had traditionally looked for portents as evidence of imminent change, particularly natural calamities and political disruptions. Edwards added to these categories that of personal spiritual renewal. The Awakening also built upon the belief that America represented a new beginning, hence had some special mission to perform in the economy of world salvation. This belief in turn interlocked with the Puritan suspicion of England as a decadent society that had lost its claim to being a divine instrument.

When in the mid-1700s the climactic struggle took place between England and France for the political division of North America, New England clerics were initially unsure how to react. On the one hand, the confrontation between Protestant England and Catholic France conformed well to English millenarian rhetoric, which identified the Pope with the Anti-Christ. On the other, it was tempting to see the struggle as between nations that differed only in their degrees of unworthiness.[20] It was difficult not to view the fall of the French fortress at Louisbourg, Cape Breton Island (1745), as the victory of God's elect: "Against the onslaught of popery and slavery the sacred cause of liberty became the banner under which New Englanders rallied ... not only had the course of providential history hallowed the rise of liberty, but the triumph of liberty would be realized in the coming of the millennium."[21]

Virtuous New England rather than corrupt England was the instrument of victory, with the implication that the arena of millenarian battle had shifted decisively from Europe to America. The gradual assimilation of political liberty to millenarian history marked "a subtle but profound shift in emphasis—the religious values that traditionally defined the ultimate goal of apocalyptic hope—the conversion of all nations to Christianity—became diluted with, and often subordinate to, the commitment to America as a new seat of liberty."[22] The implications of the shift lay not only in the new geographical locus of millenarian events but in the suggestion, hardly novel historically but new in an American context, that the millennium could be politicized. If liberty might be used as a rallying point against the French in Canada, it could and would be used against the British in America thirty years later.[23]

In fits and starts, expectation of the millennium continued through the Revolution itself. In 1775 many, particularly in New England, prepared for the Revolution as for a crusade. Whatever special role America had to perform could be accomplished only with full independence. However, with the attainment of independence, national unity gave way to political partisanship. Religious observance was on the decline in America and even more dramatically in Revolutionary France. Anti-Christ seemed to be everywhere at once. "Events had left the nature of God's plan in doubt, and millennialists addressed themselves to issues which bespoke a fear that the signs of the times were not as clear as they ought be."[24] The constitutional edifice was outwardly complete, yet if the millennium had in fact arrived, its existence was difficult to detect after the passing of revolutionary euphoria. Perhaps independence and constitutional restructuring were not enough.[25]

The significance of disillusionment was twofold. In the first place, it resulted from the prophetic disconfirmation inevitable in revolutionary situations. The postrevolutionary situation never fulfills the original prerevolutionary promise. Second, the emphasis after 1790 was increasingly upon the primacy of inner over outer change. This altered orientation avoided the disillusionment associated with the imperfections of social, economic, and political institutions. If personal transformation lay at the root of virtuous social behavior, then inner transformation must necessarily precede visible social change. This spiritual inner-directedness pushed more radical forms of transformation farther into the future, for society could scarcely be stood on its head before the spiritual odysseys of individuals had been completed. As in the Great Awakening, the instrument for these personal changes was the revival, in which prolonged soul searching in a group setting was led by preachers adept at arousing feelings of guilt and remorse. Stimulated by a sense of personal unworthiness, revival participants were offered the hope of redemption through a transformative religious experience.

THE SECOND GREAT AWAKENING

The post-1790 revivals were neither as brief nor as spatially confined as their colonial predecessors. Dating the "Second Great Awakening" permits simply a specification of its outermost boundaries and the years of maximum activity. On this basis, it began about 1795 (half a century after the First Great Awakening had ended), and lasted until some time between 1835 and about 1860, depending upon the area of the country. The Awakening "seems to have begun in different parts of the nation at different times and to have reached a series of peaks in different years in each area."[26] Geographically, the revivals reached their greatest intensity not in New England but in areas where the first generation of settlement was just ending, then regarded as "the West." That included particularly the Burned-over District and northern Ohio, areas that had received migratory streams out of Western New England. Less intense revivalism also occurred in the Ohio and Connecticut valleys.[27] In New York State, revivals occurred in every county, but most often on either side of the Erie Canal, diminishing sharply in the lower Hudson Valley. All told, at least 1,343 revivals occurred in the state between 1825 and 1835, and most frequently between 1829 and 1832.[28] Demographically, the counties implicated in the revivals were those with the highest proportion of individuals born in New England. Late eighteenth-century population movements brought New Englanders into New York State by two routes: from Connecticut and Massachusetts into the upper Mohawk Valley and western Catskills, and from Vermont above the Adirondacks into the St. Lawrence Valley and around to the eastern shore of Lake Ontario. The convergence of these streams in central New York around 1800 pushed the Yankee population directly westward into the Finger Lakes and the Genesee River Valley. The movement was sufficiently systematic to constitute the transplantation of portions of New England society: "Jefferson and St. Lawrence counties were the new Vermont. Oneida was the new Connecticut. Farther west, Genesee, Wyoming, and Chautauqua contained people of considerably mixed local New England derivation, scarcely tinged by other strains."[29]

The upstate revivals benefited from such superbly gifted orchestrators as Charles Grandison Finney, whose intuitive grasp of the psychology of conversion contributed substantially to the revivals' success. Finney and fellow revivalists systematically developed Jonathan Edwards' emphasis on inner renewal as the precondition for salvation. If fundamental transformation occurred in the hearts of believers rather than in the institutional structure of society, some traditional theological conceptions would be weakened. The first was the Calvinist insistence upon predestination, for the point of the revivals was to stimulate personal change. The saved and the damned had not been irreversibly chosen by the deity; rather, the category into which one fell was subject to willed change. Individuals might save themselves, or rather open themselves up to God's saving grace. While in theory this might happen at any time, it was more likely to happen under the prodding of a skilled revivalist, who knew how to arouse a sense of despair while at the same time holding out the possibility of transformation. As predestination reinforced the social hierarchy of the colonial village, so revivalists' conversions harmonized with the new Jacksonian social mobility. Increasingly, all things were deemed possible, including freeing the world from sin by the exercise of personal initiative.

The revivals' emphasis upon the significance of human agency held important implications for millenarianism. Traditional chiliasts had been premillennialists. That is, they believed the millennium would be preceded by the Second Coming. Only after the return of Christ would the thousand years of peace and plenty begin. Premillennialism emphasized not simply the totality of change but its suddenness. The Second Coming would abruptly sever the flow of historic time in order to purge the world of sin and evil. Themes of discontinuity and purification led premillennialists to associate the inauguration of the millennium with tumult and disaster, as divine forces destroyed all that was corrupt in earthly life.

The revivalists, more optimistic about human potentialities, inclined toward a different view. Most were postmillennialists who believed that the Second Coming would follow rather than precede the thousand-year kingdom of God on earth. The climactic moment was not likely to come in the very near future, for it had to be preceded by the conversion of those as yet unsaved. This view of history reduced the anxiety associated with a belief in imminent divine intervention; it also emphasized gradualism, a reformist approach to problems, and the importance of human effort. The world was to be made ready for the consummation of history through incremental improvements instead of by a once-and-for-all, miraculous solution. Just as human effort could redeem the state of one's soul, so it might in time redeem the outer world through the virtuous behavior of the saved. Premillennialists tended to be anxious and pessimistic, for their millennium was to be preceded by the descent of Christ in clouds and thunder. Only after the purging cataclysms would the thousand years begin.

There had already been glimpses of postmillennialism in the first Great Awakening, as the sheer fact of spiritual invigoration came to be interpreted as a sign the millennium was near. Evidence for premillennialism was generally gleaned from the state of the external world of politics and nature, but the evidentiary base for postmillennial expectation lay within the souls of believers. The fervor and spread of belief was evidence of how far humanity had traversed the ordained course of history. While this shift was implicit in the eighteenth century, it became explicit in the nineteenth.

Not surprisingly, the more revivalists learned about William Miller and his premillennialism, the less they liked it. Finney's and Miller's paths finally crossed in Boston in the Advent year, 1843. Finney took in one or two of Miller's Bible classes, and then "invited him to my room, and tried to convince him that he was in error." Initially certain he had demonstrated the internal contradictions of Miller's position, Finney succumbed in the end to uncharacteristic despair: "it was vain to reason with him, and his followers, at that time. Believing, as they most certainly did, that the advent of Christ was at hand, it was no wonder that they were too wild with excitement, to be reasoned with to any purpose."[30] Premillennialism was now so far outside the realm of accepted doctrine that a postmillennialist like Finney found belief in it incomprehensible.

POSTMILLENNIALISM IN THE NINETEENTH CENTURY

Nineteenth century postmillennialism did not, of course, exclude God from participation, but the deity's role had been altered from that of sole actor to co-participant; the emphasis shifted to human efforts, often mobilized through benevolent societies and other voluntary associations.[31] Inevitably, the concentration upon human efficacy subtly subordinated the traditional interventionist element in millenarian thought. The perfection of the world would not occur all at once through direct divine intervention, but gradually as divinely inspired individuals came to dominate society.

In postmillennialist terms, the perfection of the outer world would result from the perfection of the inner world. First, saved individuals would manifest their spiritual improvement in virtuous behavior. The more such people, the higher the moral tone of political and economic endeavor: "ethical renewal ... was prerequisite to social righteousness."[32] Second, such individuals would feel obligated to induce similar changes in others. Their own perfection carried the obligation to assist the perfection of those presently unregenerate through the active support of religious causes in general and revivalism in particular. Thus, the newly "saved" were not expected to smugly enjoy their salvation.

Putatively virtuous behavior and religious activism both encouraged a peculiar social militancy whose hallmark was the simultaneous pursuit of religious evangelism and social reform. Those touched by the revivals supported conversionary religion through financial and personal participation oriented toward reaching the unsaved. A multitude of missionary organizations and societies devoted to the publication and distribution of Bibles and religious tracts formed in pursuit of this goal. The same persons committed to these causes, however, were often involved in others of an apparently more secular character, concerned with the amelioration of social ills. Reformist efforts were sometimes aimed at improving the status of women, reducing urban poverty, or eliminating political corruption, but were most often directed at the abolition of slavery and at temperance. This "politics of benevolence," as John Hammond calls it, arose from the belief that the unregenerate could not achieve salvation if social circumstances prevented them from fully exercising free will. Since revivalist conversion was considered the product of personal choice, any condition that inhibited choice made conversion less likely. Thus it seemed natural for the saved to shoulder "the obligation to order the world in a manner that would facilitate the conversion of others."[33] There was an evident logic at work here, for once human efficacy was acknowledged in the religious sphere, there was no necessary reason to exclude it from the secular sphere (although, of course, those involved would not even have acknowledged the validity of the distinction). The logic seemed all the more compelling, inasmuch as the postmillennial fervor occurred at a time when commercial and technological growth confirmed the power of human effort and ingenuity. Postmillennialism also seemed the ideal vehicle to develop more fully the view already articulated by the eighteenth-century New England millenarians that America occupied a unique position in the divine plan of history. As the new locus of salvationist activity in the world, it would also presumably achieve a state of moral improvement before others.

THE PARADOX OF POSTMILLENNIALISM

The problem with postmillennialism lay in the fact that the more seriously it was taken, the less millenarian it became. The greater the emphasis on the human role in moral purification, the greater the belief in step-by-step solutions to social problems. The greater the commitment to incremental reform, the more remote the final goal of total perfection became. Effective problem-solving lay in the additive consequences of many small steps rather than in any capacity to achieve comprehensive solutions. And yet if this were indeed the case, what was left of the millennium itself? The total perfection of life on earth might remain an aspiration and a standard against which the present was measured, but it also took on the character of a far-off dreamy vision that none living would ever personally see.

The postmillennialism that developed from the revivals was consequently optimistic, gradualist, and human centered. Its compatibility with reform movements lent momentum to organizations devoted to the alleviation of social ills, particularly in the growing urban centers. By the same token, postmillennialists themselves found it easy to pass into a semi-secular reliance upon human good will and the growth of scientific knowledge:

> The churches and the benevolent societies connected with them were still considered important instruments of the coming kingdom [after the Civil War], but great significance was now attached to such impersonal messianic agencies as the natural and social sciences. The spirit of brotherhood was still given a major role in perfecting the world, but it was often regarded as an achievement of human evolution with only tenuous ties to a transcendent deity.[14]

James Moorehead suggests that postmillennialism was inherently unstable and might best be viewed as a transitional phenomenon, midway between the premillennialism it sought to supplant and a more naturalistic religion of uplift and social improvement. In the end, it satisfied no one, for its developmentalism managed to offend premillennialists while it remained too attached to supernaturalism for the taste of liberals. Hence it could not survive the subsequent polarization between Protestant fundamentalists and liberals in the early twentieth century.[35]

In the 1830s and 40s, however, the decline of postmillennialism lay far in the future. During the revivals of the Second Great Awakening, when evil still seemed conquerable by religious will, the postmillennialists saw no need for a flawed society to be destroyed in a supernatural conflagration. Their commitment to progressive human betterment transformed the millennium from an event that was to begin at a fixed point in time to a process capable of realization by degrees, little more than a metaphor of distant perfection. With eschatological transformation pushed into a non-specific future, there was little reason to despair of the present or to face the anxieties of imminent divine judgment. The task was not to abandon life as usual nor to await catastrophic upheaval but to push ahead with the tasks mandated by the reformist ethos.

The wide acceptance of revival-oriented evangelical Protestantism after about 1830, under such master practitioners as Finney, emphasized the importance of human effort and de-emphasized, albeit unintentionally, the importance of divine intervention. The significance of human effort in turn encouraged an incremental approach to the struggle between good and evil, decomposed now into a thousand skirmishes rather a climactic, cosmic battle. Reformers, struggling against low church attendance, alcoholism, slavery, or urban poverty, saw themselves as the instruments of whatever millennial consummation might eventually be attained in God's good time.

Postmillennialism was in two senses the victim of its own success. On the one hand, when the revival spirit was at full strength it induced an exaggerated optimism, so rapidly did religious invigoration and philanthropic endeavor seem to proceed. The fervor could not be sustained indefinitely, however, and social problems often were surprisingly stubborn, as the abolitionists found. The result could be at least temporary disillusionment. Compared to premillennialists, who could stake all on a fixed date for the "end of the world," postmillennialists found it easier to weather disappointments and learn to fight on. But they did so by pushing the millennium forward or, rather, by becoming accustomed to its continual recession into the future. This, in turn, engendered a second form of failure through success. As postmillennialism was interpreted in reformist terms, the intimate link between the millennium's realization and religious commitment weakened. If reform was a way of doing God's work on earth and bringing perfection closer, and if the instruments for perfectability consisted of organization, hard work, and knowledge, then one hardly needed to remain immersed in orthodox religious activity in order to do it.[36] Further, the postmillennial optimism permeated American culture, playing upon older conceptions of America as the "redeemer nation" destined to effect the world's salvation.[37] To the extent that most Americans remained optimistic nationalists, they partook of the postmillennial ethos in a manner that was both unconscious and uncritical, postmillennialists without realizing it. Hence, even though religious writers continued to discuss postmillennialism in theological terms, postmillennial themes of progress and uplift found their way into more secular and naturalistic interpretations.[38] Particularly after the Civil War, it might truly be said that almost all Americans with the exception of nativists, agrarian radicals, and declassed older elites had imbibed postmillennial orthodoxy in its diluted secular form. It became part of the American "civic religion," according to which the nation had a special obligation and a special capacity to develop social virtue.[39] Thus the double paradox: that the more seriously postmillennialism was taken the less explicitly millenarian it became, with the result that it could not maintain itself as an independent theological position on the fundamentalist-liberal battlefield of the 1920s. At the same time, the diffusion of postmillennial beliefs throughout American culture made it the source not only for a thousand sermons but for inspirational political rhetoric as well, such that by the very time that it succumbed in religious circles its secular version triumphed in the society at large.

2

THE RISE OF THE MILLERITES

THE INFLUENCE of postmillennialism makes the appearance of Millerism all the more curious. For if indeed doctrines of gradual improvement were becoming widespread, why return to an older tradition, so seemingly at odds with the sunny American temperament? Before an answer can be given, the history, personnel, and doctrines of Millerism must first be outlined.

THE RETURN OF PREMILLENNIALISM

The Second Great Awakening reached one of several peaks between 1838 and 1844, with particularly intense revival activity in Millerism's climactic year, 1843.[1] Thus, the most dramatic period of Millerite premillennialist activity coincided with a surge in revivalist, essentially postmillennialist, conversions. While this juxtaposition has sometimes been attributed to a vaguer and more general millenarian ambiance,[2] the distinctions already drawn between the two millenarian orientations suggest the need for a more precise explanation, especially in view of the fact that no subsequent premillennial movement approached Miller's in notoriety.

Millerism strongly resembled earlier European millenarian movements. It included a complex apparatus of Biblical exegesis, which sought to extract every concealed meaning from sacred texts; emphasis upon a specific date on which a miraculous event was to occur; the cessation of routine activity as the date drew closer; preoccupation with images of catastrophe, both as signs of the future and as instruments of the world's destruction; increasing characterization of the existing society as evil and corrupt; and the drive to take the salvationist doctrine out into that society through militant proselytizing. There were also three notable dissimilarities: First, the Millerites were apolitical. Unlike earlier millenarians, such as the Taborites, a Bohemian sect that mounted a war against unbelievers in the fifteenth century, or the Fifth Monarchy Men, Puritan extremists who tried unsuccessfully to unseat Oliver Cromwell in 1661, the Millerites made no move against the existing political order. They did not articulate obvious social protest. Thus, they did not advocate radical redistribution of wealth or power, although they found much to criticize in the status quo. Second, and not unrelated, their membership did not encompass significant numbers of the endemically poverty-stricken or oppressed. While that did not mean the Millerites were without grievances, it did mean that for the most part they did not have to worry about obtaining the necessities of life, and they certainly did not face the chronic deprivations experienced by peasant millenarians in pre-industrial Europe or Asia. Third, while William Miller offered intellectual and spiritual leadership, he was not a charismatic figure in whom followers identified superhuman gifts. Indeed, Miller insisted that anyone else who studied the Bible could reach identical conclusions. Thus the Millerites can be distinguished, on the one hand, from their postmillennialist contemporaries, and, on the other, from their doctrinally similar forebears. Why, then, should the 1840s have seen any substantial premillennialism at all, given the postmillennial ethos, and why when it came was it a premillennialism free of radical social doctrines?

These problems may best be approached by first establishing the narrative of the Millerite experience through the "Great Disappointment" of 1843–44, when the predicted Second Coming failed to occur, and then surveying the available information concerning the demographic characteristics of the movement. Millerism conveniently divides into three phases. The first from 1831 to 1839 covers Miller's early but unorganized attempts to communicate his views in Eastern New York and Western New England. Then, from 1839 until early 1843, an organization took shape under the leadership of the Reverend Joshua V. Himes, who promulgated Miller's ideas systematically through the population centers of the coastal Northeast. In the brief third phase, from the spring of 1843 through the depressing fall of 1844, Millerism spread with increasing rapidity in the Burned-over District west of Rome, New York, before the final prophetic disconfirmation.

THE RISE OF MILLERISM

Millerism occurred at the center of American consciousness, since it remained in and around the most urbanized and economically developed section of the country. While Mormonism moved progressively westward, to Ohio and Missouri in the 1830s, Illinois until the mid-1840s, and the Great Basin thereafter,[3] Millerism, because it never faced the same level of community hostility, sought the great Eastern cities. While generally accepted as "the largest and most influential early nineteenth-century pre-millennial group,"[4] the precise numbers involved will never be known. The Millerites did not compile membership lists as such, and only at a late stage did Millerites clearly break with denominational Protestantism. As knowledge of Miller's teachings spread, it also became difficult to distinguish truly committed members from sympathizers or the merely curious, although the progressive failure of his predictions presumably weeded out the less committed. The generally cited estimate of seriously committed Millerites at the movement's height is 50,000. The source of the figure was Miller's own estimate, contained in his autobiographical "Apology and Defence," written in the post-Disappointment Summer of 1845: "In nearly a thousand places Advent congregations have been raised up, numbering, as near as I can estimate, some fifty thousand believers."[5] This estimate reflects the 1844 "come-outer" movement when Millerites withdrew from churches with which they had been affiliated. Since Miller also claimed six thousand conversions obtained by his own personal effort, and since his personal modesty was legendary, 50,000 does not appear an inflated figure. It is possible that upwards of a million others were "skeptically expectant."[6]

David Rowe has suggested another, albeit indirect, measure of Millerite numbers by calculating the ratio between the movement's leaders and followers. Drawing upon letters to Miller from sympathizers in upstate New York, Rowe noted that many bore multiple signatures. Published sources provided the means for identifying signatories who were leaders of the movement. This suggests a ratio of one acknowledged leader to 23 committed members of the rank and file. On the basis of the known leadership cadre for the region, the ratio yields a committed followership of about 4,600. Rowe derives the same relative numbers from the fact that 200 Millerite meetings are known to have taken place in the Burned-over District by October 1844. Assuming conservatively that each meeting consisted of no more than 25 people, this implies an audience of about 5,000.[7]

By any means of estimation, the numbers were formidable, especially in light of the concentration of Millerism in the Northeast, with some late extension into the West (Ohio and Michigan). The entire national popula-

William Miller as he appeared in the early 1840s. He was already past sixty when the millennial date arrived, but he appears here looking fit and relatively youthful, with an expression that is both contemplative and curiously sad. The years after the "Great Disappointment" were marked by rapidly deteriorating health for Miller, and he died in 1849 at the age of sixty-seven. Source: *The Midnight Cry. Courtesy Loma Linda University Heritage Room*

tion at the time was about 19,000,000. New York State in 1840 had a population of almost two and a half million.[8]

Little in William Miller's past pointed toward the role he occupied in the early 1840s. His forebears had lived in Springfield, Massachusetts, since at least 1675, residing there until the mid-1700s, when the family moved to

Pittsfield. The date of the move by Miller's grandfather from Springfield to Pittsfield is of some significance, because Springfield was deeply involved in the revivals of the First Great Awakening. Since the elder Miller was born in Springfield in 1730, and Miller's father was born in Pittsfield at the end of 1757, the move may have occurred during the young manhood of Miller's grandfather, about 1750. That would place the family deep in Great Awakening territory during the critical years of the 1740s. Miller himself was born in Pittsfield in 1782, but the family moved once again four years later, this time to Low Hampton, New York, just across the border from Vermont[9]; as a young man he also lived briefly in the neighboring Vermont town of Poultney.

Miller fought in the War of 1812 and filled local political offices thereafter. He was a Mason, a Democrat, and a reasonably prosperous farmer. Descended from a line of preachers, he went through a youthful flirtation with deism but eventually returned to the fold as a fervent Baptist. Despite William Lloyd Garrison's charge that Miller was illiterate, he seems to have been reasonably well-read. Though scarcely scholarly, his religious skepticism coincided with attempts by Poultney deists to broaden his intellectual horizons. Foremost among them was the renegade politician, Matthew Lyon, whose anti-Federalist activities as a Congressman had led to conviction under the Sedition Act. Although Lyon was probably an Episcopalian by birth, he held to the deism of Ethan Allen, under whom he had fought in the Revolution. During the time that Lyon lived in Poultney, he accumulated a formidable personal library, which he generously shared with his neighbors, including Miller.[10] It was doubtless with Lyon in mind that Miller wrote of the Poultney rationalists: "They put into my hands the works of Voltaire, Hume, Paine, Ethan Allen, and other deistical writers."[11] If so, they left little enduring mark on his style, and he looked back upon this period with the ruefulness others might reserve for the sexual pecadillos of youth.

The episode with Lyon was the late stage of a long process of self-education. Miller's formal education was of the patchy sort typical of a modest rural childhood. From nine until fourteen he received three months' formal education a year, of whatever sort the common school in Low Hampton could provide. His home contained only three books, the Bible, the Psalter, and a hymnal, which his mother taught him to read. Beyond that, he was an autodidact. The full extent of his reading is not known, beyond the references to deistic writers. Joshua Himes claimed that in late adolescence Miller also devoured "ancient and modern history," perhaps in Lyon's library.[12] However, Miller's writings, particularly the earliest, rely far more heavily on Biblical citations than upon any secular authorities, and his own reminiscences suggest that questions of Biblical interpretation led him to history rather than the other way around.[13]

His gradually developing religious ideas bore close resemblance to those of British chiliasts both prior to and contemporary with him. The ideas of Joanna Southcott (1750–1814) in particular resembled Miller's, as Millerites subsequently found on a visit to England after the Great Disappointment.[14] Yet Miller does not seem to have participated in any known trans-Atlantic millenarian contacts, although there was a good deal of international communication among millenarians from the late eighteenth century onwards.[15] Independent invention rather than diffusion seems responsible for the similarities. Miller may also have drawn ideas from the popular religion of the area. He lived in or near the area of the First Great Awakening. Small but emotionally charged millenarian movements flickered spasmodically in the Vermont counties that bordered Lake Champlain, adjacent to Miller's home.[16] Although to all appearances theologically self-taught, the congruence between his Biblical interpretations and older readings of millenarian symbols strongly implies access to an oral if not a written exegetical tradition.

An exhaustive reader of the Bible, he labored with a concordance in relative seclusion for fourteen years. He became convinced that the Second Advent was imminent and began in 1831 to preach it locally. Word gradually spread from the Low Hampton locality to adjacent areas of Western New England and Eastern New York. Miller did not draw a following then or later by virtue of any "personal magnetism" or the attribution of extraordinary gifts. He was not, in a word, "charismatic" in either a theological, Weberian, or common-usage sense. His expanding influence in the 1830s was due in part to exogenous social factors to be dealt with in due course, in part to his indefatigible itinerant preaching, and in part to the "fit" of his conclusions regarding the Second Coming with the intellectual framework of scholarly millenarianism which had remained intact through the revival periods.

Miller claimed to have lectured 800 times between June 9, 1834, and June 10, 1839, and 4,000 times over the whole of his public career up until 1845.[17] Whether exaggerated or not, his early biographer, Sylvester Bliss, mentions more than 230 communities in which Miller spoke between 1831 and 1844, and since in many he delivered a series of lectures, the number of total appearances was considerable by any calculation.[18] More revealing than sheer numbers is the pattern of geographical dispersion. Before 1839, he appeared exclusively in New York and Vermont. Although he spoke in Rome, New York, in 1838, almost all his New York State appearances were in the Champlain Valley, Adirondack foothills, and Albany-Troy areas. He reached Massachusetts and southern New Hampshire in 1839, the year he met Joshua Himes. The pre-1839 areas were, not surprisingly, those closest to his home and, in New York, were those which at the time had the largest proportion of New England-born inhabitants.[19] In about 1834, Miller's views were published in a sixty-four-page pamphlet, issued in Brandon, Vermont, in a printing of unknown size. In 1835 a second printing of 1,500 was issued. Since he distributed most of these pamphlets himself when he lectured or in response to letters, the area of their immediate circulation coincided with the area in which his name was already known through other means.[20]

During the peripatetic years of the 1830s, Miller's teachings were geographically confined, and there was nothing resembling a "Millerite movement." Miller functioned as an advocate rather than as an organizer, as yet another revivalist, albeit one with an idiosyncratic message. Geographical expansion and organization began simultaneously after his 1839 meeting with Himes, a Boston minister already enmeshed in causes that ranged from temperance to abolitionism. Himes's eventual defection from abolitionism to Adventism was taken more in sadness than in anger by his friend William Lloyd Garrison, who wrote in The Liberator: "I am somewhat intimately acquainted with Mr. Himes. I am sorry that he has become the victim of an absurd theory, but I still regard him as a sincere and worthy man."[21] In a less guarded moment, his underlying resentment emerged: "A considerable number of worthy abolitionists have been carried away by it [Adventism], and for the time being, are rendered completely useless to our cause. But the delusion has not long to run, and let us rejoice."[22]

It is not clear how Himes first heard of Miller. The most likely explanations are word-of-mouth or through the circulation of Miller's printed materials. Miller had by this time preached in Southern New Hampshire and the small towns around Boston. In any case, Himes first saw Miller in Exeter, New Hampshire, at a Christian convention where Miller spoke. On the basis of those lectures, Himes brought Miller to his Chardon Street Chapel in Boston beginning December 9, 1839, Miller's first appearance in a major American city. The Boston appearance opened a new phase, not simply because of the urban setting, but because Himes quickly took on the responsibility of systematically spreading Miller's message throughout the Northeast. The results were equivocal. On the positive side, Himes thrust Miller's views beyond eastern New York—western New England, with special attention to urban areas. In addition to Boston, Miller or his followers appeared in Portland, Maine; New York City; and Philadelphia.

Himes's greatest organizational contribution lay, however, in his adaptation of the camp meeting, which had been invented by the Presbyte-

Millerite camp meetings in the Northeast centered about the "Great Tent," imposing even in this rendering that appeared in one of the movement's main detractors, the *New York Herald*. With its combination of size and impermanence, the tent might almost serve as a metaphor for Millerism itself. Source: *New York Herald*, November 14, 1842. *Courtesy Loma Linda University Heritage Room*

rians at Cane Ridge, Kentucky, in 1801, and was utilized extensively during the Second Great Awakening.[23] The virtue of the camp meeting lay in the creation of a total environment, where participants were insulated from the distractions of mundane existence. The value of such a device may be appreciated in light of Miller's and Himes's initial reception in New York City. While Miller's audiences eventually increased, the two millenarians first entered a friendless city where lack of funds and supporters obliged them to sleep in an anteroom off the lecture hall.[24] The Millerite version of the camp meeting was the "Great Tent." Himes's promotional genius had hit upon the idea of a mammoth tent, 55 feet high at the center, 300 feet around the circumference, with a capacity of 3,000–4,000.[25] With or without the famous tent, Millerite camp meetings sprang up throughout the Northeast. The camp meeting, in effect, built a temporary artificial environment. Thus, the initial site at East Kingston, New Hampshire, was accessible by rail from Boston and New York, yet sufficiently isolated so that those who attended were a self-selected group of believers and potential believers, perhaps 10,000 in all. During a four-month period in 1842, thirty such meetings were held.[26] Through Himes's carefully orchestrated efforts, Millerite doctrines spread as far south as Washington, north to Montreal, and west to Cincinnati.

Millerism's distinguishing characteristic was, of course, its willingness to make a specific prediction concerning the timing of the Second Coming. Yet in this respect at least, Miller himself was a reluctant as well as an unsuccessful prophet. He was not initially willing to venture a date, yet succumbed under pressure from expectant followers. In the early 1830s, he gave the time as "sometime in 1843." In early 1843, he modified that view and spoke of "the Jewish year, 1843," by which he meant the period from March 21, 1843, to March 21, 1844. Bitterly disappointed Adventists sought some way out of the disillusionment and ridicule of failure, and thus in August 1844 Samuel S. Snow proposed a new chronology which reset the date at October 22, 1844. Miller, depressed and ill, was reluctant to endorse Snow's recalculation. The new date, however, swept Adventist circles, and, under Himes's prodding, Miller finally endorsed the new prediction.[27]

As the first millennial date approached, Millerism grew at an accelerating rate. The formerly skeptical wondered whether Miller might not be correct after all. In any case, by that time Himes's incessant propagandizing had made Miller's name a household word. Nonetheless, the aggressive move into urban areas was in fact double-edged, exposing Millerism to scoffers as well as to potential converts, for it coincided with the first great American newspaper circulation war, between James Gordon Bennett's *Herald* and Horace Greeley's *Tribune*. Bennett seized upon the Millerite camp meeting at Newark in November 1842 to run a sensational ten-installment feature with accompanying cartoons, later reprinted as an eight-page tabloid "extra." The "end of the world" theme proved an excellent circulation builder, and for the next two years Millerism was caricatured, lampooned, and defamed in the mass press.[28] Despite the *Herald*'s attacks on "prophetic fevers and millennium inflammations," Joshua Himes sent the paper a letter of thanks, presumably on the principle that any publicity is good publicity; and, indeed, the Newark meeting, for whatever reason, attracted 6,000.

While the *Tribune* was equally hostile to Miller's ideas, Greeley mounted the attack in a far different manner. On March 2, 1843—nineteen days before the period of Advent expectation was to begin—Greeley devoted an entire issue to rebuttal. Most of the front page was given over to a reproduction of one of the Millerites' famous chronological charts, with vivid engravings of the beasts and trumpeters of Revelation. Unable to accommodate the chart in a standard vertical orientation, the *Tribune* reproduced it on its side. Since the paper's front page hardly ever bore visual material more arresting than a one-column headline, one may imagine readers' reactions to the lopsided Biblical menagerie. However, the accompanying essay by a Baptist clergyman from Providence was as turgid a treatment of Scriptural texts as Miller's own. Clearly, for Greeley, Miller's views were too important to poke fun at. The press was equally hostile in Boston, as well as in the smaller cities of the Burned-over District itself.[29]

The more significant expansion of Millerism, however, was through the Burned-over District itself. Under the pressure of ridicule such as Bennett's, Millerism could make relatively little headway after its initial appeal to the curious. In the rural counties of Western New York, however, the climate was more sympathetic. Beginning in the Spring of 1843, Himes and his and Miller's lieutenants finally took their message into the relatively untouched area west of Rome. The short but rapid diffusion of Millerism westward in the third phase effectively shifted its center of gravity away from the large but skeptical Eastern cities.

The more Millerism grew and the closer the final prediction came, the more it resembled a social movement rather than simply a set of deviant beliefs. On the one hand, conventional churchmen became increasingly alarmed at both the beliefs and the sheer numbers of Millerites. With apprehension came hostility; Miller was a competitor, not a colleague. The other side of rejection by the orthodox was the Millerites' own increasing discomfort at remaining affiliated with religious institutions that seemingly were unable to recognize the truth. By 1843, Second Adventists such as Charles Fitch, who considered Millerism's opponents to be Antichrist, urged the faithful to separate from their churches: "If you are a Christian, *come out of Babylon.* If you intend to be found a Christian when Christ appears, *come out of Babylon,* and come out *Now.*"[30] This appeal inaugurated a sectarian phase in which large numbers of Adventists participated.

The failed predictions of 1843–44 progressively and drastically diminished the movement's size. Unfortunately, precise measures of the falloff do not exist, for the period of sectarian development in 1843–44 was too brief to permit the introduction of accurate record-keeping. Those who remained faithful constructed elaborate structures of rationalization, such as Apollos Hale's and Joseph Turner's "closed door" theory, according to which God closed the "door of mercy" on unbelievers on October 22, 1844.[31] Among unbelievers, the Great Disappointment became the lurid stuff of legend. Adventists allegedly put on white "ascension robes," and waited on hilltops for translation into Heaven; sold off or abandoned their property in expectation of the great day; and, most prominently, went mad from disillusionment and despair.

The folklore of Adventism has presented particular problems for the two major modern Adventist churches, the Seventh Day Adventists and the Advent Christians, and nowhere more than on the issue of insanity. Hence one of Millerism's foremost modern apologists, Francis Nichol, contended in 1944 that an examination of New England asylum records showed Millerism to be implicated in only 39 of 1,516 cases, and then almost certainly as a result of error or intolerance.[32] In fact, the psychiatric profession in the 1840s took an exceedingly dim view of any activity that produced "excessive" mental or sensory stimulation. Revival religion, with its strong emotional component, was particularly suspect, and the *American Journal of Insanity* suggested as late as 1845 that Millerism was a greater danger to public health than yellow fever or cholera.[33]

Yet a recent examination of asylum records demonstrates that the relationship between Millerism and insanity may have been more complex than partisans on either side have recognized. Ronald and Janet Numbers found records of 170 admissions for causes related to Millerism. An extensive analysis of case records at three asylums in New Hampshire, Massachusetts, and New York disclosed, on the one hand, that the disappointed predictions did not precipitate breakdowns, but, on the other, that physicians made the admissions on the basis of patients' overt behavior, not because of their beliefs. Millerism could not be held responsible in the majority of the cases, which involved chronic mental disorders, except in the indirect sense that some already disordered persons may have self-selected it. But in approximately 18 percent of the Millerite cases, involving acute, short-term illness,

> Millerism [might] have been a contributing cause of mental disease. The intense emotional excitement of the movement, the inner conflict and confusion induced by dashed hopes and hellish fears, and the exhausting toll on body and mind taken by prolonged exposure to noise, fasting, or deprivation of sleep . . . might well have caused the emotionally vulnerable to crack under the strain.[34]

These individuals clearly constituted a minority of Millerite asylum admissions and a far smaller minority of the movement's rank and file. A far clearer picture of Second Adventism emerges by turning from the disoriented few to the anxious but coping many.

DEMOGRAPHIC CHARACTERISTICS OF THE MILLERITES

Although Millerism began in Eastern New York and enjoyed its early successes there and in New England, the center of gravity of the movement shifted westward to the Burned-over District. At least as many individuals seem to have accepted Miller's teachings in the District as in New England,[35] particularly remarkable in the light of the disparity in size of the two areas. The shift to Western New York State can be documented by the number of towns introduced to Millerism on either side of a north-south line through Rome. Through 1842, contact had been made in fifty-six communities east of Rome and only twenty-seven to the west. Between 1843 and 1845, the relative magnitudes are reversed: fifty-seven east, as against 154 west.[36] In 1843 Miller appeared in Utica, Rochester, Lockport, Buffalo, and Lewiston; lectures in Rochester, Buffalo, and Lockport followed in 1844.

Millerite organizers, particularly Himes, sought to reach the largest possible audiences. The distribution of tracts, the itineraries of lecturers, and the march of the Great Tent tended to be in areas of high population density. When Second Adventism began moving away from the coastal cities, it followed the railroads and canals, where the largest audiences could be assured. Rochester, well situated on transportation arteries and already filled with religious and reformist enterprises, became the center for missionary efforts in the Burned-over District.[37]

In light of the systematic orientation toward urban areas, it is noteworthy that the most intense and enduring Millerite affiliations in fact occurred in relatively under-propagandized rural areas and small towns. The significance of smaller communities became apparent in Millerism's final phase, particularly in 1844–45. Even before the disillusionment of October 1844, conversions in urban areas such as Rochester declined as the most easily reachable audiences were exhausted.[38] Just as the saturation of Eastern New York mandated attention to the West, the saturation of urban areas made the less immediately reachable small-town and rural populations more attractive. In this respect, Millerism follows a pattern apparent in most millenarian movements across many cultures and time periods until the twentieth century—the ascendancy of rural over urban areas.[39] There the faithful benefitted from the greater intimacy of personal relationships, the greater homogeneity of the population, and the relative insulation from systematic opposition.

The strength of Burned-over District rural areas was especially evident as predictions came and went. Members least likely to leave the movement were those in the small towns of Western New York. Indeed, the movement actually continued to grow there after October 1844 and into 1845.

These back-country sanctuaries appear to have maintained themselves in part through the out-migration of committed Millerites from major cities, where ridicule and even mob violence prevented the holding of public meetings.[40] Millerites were able to maintain a critical mass of committed members more readily in sparsely settled and less sophisticated areas.

Not all rural areas were equally affected. The counties on the Pennsylvania border, known as the Southern Tier, were almost wholly unaffected, and although Miller had begun in the eastern part of the state, the Hudson Valley was untouched. Geographical distribution was strongly related to migration patterns. The Southern Tier counties, for example, were populated heavily by persons who had migrated from Pennsylvania. The Hudson Valley was a long-settled area, whose population was already stable and indigenous at the beginning of the nineteenth century. Millerite areas, by contrast, were peopled by recent migrants of New England origins. Although transportation of Western New England had only begun about 1790, by 1830 the Yankee character of the Burned-over District was already established.[41]

The geographical distribution of Millerism provides clues to its social composition. Finneyite revivals were particularly attractive to the newly affluent urban middle class.[42] Millerism seems to have had a special appeal for solid but somewhat less-well-off citizens. David Rowe's analysis of 116 Millerite leaders in the Burned-over District suggests that even its elite blended rural and urban, farmers, artisans, and merchants. Indeed, their occupations as recorded in the 1850 census (albeit several years after the event) show that almost 20 percent were farmers, as against 6 percent who were merchants, and 13 percent craftsmen. About half—45 percent—were identified as ministers, a figure which almost certainly reflects the disproportionate number of clergy in the leadership stratum, and may not adequately reflect their actual sources of livelihood. Twenty percent were engaged in occupations that were clearly non-rural, and 2.4 percent were professionals.[43] It is reasonable to assume that individuals who took community leadership roles possessed higher social status than other Millerites whose names are lost to the historical record. The high proportions of farmers and artisans parallels the composition of Mormonism in its early Burned-over District phase.[44]

Second Adventism thus struck its deepest roots among rural and small-town New Yorkers of New England birth or ancestry. They were neither conspicuously rich nor strikingly poor. Rather, they were solid, established individuals, with places in the community, skilled enough to prosper in reasonably good times. Like so many participants in pre-industrial social movements their most striking characteristic was their very typicality.

AWAY FROM THE GREAT DISAPPOINTMENT

Millerites took three routes away from the failed predictions of 1843–44. Presumably the greatest number found their way back into conventional religious denominations, although we shall never know how large a proportion simply melted back into American Protestantism. A far smaller number of confirmed Adventists, accepting rationalizations for the failed predictions, sought some enduring mode of organization. The most significant of these groups became, under the leadership of James White, Joseph Bates, and, later, Ellen G. White, the Seventh Day Adventist Church, which grew from 200 members in 1850 to 3,500 at the point of its formal organization in 1863.[45]

The third route is in many respects the most interesting, for it was traversed by those Adventists traumatized by the failures yet yearning for a continued sense of millennial mission within an enclosed community. Those who did so by migrating to already existing utopian communities, notably the Shakers, will be considered in a later chapter. Here it remains to describe those who confronted failed predictions by creating separate communities of their own. At least three such communities can be identified: the Germania Company (1856–79), in Germania, Marquette County, Wisconsin; Adonai Shomo, also known as the Community of Fullerites, (1861–97) in Worcester County, Massachusetts; and Celesta (1863–64) in Sullivan County, Pennsylvania.

Like many utopian communities, the Germania Company and Adonai Shomo left few traces. Both appear to have grown out of contacts made at an Adventist camp meeting held in Groton, Massachusetts, in 1855, eleven years after the Great Disappointment. The insubstantial evidence that remains is in part attributable to their exceedingly small size, for Adonai Shomo began with about 10 members and grew to only 25 or 30, while Germania began with 6 families and 5 single members.[46] By the end of the century, Adonai Shomo did not seem identifiably Millerite. Materials collected by the Oneida Community scholar of communitarianism, William Hinds, emphasize its "seventh day Sabbath" and vegetarianism. This suggests that the doctrines of Ellen White, one of the founders of Seventh-day Adventism, dominated.[47] White had combined Adventist theology with a seventh-day (i.e., Saturday) Sabbath and a strong emphasis on health and diet reform as religious obligations.

The shortest-lived community, Celesta, maintained the clearest ties to Millerite teachings. Its founder, Peter Armstrong, sought to establish a mountain retreat where the 144,000 saints of the Book of Revelation would gather at the Judgment. Although the community itself was very small, its newspaper, *The Day Star of Zion,* was widely distributed. Its first issue claimed a printing of 3,000 copies and 1,200 subscribers, and lists of financial contributors contain individuals as far distant as Minnesota, Oregon, and England.[48] Early issues were heavily concerned with attempts to fend off the attentions of government. Believing that the Advent had not occurred only because too few believed in it, the stalwart Armstrong asserted that "we are no longer in subjection to earthly governments." This produced some practical problems, not the least of which was the necessity of ignoring Civil War conscription. The failure of the subsequent prosecution led Armstrong to assume the operations of a higher power: "Why did not the war department put our faith to the test. The answer is obvious.—Their times are ended." Lest any other arms of the state become similarly intrusive, Celesta petitioned the Pennsylvania legislature to be considered "peaceable aliens and religious wilderness exiles from the rest of the Commonwealth of Pennsylvania."[49]

Although none of the Millerite communities was in the Burned-over District, at least two of the three had considerable ties with New York State. The Germania Co. appears to have been composed at the outset of groups from Rochester, N.Y., and from Massachusetts. By the 1940s, however, it had completely assimilated to its Midwestern religious environment. The later members included both Lutherans and Catholics, and the community itself built the local Methodist Episcopal church.[50] As for Celesta, indirect evidence is available from the lists of contributors published in the *Day Star,* for whom state of residence is given. The 1864 issues list 245 contributors spread over 20 states and England. The vast majority, as might be imagined, were from the Northeast and Middle West. But, there were more New Yorkers (33) than those of any other state, followed by Maine (26), Connecticut (25), and Massachusetts (17). Curiously, only 15 were Pennsylvanians.

There may have been a fourth Millerite community with Burned-over District origins. In about 1850, Thomas Lake Harris and more than a hundred followers established the Second Adventist community of Mountain Cove in Fayette County, Virginia (now West Virginia). The group dissolved in about 1853. Harris went on to become well known as a prolific writer of spiritualist literature and as the founder of more stable spiritualist communities later in the century. The possibility of Millerite influence at Mountain Cove derives not only from the community's known Adventist expectations but from its proximity to the Great Disappointment and from the origins of its moving figures. Harris had grown up in Utica, while another leader at Mountain Cove, James L. Scott, came from Auburn, New

York. However, unlike Harris' later ventures, which generated a sea of published and unpublished writings, Mountain Cove vanished leaving little trace.[51]

Millerism was thus a movement of abrupt rhythms. It appeared to come out of nowhere, since few other than those in Miller's home territory knew his ideas until the great Himes-directed campaigns. Onlookers, observing Millerism at its zenith, perceived its growth to be as rapid (and as apparently irrational) as fashion. The collapse of Miller's predictions seemed to be followed by the rapid collapse of the movement, although the actual magnitude of the reduction is difficult to measure and, as we shall see, invalidated predictions may have been the least of its problems.

What unquestionably increased public fascination was that so many should rally so quickly behind so colorless a figure as Miller. While contemporary descriptions note the depth and sincerity of his personal commitment, he seems utterly lacking in glamour and magnetism. How then could he have drawn so many from their accustomed beliefs and behavior? An important part of his and the movement's appeal lay in situational factors which predisposed the otherwise skeptical. We shall examine those factors in detail in chapters six and seven. Environmental forces increased the plausibility and legitimacy of Miller's message, and without that message, the environmental factors alone would not have produced a distinctly millenarian response. If people did not respond dramatically to Miller's personality, they did grasp excitedly at his ideas, and it is to the intellectual framework of Millerism that we now turn.

3

THE IMAGERY OF APOCALYPSE

 WILLIAM MILLER'S own writings were singularly free of rhetorical excess. His principal work, *Evidence From Scripture and History of the Second Coming of Christ About the Year 1843,*[1] advances its argument with plodding deliberateness. Miller manipulated Biblical chronology with the familiarity of one who had pondered many years before putting pen to paper, but, perhaps because he was an autodidact, meticulous concern for detail overrode emotion. His obsessive interest in the books of Daniel and Revelation resulted from the belief that their ambiguous symbols could be decoded in order to yield a chronology from Creation to the Last Judgment. Miller rarely wrote about modern events and only then as validations of Biblical prophecies. The Millerite press, on the other hand, consistently sought to validate prophecies by recourse to the news of the day. Hardly an issue of *Signs of the Times* or *The Midnight Cry* went by without a digest of recent events filled with millennial import.

The Millerite publications thus continued the search for portents that had occupied millenarians since the Middle Ages. They reasoned that since God acted in history, historical events carried double meanings. On one level they had consequences for human beings in the affairs of everyday life; what happened in the world necessarily made some people better off and others worse. On a second level, they constituted a code. Just as the symbols in sacred books required translation so that their deeper significance could be understood, so seemingly mundane events needed to be decoded so that their spiritual messages could be read.

Always in search of techniques for reaching out to the public, Miller-ism's most arresting form of pedagogy was the chart, in which a combination of words and pictures described the correlations Miller had drawn between Biblical time and world history. The awesome imagery of the Book Revelation, with its beasts and trumpeters, here takes on an almost whimsical appearance. *Courtesy Loma Linda University Heritage Room*

The New Testament Book of Revelation was perhaps the critical text in this enterprise, for it combined a dramatic apocalyptic scenario with symbols that were as ambiguous as they were vivid. With its seven seals, seven angel trumpeters, and seven bowls of wrath, Revelation simultaneously beckoned and frustrated generations of interpreters. Yet its climactic vision of "a new heaven and a new earth" implied that if its enigmas could be solved, the solution would reveal with exactitude the timing of the millennium. For once the meaning of the text was clarified, it would then establish the eschatological import of real-world events. Integral to the millenarian world view was the belief that out of the welter of life on earth, a special category of events existed whose significance was simultaneously mundane and transcendant. To capture the transcendant significance, the role of these events in the divine scheme, it was necessary first to know the divine plan. Since that plan was set out in canonical texts, only after the texts had been penetrated could the cosmic chronology of world events be established.

Hence millenarian writings reflect a double decoding process, one aspect of which involved ambiguous scriptural passages, the other of which involved equally ambiguous real world events. Neither could be done successfully without the other. Biblical symbols disclosed their meanings by an application of exegetical rules (such as the "year-day" rule according to which each day mentioned in a text constituted a year of historic time), and by the judicious selection of historic figures and events to correspond to the symbols. But events alone were an unordered chaos that had to be reduced to manageable proportions, and a knowledge of Biblical categories aided in this winnowing process. Miller himself began with the text, and moved from them to events. The testimony of Second Adventist periodicals suggests that the followership was far more concerned with the ambiguity of events, doubtless because Miller's Biblical interpretations had reduced their scriptural uncertainty, but also because temporal events continually emphasized the disordered state of the empirical world.

Millerites tried to reduce the disorder by distinguishing between those events that carried a divine message and those that did not. Most events were not deemed to be portents and could be safely disregarded. Those that remained were of truly momentous significance, for, if properly understood, they held the secret of the end-time. On the strength of Biblical precedents, Second Adventists recognized two categories of portents: political upheavals and disturbances in the natural world. War, civil strife, and the toppling of governments counted heavily among portentous events; so too did natural disasters such as earthquakes, storms, and volcanic eruptions. What was omitted was as significant as what was included. Social and economic conditions were important only insofar as they might have direct political consequences. The depression of the late 1830s and early 1840s was mentioned only in passing, and slavery scarcely alluded to, despite Miller's well-known abolitionist views. The plight of the urban poor, when noted at all, was often viewed through the lens of anti-Catholic nativism.

WAR AND RUMORS OF WAR

Millerite commentaries on threats to peace were of two kinds: On the one hand, Adventists were always on the alert for war between major European powers. The more likely a continent-wide conflagration, the nearer the Second Coming must be. On the other hand, there was a more specialized concern, particularly intense in 1840–41, for the fate of the Ottoman Empire. The Empire occupied a special position in Millerite calculations because of the belief that a significant Ottoman defeat was the empirical correlate of events described in the Book of Revelation.

War between the Great Powers always seemed imminent, yet always was avoided at the last moment: "The late accounts from Europe and Asia, relating to the unprecedented preparations for war, and particularly the dissensions among the principle nations of Europe, we think very clearly shows that the 'spirits of devils' has actually gone forth to the kings of the earth to gather them to battle."[2]

If this seemed the case in May 1840, the final combat appeared even closer in March of the following year, when "it now requires but a spark to set the whole world in a blaze!" In large part, the expectation of war lay in the belief that Catholic and Protestant powers were set implacably against one another, a common seventeenth-century millenarian theme now transposed, ironically, to the era of the post-Napoleonic balance of power: "Let things run on in this train a few years longer, and the points of exasperating collision continue to multiply ... and such a popular feeling will be raised as will merge all other conflicting interests in itself, and range the several nations in a general war, for and against popery; such a war as prophecy makes that to be, which is immediately to precede the universal peace."[3]

The hoped-for war did not of course come in 1841, or in 1842. Yet in 1843 expectation remained high enough so that even the harmonious course of international relations could be reinterpreted as "the calm that precedes the hurricane." "Things cannot long thus continue," *Signs of the Times* wrote. "Affairs must soon arrive at a crisis."[4] Peace was a matter of appearances that could not endure: "While the war-like attitude of nations has waxed and waned, and at times almost, (apparently) settled down with a guarantee of peace ... a change has again spread a cloud over the world's civil and political horizon, which, at each recurrence has become more dark and foreboding."[5]

The same unquenchable faith was evident in discussions of "the Eastern question," the Great Power rivalries in the Levant. Operating on "the worse, the better" logic favored by premillennialists, Millerites kept close track of deteriorating conditions in the Ottoman Empire. Fear of Russian influence in Constantinople and of potential Russian control of the Straits brought Britain, France, Austria, and Prussia into the convoluted politics of the Empire. During the Summer and Fall of 1840, the powers jockeyed for position. The French, supporting Muhammed Ali, the rebellious Ottoman governor of Egypt, were arrayed against the Russians, Austrians, Prussians, and the Sultan, all anxious for their own reasons to quash Muhammed Ali's separatist ambitions. An Anglo-Austrian attack on Syria and Lebanon was required to root out Ali's forces. In the end the Sultan's throne was nominally secured, the five European powers all became equally involved in the Empire's politics, and the Straits were closed to warships of all nations.[6]

Before the 1841 settlement, however, the outcome was not so clear. As the lines of battle were drawn, the most audacious Millerite interpretation came from the pen of Josiah Litch, a young Methodist minister who had embraced Second Adventism. On August 1, 1840, Litch predicted that the Ottoman Empire would in fact fall August 11.[7] Like millenarians before and after, he sought to place these events within the ambiguous scenario provided by the New Testament Book of Revelation. Revelation's author, proceeding through traditional sequences of seven's, placed the apocalypse at the end of the breaking of seven seals, the sounding of seven angel trumpeters, and the pouring of seven bowls of wrath. Litch identified the defeat of the Ottomans with the conclusion of the sixth angel's trumpet blast, which would leave only the seventh angel's call before the literal beginning of the end (Revelation, chpt. 11). August 11 came and went. An English-Austrian-Ottoman force bombarded Ali's troops in Beirut and landed in early October 1840. The *Signs of the Times* greeted the Beirut attack with the observation that "a general war is inevitable; the kings of the earth and the whole world will be involved."[8] Litch could hardly contain himself. He wrote Himes: "What a prospect! Nothing short of one universal blaze of war all over the world can be anticipated."[9]

By the time calm returned to the Eastern Mediterranean, Millerites had to face the question of what it had all meant. Despite the small matter of August 11, Litch remained confident, explaining that what actually had happened on the eleventh was the beginning of the Ottomans' irreversible political decline: "I am entirely satisfied that on the 11th of August, 1840, *The Ottoman power according to previous calculation,* DEPARTED TO RETURN NO MORE. I can now say with the utmost confidence, 'the second woe is past and behold the third woe cometh quickly.'"[10] Litch argued that on August 11, the European powers had tendered an ultimatum to Ali to end his rebellion, thus assuming effective control over the internal affairs of the Empire. Unfortunately, as Eric Anderson has pointed out, Litch's hypothesis was non-falsifiable, for it was validated if the powers intervened effectively, but also would have been validated if Ali's rebellion had succeeded, for that too would have diminished the Sultan's power.[11] Matters never being as they seemed, Adventists were still writing in 1843 that "every indication ... is that the nations of the eastern world are fast approaching a crisis the result of which man cannot predict."[12]

The great apocalyptic war never came, of course, in the Near East or in Europe, at least not in the Millerites' lifetimes. Indeed, there was scarcely a worse time to indulge in such predictions than the 1840s, since the 1815 settlement at Vienna still held fast and limited war remained the rule. Thus, in a period of unprecedented international order, Millerites were reduced to chasing alarms of war and then rationalizing away its non-appearance.

SOCIAL AND POLITICAL INSTABILITY

The two major Millerite periodicals—*Signs of the Times* in Boston and *The Midnight Cry* in New York—paid close attention to social and political instability. Generally, however, poverty and civil strife were not considered to be themselves portents of millennial transformation. Rather, they were moderately useful data from which the imminence of revolution might be inferred, or simply additional evidence of the general moral decline presumed to accompany the "latter days." Although most such information was consequently cast in a subordinate role, a major exception was the influx of poor Catholic immigrants and the rise of an American Catholic Church. Both publications took up the hackneyed theme of Protestant nativism.

Direct references to poverty were relatively rare in the Adventist press, despite the economic pressures of the early 1840s. There were occasional queries as to why "distress, despondency and gloom" should persist "while we have means of prosperity and happiness so abundant," but the anonymous author took these social speculations no further.[13] A more eloquent yet resigned statement came from a postmaster writing from Steuben

County in southern New York State: "Nearly half of our population want bread. What grain there is, is principally in speculators' hands, and can't be had without money, and that is not to be had. ... Such things will be in the latter days."[14] This letter is remarkable not only for its description of rural poverty but because it is one of the few Millerite writings that suggests any interest in the fiscal and economic forces at work in American society.

Millerites were in fact far more interested in English than American poverty: "The gloom that overspreads the manufacturing districts of England is apparently increasing rather than diminishing. ... Thus, the distress of nations is accumulating on every hand."[15] The civil strife of early industrial England received extended coverage, less because of the human suffering than because of the revolution it portended: "The internal state of England is like a vast volcano that may at any moment explode."[16] This was a matter of some consequence not simply because armed violence was generally portentous, but because the fate of great powers was especially important. All other things being equal, therefore, an event in England was more noteworthy than the same event in America. In noting poverty and social unrest in England in the Summer of 1843, *The Midnight Cry* observed: "the Lord is calling us to look at the fulfillment of prophecy in the greatest government of the world, one which takes the lead among the so-called civilized and Christian nations."[17] Millenarians generally dwelt on themes of social and political inversion: "the last shall be first and the first shall be last." Consequently, any news that might suggest the imminent fall of the mighty was important; poverty and social unrest were not nearly as significant when they occurred in America.

Notwithstanding the importance accorded foreign news, political disturbances in America were duly noted, although Millerite observers were not always sure precisely what they meant. No Josiah Litch arose to correlate American politics with the Book of Revelation. In response to the disarray of political parties under President John Tyler, *Signs of the Times* could only conclude: "What will be the end of these things, it is impossible to foresee. But one lesson we may all learn from this state of things, and that is, 'not to put our trust in princes.' "[18]

Perhaps because *Signs of the Times* was published in Boston, the constitutional crisis known as the "Dorr Rebellion" was the subject of extensive reporting and comment during the Spring and Summer of 1842. Opposed to the restrictive franchise in Rhode Island, Thomas Dorr and his followers sought to introduce and implement a new state constitutional document to replace the existing one, which scarcely differed from the old colonial charter. The rift between the Dorr forces, advancing their unofficial "constitution," and the legislature, at first willing to make only token vot-

ing reforms, led to virtual civil war, which ended in the defeat of the Dor-
rites. The Dorr Rebellion was important primarily as an indicator of the
public's nervous irritability: "It may be considered one of the signs of the
times—of the combustible material of which the present age is composed
... such is the intolerance, irritability, recklessness, and feverish state of the
public mind, that aside from Miller's views, many are predicting and expecting, near at hand, some terrible convulsion in the moral, if not the natural world."[19]

In the same way, mob violence in America meant something, yet Millerites were never sure quite what: "How far this spirit of violence may be
considered portentous of the final overthrow and destruction of a world of
wickedness, by a justly offended God, every one of course will be left to form
his own opinion."[20]

Where Catholics were concerned, however, there was neither coyness
nor mere generalities. The identification of the Pope with the Antichrist had
become a convention of Protestant chiliasts, imported to America along
with other Reformation motifs. Millerite excoriations of the Pope consequently fell within the mainstream of Protestant millenarian thought: "He
[the Pope] will continue to make war with the true saints until Christ shall
come a second time without sin unto salvation. Then the Beast, False
Prophet, and Dragon will be destroyed together, and the millennial reign
will commence."[21]

Anti-Catholic themes received a new edge from the Catholic immigration which began in the 1820s. The anti-Catholicism of Protestant millennialists, virtually unchanged since the sixteenth and seventeenth centuries, now fused with the economic, social, and political resentments of
American nativists, who saw in the Catholic immigrants an alien, unas-
similable element. One had only to open the floodgates for America to be
drowned in a sea of politically ambitious yet devious Catholics:

> Give the Catholics the power and the occasion, which is never long
> wanted, and *submission or death would be the only alternatives!*

> The Roman Catholics already number their millions in the United
> States, and nearly 100,000 are added to the number yearly by emigra-
> tion. They already vaunt loudly, ask strong favors of state governments,
> and are getting them allowed. Papacy is almost wholly allied with one
> of the corrupt political parties in our land [presumably the Democrats],
> which bids fair to control the nation.[22]

The Midnight Cry displayed a special fondness for the melodramatic "Mississippi Valley conspiracy," according to which Catholic secret societies

would attempt to convert the apparently gullible inhabitants of the Valley, flood it with pliable Irish Catholic immigrants, and politically separate it from the rest of the country. Although this particular nativist fairytale had its vogue in the 1830s, Millerites reprinted it from the nativist press a decade later.[23]

DISTURBANCES IN THE NATURAL WORLD

For millenarians the world was a slate upon which God wrote for those who knew how to decipher the message. That message sometimes took the form of the fate assigned to nations in war and revolution. But the physical world, too, contained these putatively divine communications. Two types of natural phenomena drew Millerites' attention—astronomical anomalies and natural disasters.

A tradition connecting the end of the world with unusual natural occurrences had persisted through the early nineteenth century. Dire implications were drawn from sudden darkening of the mid-day sky on November 12, 1807; the total solar eclipse of June 16, 1808; the spectacular auroral display of 1827; and the dramatic meteor shower of November 13, 1833.[24] Millerism consequently reinforced a pre-existing popular apprehension concerning untoward natural events.

Several such events conveniently occurred in 1843. Some thought they saw a cross on the face of the moon. Others noted lights and haloes around Venus and Jupiter.[25] The most dramatic sign of all was the comet that came in February, and prompted one Signs of the Times reader to comment, "I could not but think of 'the Signs of the Son of Man in Heaven.' "[26]

Not content merely to catalog contemporary occurrences, Millerites combed past records for puzzling celestial phenomena. They claimed to find evidence that fixed stars were disappearing and that the Northern Lights had only become visible in the 1700s.[27] They were particularly fascinated by reports of the earlier "Dark Day," when on May 19, 1780, the daylight sky had gone to near blackness from eastern New York to Maine. Ezra Stiles had attributed the "Dark Day" to the smoke of forest fires. A stationary weather front seems to have trapped the polluted air until it cut off the sun's rays. Stiles likened the sudden darkness to "the miraculous Eclipse at the Crucifixion of our Blessed Savior."[28] In the revivalist atmosphere of the time, the "Dark Day" was an unimpeachable sign to many of the nearing end and was in fact the stimulus for the first major Shaker missionary campaign in New England.[29]

The Millerites collected such nuggets with the same eagerness with which they greeted the rise in international tensions. Yet they were at the same time troubled by the fact that neither past nor present celestial events had the desired effect on the general population: "Many years ago these signs were noticed but not sneered at. Now, when they are more numerous, and better authenticated, they are either denied or laughed at."[30] The popular skepticism was especially vexing, since heavenly portents seemed to be incontrovertible public proof. "Many ask for more signs [of the Second Advent], but the more they are multiplied, the less effect they will produce."[31]

Some portents were simply marvels, meant to astonish and disconcert humanity. Others, however, touched human lives through their power to kill and destroy. The portentous significance of disasters was not lost on the Millerites, who habitually linked political and natural disturbances. Thus under the headline "Earthquakes, Conflagrations, and Moral and Political Convulsions," one Adventist wrote that they were "signs of the times, which were foretold to take place in the latter days."[32] This led to a dogged selectivity with which the news of the day was read, for it appeared to constitute an endless litany of misfortune: "The pen grows weary in recording—and the press in publishing the daily records of desolating earthquakes, sweeping fires, distressing poverty, natural perplexity, political profligacy, private bankruptcy, and wide-spread immorality, which abound in these last days."[33]

While fires and volcanic eruptions were given their due, great storms and earthquakes seemed to have the greatest power to rouse even the most fatalistic collector of dour events. A collection of shipwreck and storm tales bore the brisk Biblical heading, "The Sea and the Waves Roaring,"[34] and the Lisbon earthquake, although it had taken place eighty-eight years earlier, was still well remembered, for with it Revelation's sixth seal was thought to have been opened.[35]

The most difficult problem with earthquakes lay in their prediction. Actual earthquakes begat prophecies of future earthquakes. London, for example, had experienced two moderately strong earthquakes four weeks apart in 1750, and panic overtook many people four weeks later in the expectation of a third, which never occurred.[36] The Millerites' own earthquake predicament was somewhat more complicated. They were not living in a place or time when earthquakes were frequent, and none seem to have occurred in America during the years of high Millerite activity. On the other hand, Adventists believed that they possessed independent and altogether reliable evidence that the millennium was imminent; and if the millennium *was* imminent, then earthquakes *should* occur. The theoretical framework within which Millerites operated thus made earthquake prediction plausible and tempting. The difficulty, as they well recognized, was that previous earthquake predictions had often been incorrect, and that a false prediction on a matter of such high public interest and visibility could only increase the ridicule from which they already suffered in the popular and religious press. Their vulnerability does not appear to have been lost upon their adversaries, for in early 1843 anonymous handbills in Boston prophesied an imminent tremor. An Ohio Adventist who had heard about the handbills implored "our Second Advent friends at the east tell us what is true respecting the matter." The editors of *The Midnight Cry* replied that it was simply "too clumsy a hoax to require notice ... utterly without foundation."[37] Yet the very issue that contained this lofty disclaimer also carried an article on the contemporary frequency of earthquakes.

As it had been for the chiliasts of earlier centuries, the world was filled with mysterious but decipherable correspondences: Biblical texts could be joined with past and present events, and politics and morals were reflected in the movements of earth, sea, and sky. Seemingly discrete or random events took their places for initiates in an elaborate web of divinely guided interconnections. There could be correlations but not coincidences.

Some events might be so inherently dramatic, such as the "Dark Day," that most individuals might be driven by them to reflect upon the state of the world. But the language of portents was in its own way a technical vocabulary whose manipulation depended upon a knowledge of sacred texts and an ability to sort out the portentous from the trivial. In the hands of devoted and virtuosic practitioners, these manipulations produced a view of the world quite different from that of skeptics. William Lloyd Garrison, apparently at least an occasional reader of *Signs of the Times*, wrote:

> It is amusing to see how the most ordinary events are cited by the advocates of this new theory [Millerism], as proofs that "the day of the Lord is at hand." The fire at Hamburgh—the earthquake at Cape Haitien—falling of the chandelier in the U.S. House of Representatives— the pecuniary embarrassments of the times—these, and many other equally *remarkable* occurrences, are set forth as solemn warnings.[38]

Garrison's heavy-handed sarcasm aside, the point was that events deemed "most ordinary" by unbelievers were "extraordinary" to the Millerites, believing themselves in possession of the means to decode the news of the day.

The events of daily life are inherently ambiguous. Devoid of inherent meaning, significance must be given to them by both spectators and participants. In the usual transactions that constitute normal social life, the act of

ascribing meaning takes place so frequently and is so facilitated by a reper-
toire of cultural categories that we are scarcely aware it occurs at all. The
ascription of meaning becomes a conscious process for those who possess
an unorthodox system of beliefs, as well as for those who battle ideological
deviants, as Garrison had to reassert the criteria of "ordinariness" in the
face of Adventist claims.

Belief in divine providence was scarcely absent from American society
in the 1840s, when evangelical Protestantism was a vital force. Yet two significant historic shifts had given most Protestants a world view antagonistic
to traditional portents. In the first place, postmillennialism, anchored in a
commitment to free will, made the individual soul rather than the external
environment the primary arena for the clash between good and evil. In the
second place, a growing naturalism allied to the growth of the sciences in-
vested the natural order with a harmony reflective of divine design. Postmillennialism made gradual spiritual advancement crucial, rather than a
mechanistic scheme of abrupt, stepwise ascents. Naturalism altered the significance of portents. Where millenarians were once accustomed to emphasizing breaks in the pattern—prodigies and disasters—now the very pattern itself bespoke divine concern.

The Millerite framework for organizing reality was thus at odds with
those cultural forces most closely linked to American optimism—belief in
the power of the individual will and confidence in the cumulative effects of
gradual improvement. Saving souls could alter individual fates at the time
of judgment, but it could not alter the timetable itself. In like manner, the
reformers' scale of improvement seemed pathetically modest beside the Millerites' cataclysmic overturning.

In the end it was a question of who offered the more convincing construction of reality, the Millerites with their savior descending from the
clouds or their postmillennialist adversaries urging that effort and patience
would reap an eventual reward, even if the generation now living would
never see it. While it is a gross oversimplification to characterize the debate
as between optimists and pessimists, each emphasized different kinds of
evidence and envisioned the future in different terms. Second Adventism offered a world view drastically different than that of the postmillennial revivalists, a world view in which progress was a mirage, calamity and conflict
the norm, and stability an illusion. Second Adventism took nothing about
the present for granted except that it would become continually less stable
until it ceased to exist altogether.

IMPLICATIONS OF MILLERISM

The brevity of Millerism, together with its unconventional beliefs, have given it the character of a historical footnote—a brief, atypical episode neither related to nor consequential for the shaping flow of events. Yet Millerism also demands to be taken seriously, if only as a function of its size and notoriety. In doing so, we would do well to bear in mind Christopher Hill's advice to scholars of Puritan millenarianism: "Each generation ... rescues a new area from what its predecessors arrogantly and snobbishly dismissed as 'the lunatic fringe.' "[39]

The Millerites were ironically the victims of their own success. The Great Disappointment was, of course, a major cause of rapidly dropping membership, yet prophetic disconfirmation does not fully explain their decline. The continuation of an Adventist cadre after 1844 begs the question: If some members found it possible to continue on the basis of post-October 1844 rationalizations, why were more not able to do so? The problem is already well-known in millenarian studies, on the basis of the cognitive dissonance argument offered by Festinger, Riecken, and Schachter, who argue that a contradiction between strongly held beliefs and disconfirming evidence produces tension which the individual wishes to resolve. He or she may do so by either explaining away the disturbing evidence or accepting the more traumatic necessity of jettisoning the beliefs. The analysis of Millerism by Festinger et al. produced curiously mixed conclusions, in large part attributable to the incomplete data from which they worked. Looking back on the 1843–44 sequence of prediction-disappointment-new prediction, they saw the new prediction as evidence of the tenacity of millenarian beliefs. They saw in its post-1844 failure evidence of the final power of irrefutable evidence: "Although there is a limit beyond which belief will not withstand disconfirmation, it is clear that the introduction of contrary evidence can serve to increase the conviction and enthusiasm of a believer."[40] Each disappointment was a stimulus to new predictions until multiplying disconfirmations broke the cycle. The cycle was broken, they added, because rank-and-file Millerites did not utilize the single device that can most successfully fend off disillusionment—the search for converts. From a social psychological viewpoint, "if more and more people can be persuaded that the system of beliefs is correct, then clearly it must, after all, be correct. ... If everyone in the whole world believed something there would be no question at all as to the validity of this belief."[41]

Millerite proselytizing did apparently fall off by late 1844. On the other hand, there had earlier been enough itinerant, unofficial Adventist preachers to suggest that many Millerites had a heavy psychological investment in their beliefs. When the final disappointment came, the movement turned inward. In part, this was a consequence of the movement's headlong growth earlier, which produced adherents faster than the organization could absorb them and led to factionalism, particularly through the militancy of Burned-over District members. After October, the attention of remaining Millerites turned to questions of internal control and the resolution of factional strife. Himes, ever the organizer, was clearly more interested in the future locus of decision-making within the small surviving movement than in embarking upon a new campaign for converts. Miller, ill and disappointed, played a diminished role in the mid-1840s.

Beyond questions of personality, the movement's declining energy was related to its spatial distribution. Himes's masterly command of communications media dictated the search for urban converts, yet in the end it was the rural areas that held on. Clearly, as astute as Himes was in raising public enthusiasm, he had somehow misjudged his audiences. The communications media that produced proselytes could also produce ridicule and even violent attacks. Miller had begun in small-town America, and in a real sense that is where Millerism ended.

Finally, the abrupt end of Millerism raises issues concerned with millenarianism and social protest. Millerites had few qualms about attacking the evil in the world, yet they did so without addressing political issues. Although many had had experience in movements of social reform, they did not steer Millerism into such well-worn channels as abolitionism. Financially pressed though Millerite farmers apparently were, one searches in vain for overt themes of agrarian radicalism. These were not Populists obsessed with conspiracies or fiscal panaceas. The evil of the world lay in its inattentiveness to moral precepts and its lack of religious observance rather than in the oppressive use of power by one group against another. Those drawn to Miller came because they thought he was right rather than because they felt his prophecies would advance their personal interests. Elites in the communities Millerism touched were sometimes patronizing but were often curious and sympathetic, suggesting little fear of social upheaval.

The Second Adventists' disdain for social protest was particularly surprising since many were victims of economic dislocations and had much to be angry about. The absence of anger in the movement does not suggest that its members enjoyed an extraordinary sense of well-being or that they possessed a stoicism their neighbors lacked. Rather, Millerism's apolitical tone was a direct consequence of the system of portent analysis described in this chapter.

Millerism had no room for social protest because its intellectual structure could accommodate only the stereotypical events of the latter days—

the wars, celestial marvels, and natural disasters already identified as the essential eschatological signs. Occurrences that failed to fit within these categories might be personally significant, but they were theologically trivial.

The anxieties of the 1840s were thus discharged by a circuitous route. The stuff of protest was transmuted into the elaborate and archaic language of chiliastic expectation. The imagery of war and disaster was, like referred pain, an expression of troubles that lay elsewhere.

THE GROWTH OF UTOPIAN COMMUNITIES

THE UTOPIAN ALTERNATIVE

 THE ESCHATOLOGICAL DRAMA of the 1840s did not revolve exclusively around Millerism. A very different kind of millenarian activity appeared alongside Second Adventism: utopian communities. These social experiments occurred in approximately the same region as the religious excitations, but their small size and indrawn character bespoke a quite different style. The communities did not have the capacity to absorb large numbers, even where, as in the case of the Shakers, they actively sought new members. Despite their small size, they attracted attention far out of proportion to their numbers.

Many of the communities were shaped by religious goals. They sought to preserve distinctive forms of worship and unorthodox theologies. Nonetheless, even the manifestly religious groups contained secular elements. The best-known utopian practices involved more than narrowly religious subjects and addressed the role of women, the structure of the family, the organization of work, the distribution of property, and the regulation of sexual expression. Although conventional, non-communitarian religious groups often held strong beliefs about these issues, their beliefs tended to support prevailing social practices, such as the subordination of women, the primacy of the nuclear family, wage labor, private property, and sex within marriage. The utopian communities, on the other hand, radically challenged them. Their translation of heterodox beliefs into action necessarily involved the justification of new forms of social and economic organization at least as much as the justification of new theological dogmas.

63

This fusion of belief and practice implied a distinctive attitude toward the efficacy of human actions. The postmillennialists projected the perfect society into the future as the cumulative consequence of incremental improvement. The receptivity of postmillennialists to a "politics of benevolence" reflected their confidence that the world could be perfected by a combination of religious observance and social reform. The premillennialists, on the other hand, assumed that the final consummation was an imminent rather than a relatively remote event. The overturning of human institutions consequently would take place in the immediate future. This allowed no time for remedial action, which was in any case considered inadequate to the task. The millennium would be the product of direct divine intervention. The function of human effort was to warn as many as possible, and in so doing to gather a "saving remnant" that would enjoy the fruits of the millennial kingdom.

Utopians fell uneasily into this scheme of classification. On the one hand, the very act of establishing self-contained communities suggested a confidence in human action, for the creation of new institutions made sense only as instruments for the advancement of their members. Although not all utopians subscribed to the belief that a sinless society could be achieved on earth—a tenet of both the Shakers and the Oneida Community—all believed that communal living promoted higher states of individual virtue. A few communities, among them the Adventist Communal groups described in Chapter Two, explicitly saw themselves as anterooms in which the faithful could cluster before entrance into the millennial age.

The Shakers and the Oneida Perfectionists were neither premillennialists nor postmillennialists in any clear sense of the terms. Both have been described, somewhat inelegantly, as "intermillennialist," suggesting that they viewed the present as farther on the road to perfection than did postmillennialists, but the final consummation as more distant than premillennialists claimed.[1]

The Shakers, "Believers in Christ's Second Appearing," incorporated idiosyncratic conceptions of the Second Coming. Their foundress, Mother Ann Lee, had experienced a vision of Christ during the Summer of 1770 in her English prison cell. She had been jailed for "disturbing the peace" in emotional religious services. In the course of the vision, she reported, Christ had urged her to spread the truth she had earlier discovered, that the source of human evil, and the act of disobedience in the Garden of Eden, was sexual intercourse.[2] The Shaker commitment to total celibacy thus figuratively placed Shakers in Eden before the Fall, the perfection which had been lost and must now be regained. As a result of the commitment to celibacy, Shakerism was destined to rely entirely on converts to maintain itself.

Another more controversial Second Adventist doctrine may have developed among Ann's followers after her group moved to America in 1774. That was the claim that just as God had taken male form in the person of Jesus, so the spirit of the divinity was subsequently embodied in Ann Lee.[3] Valentine Rathbun, a Shaker apostate, wrote in 1780, four years before Ann's death, that her followers believed "all God's elect must be born through her; yes, that Christ through her is born the second time."[4] There is no clear evidence that Ann herself held this view, but since much the greater part of Shaker history took place after her death, followers' beliefs may be more significant than her own.

John Humphrey Noyes's millennialism was far more complex and infinitely better recorded through his own voluminous writings and the remarkably candid letters of him and his family. In the summer of 1833, when Noyes was twenty-two, he came to the view that Christ had appeared spiritually to the apostles in A.D. 70, when the Temple in Jerusalem was destroyed by the Romans.[5] Having placed this invisible Second Coming in the past, he accounted for the sadly flawed state of the world by arguing for a distinction between the apostolic church, which had ascended to heaven, and the temporal church, which perpetuated error on earth.[6]

The more serious problems concerned the relationship between the Second Coming of A.D. 70 and the millennium. Had the millennium already occurred? Was it even now in progress? Or had it somehow been deferred? These complications made Noyes ambivalent and defensive in the presence of more decisive premillenarian views.[7] Noyes conceded that "The Devil ... still reigns. ... That great day of the Lord Almighty is yet future." But as he saw it in 1835, "when that day will fully come, knoweth no man, save the Father only, but looking at prophecy and the movements of his providential hand in waking up the world, we cannot but regard it as near."[8] This line of argument, which placed the Second Coming in the distant past and the millennium in the near future, led Noyes to suggest that "a *third* appearance of Christ is approaching."[9] When he came later to rebut Miller, he chose not to emphasize this point, lest he and Miller appear to be arguing simply about numbering. The passage of time seems merely to have increased Noyes's perplexity, and he confessed to one correspondent in 1840 that he was still reluctant to deal with the millennium in print.[10]

These theological concerns were shadowed by Noyes's personal crises. During a protracted nervous breakdown in spring 1834, Noyes was left shaken by a dramatic vision of a physical Second Coming at odds with his own beliefs. Described by Noyes in his *Confessions* fifteen years after the event, the account is worth quoting at length:

I received a baptism of that spirit which has since manifested itself extensively in the form of Millerism. My *doctrinal* views had no affinity with Miller's theory of the Second Advent. I knew that the first judgment took place immediately after the destruction of Jerusalem, and that it was a transaction in the spiritual world. Yet I expected a second judgment at the end of the times of the Gentiles, or rather a second manifestation of the first judgment, i.e., an extension of it to the visible world. The spirit which now came upon me produced an irresistible impression that this manifestation was about to take place immediately. It was a terrible moment. ... After several similar crises, the impression left me, and I received in its stead a persuasion that the judgment of the world will be a gradual spiritual operation, effected by truth and invisible power, without any of the physical machinery which alarms the imaginations of most expectants of the great day.[11]

The experience made a profound impression upon Noyes, terrified by this sudden cataclysmic vision which he was temporarily incapable of throwing off. At about the same time, and apparently still in the vision's grip, he wrote a semi-coherent Adventist letter to his mother: "Do your hearts fail? It [sic] tell you another coming of the Son of Man is at hand. As the lightening shinest from the east even unto the west, so shall his coming be ... Dear Mother, do your hearts fail? If you love God with all your heart Do you keep his commandments? If so, you will stand in the evil day."[12]

Noyes had a second breakdown exactly a year later in New Haven, Connecticut, where his sister Joanna lived. The visit left her certain her brother was deranged "when he begins to talk about his suffering for the world, and that he is immortal, &c."[13] This tantalizing suggestion of identification with Christ occurs nowhere else in documents by or about Noyes. Nonetheless, Joanna's letters show her to be a sober witness whose overriding concern was John's mental health. If her account is accurate, then Noyes was at that time far more similar to Ann Lee than has been thought. Given Noyes's vague but persistent references to a "third coming," he may in 1835 have considered that he himself embodied it, as Ann Lee's followers (and perhaps Ann herself) considered the Shaker Mother to have embodied the Second.

Noyes did not establish his communal group at Putney, Vermont, until 1841, and in Oneida County, New York, until 1848, by which times these episodes were past. Nonetheless, his earlier views of the millennium and Second Coming suggest the tormented chiliast more than they do the clear-eyed planner. Noyes the socioeconomic innovator and community builder replaced but could never obliterate the image of Noyes the reckless spiritual voyager.[14]

The Fourierists, for their part, eschewed the more elaborate forms of chiliastic speculation even as they remained totally committed to the millennium. This avoidance was due to the fact that some were deists, beginning with their French master, Charles Fourier, himself, and including his leading American disciple, Albert Brisbane, while others were liberal Christian ministers, including George Ripley and William Henry Channing.[15]

In any case, the movement required alterations in Fourier's original doctrines, which were bizarre where they were not impenetrable. Since Fourier believed he had discovered nothing less than the secret of the universe (modesty not being his strongest suit), American "Associationists," as they called themselves, tried to prune away elements of his thought that seemed irrelevant to community-building or were unpalatable to Americans. In particular, they tactfully omitted Fourier's discussions of the sexual benefits of utopia, which ranged from virginity for those who wanted it to polymorphous perversity.[16] The master's death in 1837 doubtless made these omissions easier.

The American Fourierism which remained was firmly fixed upon the details of utopian communities themselves, the "phalanxes." But behind the mundane details of social engineering lay a clear commitment to a millennial perfection that the phalanxes would soon realize. As Charles Dana candidly put it in 1844: "Our ulterior aim is nothing less than Heaven on earth."[17] This view was shared by other Fourierists of a religious cast, such as the Pittsburgh theologian H. H. van Amringe, who was in the midst of writing a millenarian tract when he discovered and embraced Associationism: "We ourselves, in this age of the world, are on the eve of . . . a great and terrible day of the Lord," he wrote, but at the same time the Advent, like Noyes's, would be a spiritual rather than a physical event.[18]

Although Albert Brisbane did not employ the conventional millenarian style in his own writings, their millenarian substance is never in doubt. In his old age he recalled the first flood of the Fourierist vision: "I had a vivid conception of a great function as the destiny of . . . humanity; I saw the association of our globe and the humanities upon it with the Cosmic Whole to which they belong."[19] These recollections, although not always correct in detail, faithfully record the millenarianism of Brisbane's past, for much the same lyrical mysticism infused his 1840 essay, *Social Destiny of Man:* "The terrestrial Destiny of man is TO OVERSEE the globe, which is a vast domain confided in his care. . . . If man performs well the noble task delegated to him, he is rewarded for it by the satisfaction of the leading desires of his nature, by: 'General riches, Individual happiness, Reign of Justice, UNITY OF ACTION.' "[20]

Brisbane's appeal lay in the shrewd interweaving of pre- and postmillenarian themes, as well as in the fusion of religious and secular. The possibility of radical, imminent change blended with a Victorian evocation of inevitable progress, and without removing God from the picture, Brisbane effectively emphasized the importance of human effort. The effort required was the unraveling of the divine "social Code," "pre-existing, in the mind of God prior to the creation of each globe."[21] To do Fourier's work was thus to do God's. Brisbane rhapsodically anticipated that "the boon—the Paradise itself will be the Moral Harmony of the Passions in Associative Unity—the Kingdom of Heaven which comes to us in this terrestrial world."[22] It was up to those in this world to grasp the doctrine Fourier and his disciples made available to them and achieve for themselves in one stroke what the premillennialists depended upon God to produce and what the postmillennialists deferred to a distant future.

It has been commonplace to view American utopian experiments as social laboratories in which tinkerers redesigned institutions as inventors might modify machines. One of the communities' most important chroniclers, Arthur Bestor, referred to them as "patent office models of society."[23] While the development of new arrangements for productivity and daily life were surely significant elements of the utopian enterprise, they derived their value, as far as many utopians were concerned, from the fact that they were instruments bringing the millennium nearer. It could be achieved here and now, if only in miniature.

THE RELIGIOUS ORIGINS OF UTOPIAN COMMUNITIES

The millennialism of Shaker, Perfectionist, and Fourierist communities continued a long association of utopian experiments with religious radicalism. The roots of the earliest American communalism lay in European heresy and religious dissent. A heresy-prone region lay diagonally across central and western Europe, stretching from what is now Czechoslovakia through western Germany and into the Low Countries, bridging the Channel to England.[24] Within this zone of endemic religious unrest lay many millenarian sects, whose commitment to total change had sometimes drawn them into physical combat during the religious wars of the Reformation. Defeat tamed them, however, and those that survived did so by learning virtues of political accommodation or withdrawal from temporal affairs. The bellicose Taborites merged into the Moravian Brethren, the once feared Anabaptists who had seized Münster in 1534–35 became Mennonites, and the anti-Cromwellian Fifth Monarchists dissolved into Quakerism.

Beginning in the second half of the seventeenth century, significant numbers of schismatics from this area began to arrive in America.[25] Already politically quiescent, they wished only to be left alone, a predisposition reinforced by linguistic barriers for those who came from German-speaking areas. Even had they wished to resume political militancy, the colonial ambiance did not encourage it. Such old targets as the Papacy were distant, and with neither the means nor the opportunity to strike out at former adversaries, the sectarians threw their energies into the maintenance of enclave communities to preserve their traditional lifestyles. Indeed, "the sect that clung with religious fidelity to its ideal of a completely reconstructed society became more positively communitarian in outlook and policy than it had been in Europe."[26] Eastern Pennsylvania in particular drew German-speaking settlements whose energy and strength of will inspired more secular-minded communitarians later, and brought grudging admiration from their neighbors. The Ephrata Cloister, the Harmonie Society, and Zoar—all founded before 1820—were simply the most conspicuous manifestations of sectarian migration. In larger measure, the whole world of the "Pennsylvania Dutch," both communitarian and non-communitarian, involved the transplantation of the now-docile "radical Reformation." Varying degrees of community separateness were thus a result of neither social planning nor social theorizing; rather, they were the pragmatic outgrowth of the desire to perpetuate distinctive ways of life. Nearly a dozen foreign-language communities were founded before 1825, a growth not to be matched until a renewal of linguistic separatism in the 1840s with the beginnings of mass immigration.[27]

Since only eight believers journeyed to America in 1774, the Shakers can scarcely be considered a transplanted European sect. Nonetheless, Shakerism too could claim ties, however tenuous, with Reformation radicalism. The Edict of Nantes (1598) granted legal protections to French Protestants (Huguenots). When the Edict was revoked in 1685, the subsequent persecutions led the "Camisards," Huguenots in the Cévennes south of Lyons, to attempt to retain their autonomy by force of arms. They held out through a quarter century of ecstatic prophecy and guerrilla warfare, but with the defeat of their insurrection, a remnant migrated to the presumably more hospitable atmosphere of Protestant England.[28] These "French Prophets" managed to antagonize most of their English coreligionists with predictions of miracles and the end of the world, neither of which they were able to bring about. Nonetheless, their hostility to the corruption of church and state may well have found a more lasting home in Shakerism, to which some of their sparse following repaired. The major influence on Ann Lee was surely Quakerism but the legacy of the "French Prophets" cannot be ignored.[29]

The German-speaking sects and, to a lesser extent, the Shakers constituted instances of what Bernard Siegel has referred to as "defensive structuring"—social organization based upon the desire to draw boundaries between one's own group and an environment perceived as threatening or corrupt. The function of such boundaries is to reduce to the minimum transactions between the two, neither adopting the society's values nor incurring its displeasure. Essential negotiations are generally placed in the hands of a small number of community functionaries, leaving the bulk of the population unsullied by direct contact.[30] Historically, those groups that have most successfully claimed such a right to separation have been religious groups without political ambitions. Given the pluralistic character of American society, it has seemed more conducive to social equilibrium to accept most such claims even when groups have deviated significantly from accepted norms.[31]

The successful invocation of quasi-separatist claims in the early decades of American communalism owes much to the fact that the groups that were claiming it appeared clearly to be seeking separation on religious grounds, even where other motives existed, as, for example, the desire to preserve a language other than English. However, by the 1820s, an increasing proportion of communal ventures were animated in whole or in part by more secular concerns, as in the case of Robert Owen's and the Owenites' desire to create a social structure that would eliminate a pauper class. From the time of the founding of the first Owenite community at New Harmony, Indiana, in 1825, the basis of utopian experimentation was significantly expanded beyond religion.

Nonetheless, the process of secularization was neither abrupt nor complete. Robert Owen, despite his public abhorrence of religion, still found it useful and somehow natural to call his organizers "social missionaries," just as Friedrich Engels could ignore Shaker theology sufficiently to commend their communities as models German workers would do well to emulate.[32] Utopian experimentation began to exhibit a new category of motives. Until the 1820s pre-existing groups had merely wanted to maintain their identity and cohesion in an environment whose values they rejected. They brought with them into their communities clearly formulated religious beliefs and, often, complex patterns of daily living. Secularizing tendencies brought new elements of conscious social design. The more secular the community, the more likely that its members had had little contact with one another prior to the community's founding. They desired not to preserve a threatened way of life but to create a way of life for which there was little existing precedent.

In this, as in other respects, the Shakers were transitional. The loyalty to Shaker religious doctrine was as central as were the creeds of the German-speaking sects. Yet apart from very small numbers of English members, inhabitants of Shaker communities had had no experience of Shakerism outside the communities. While Shaker "families," the group's 30-to-150-member units, existed to preserve a belief system, they also existed to create a way of life where none had existed before. The plasticity of their early social forms perhaps explains the extraordinary attraction they held, not simply for millenarians such as Noyes but for secular social reformers. Indeed, as the century progressed this attractiveness caused Shakerism to exhibit its own secularizing tendencies as it attracted members more intrigued by institutional ingenuity than by doctrines. Shakerism pointed simultaneously back to the millenarian sects of the radical Reformation and ahead to the political sectarianism of nascent socialism.

THE OWENITE PROLOGUE

Although the great burst of community building occurred in the 1840s, it built upon the efforts of Robert Owen and his followers two decades earlier. Owen had begun in a more conventionally philanthropic vein as the benignly paternalistic master of his rural textile mill at New Lanark, Scotland. As a laboratory for innovation in education, housing, and work organization, New Lanark was a mandatory stop on the itineraries of touring social reformers. The New Lanark reforms were possible because as an industrial enterprise dependent upon water power, it was sited in the countryside rather than the blighted city: "it was not so 'advanced' as Manchester [and] it might be possible to preserve something of the spirit of community and close industrial relationships that had been lost in the larger city." Just as Owen rejected the city as a locus for effective change, he came in time to leave New Lanark as well, in the belief that no community built upon industrial production could achieve the desired harmonization of interests.[33]

By about 1817, Owen had acquired a nonreligious millenarian conception of the future, seeking, as one of his followers wrote, "the construction of a great social and moral machine, calculated to produce wealth, knowledge, and happiness, with unprecedented precision and rapidity."[34] With curious ambivalence, Owen exiled industry from his communities, yet built his millennial vision upon the assumption that technology might free humanity from toil.[35] His public pronouncements in the summer of 1817 may not have "aroused the attention of the civilized world, alarmed the governments, astounded the religious sects of every denomination, and created an excitement in all classes," as he later asserted,[36] but they marked Owen's public emergence as a full-fledged millenarian figure instead of merely a philanthropic reformer, and they articulated a millennium based explicitly on reasoned analysis of social ills rather than upon religious revelation. His pugnacious opposition to religion did not, however, inhibit him from appropriating its language. Looking back upon the addresses of 1817 with forty years' hindsight, he wrote that their message

> will now advance without retrogression until they shall so regenerate the human mind, that it shall be "born again," and will entirely change society over the world, in spirit, principle, and practice, giving new surroundings to all nations, until not one stone of the present surroundings of society shall be left upon another. For in consequence of this change "old things will entirely pass away and all will become new."[37]

Owen's millennium would simultaneously free humanity from the toil and the novel oppressions of the factory system, while it liberated individuals from the selfishness of the nuclear family. The result would combine material satisfaction, individual fulfillment, and community cohesion.

Owen was already familiar with the communal religious sects long before his own utopian experiments. He knew of, admired, and wrote about the Shakers as early as 1818, and was particularly impressed by their ability to neutralize family loyalties—a result of strict sex segregation and the separation of parents and children—and their economic self-sufficiency, which "he triumphantly cited ... as proof that the principles of communitarianism were sound."[38]

An indifferent speaker but a prolific and powerful writer, Owen was already an international celebrity by the time of his first trip to America in 1824. The tangible product of the American visit, into which he ploughed much of his mill-owner's fortune, was seven communities founded in 1825–26 by him or his disciples. The most famous, at New Harmony, Indiana, had had an earlier life as a religious community of the German Rappite sect. But Owen's American visit was clearly as important for the vision it imparted as for the communities themselves. His 1825 lectures before the House of Representatives seemed interminable, but John Quincy Adams, James Monroe, and assorted legislators, cabinet officers, and jurists all dutifully attended.[39] Owen was otherwise occupied in England when his

American communities foundered. Among their human debris was Frederick Evans, who, in search of a more stable group life, converted to Shakerism in 1828. Evans rose in time to the post of Elder and worked to link the Shakers with the proto-socialism of his Owenite youth. In the later years of the nineteenth century he assiduously cultivated relationships with figures as diverse as Leo Tolstoy, with whom he held a lengthy correspondence, and the aging John Humphrey Noyes, who treated him with uncharacteristic deference.[40]

THE ONEIDA COMMUNITY

By the end of the 1840s, Owenite communalism had lost its momentum. In its place stood the Oneida Community with its satellite groups, its vigorous publications program, and the charismatic figure of Noyes; the Fourierists, with their elaborate system of support organizations and dizzying rate of community foundation; and the Shakers who, virtually alone of the sectarians, were prepared to reach out for new members.

After the psychological crises of his youth, John Humphrey Noyes had returned to his family's home in Putney, Vermont. In this benign atmosphere, Noyes commenced to put into practice his belief in "perfectionism," the possibility of living free of sin in this life. Perfect holiness dissolved exclusive personal bonds into a single community, and nowhere more dramatically than in relations between men and women. As early as 1837, Noyes had written in the "Battle-Axe Letter" that "When the will of God is done on earth, as it is in heaven, *there will be no marriage.* . . . In a holy community, there is no more reason why sexual intercourse should be restricted by law, than why eating and drinking should."[41] By the power of his advocacy and the strength of his personality, Noyes soon surrounded himself at Putney with a core of believing friends and family members, who by about 1841 had formed a *de facto* communal living arrangement. The group was small—fewer than fifty, including children.[42]

Communal ownership of property emerged in response to economic pressures rather than ideological commitment. By early 1844 the group seemed better supported by pooling of privately held resources than by soliciting contributions. By 1845 economic arrangements involved full sharing of property, although the ideological statement of "Bible communism" did not appear until four years later.[43]

The full introduction of "complex marriage" (non-exclusive sexual

John Humphrey Noyes in one of his earliest photographs, probably a daguerreotype of the 1840s, when Noyes was in his early thirties. During this period, Noyes organized his first communal group in Putney, Vermont, and at the same time conducted a one-man campaign against Millerism. *Courtesy Oneida Community Historical Committee*

relationships) was far more delicate both within and outside the community. Noyes initially revealed and practiced the doctrine only among his closest followers but in 1846–47 began its systematic promulgation. By unanimous agreement, in a meeting June 1, 1847, the community answered in the affirmative Noyes's question: "Is not now the time for us to commence the testimony that the Kingdom of God has come?"[44] By this time, however, the breath of scandal had made continued residence in the Putney area untenable, and the community prepared to reassemble around a small existing perfectionist coterie in Oneida County, New York.

In the Oneida Community, Noyes artfully interwove pre-Marxian socialism, the nascent women's movement, an overriding concern for social solidarity, and a benign industrialism. Where Owen had proscribed industrialization, recreating an arcadian atmosphere, Noyes encouraged mechanization combined with a job-rotation system to discourage boredom and status distinctions. The center of Noyes's labors remained Oneida, but as the Oneida Community prospered, branches were established in Wallingford, Connecticut; Manlius, New York; Brooklyn, New York; Cambridge, Vermont; Newark, New Jersey; and (once again) Putney. Wallingford lasted as long as its parent, formally until 1881, but the others lacked an adequate economic base and were disbanded in the 1850s, their members absorbed into the main group.[45] Noyes himself spent long periods with the Brooklyn group, but he remained the dominant force at Oneida even during absences at Brooklyn, other branches, and abroad.

The Oneida Community's cohesion was the product of Noyes's increasingly elaborate theories of sexuality. By 1844 he had come to accept Robert Dale Owen's distinction between the pleasurable aspect of sex (its "amative" function) and its reproductive aspect (the "propagative" function).[46] Robert Dale Owen, Robert Owen's eldest son, had remained in New Harmony after his father left and after the communal phase of the town's life had ended, and though never directly involved in communitarian activities, he joined a wide range of reformist causes. The younger Owen drew from his distinction the corollary that birth control was best accomplished through male continence (coitus interruptus). This perfectly fitted Noyes's view of sexual union as a religious act, for complex marriage could now go forward without burdening the woman with unwanted offspring. Sexual relations without ejaculation served as a means by which less perfect individuals could reach higher degrees of perfection through intimacy with more spiritually advanced (usually older) partners. At the same time, the web of non-reproductive unions gave physical form to the belief that the community consisted of a marriage of each to all.[47]

Sustained by successful light industrial enterprises, the Oneida Community eventually afforded its members a comfortably bourgeois style of material life. At the social level, it functioned as a vast extended family. In the words of one of its hymns:

This daguerreotype of John Humphrey Noyes can be dated only approximately. It appears to have been taken sometime between 1845 and 1855, at about the time Noyes took his little community to what was to become its permanent headquarters in Oneida County, N.Y. *Courtesy Oneida Community Historical Committee*

We will build us a dome
on our beautiful plantation,
And we'll all have a home
and one family relation[48]

As Lawrence Foster has pointed out, the family metaphor gave Oneida a striking resemblance to the Shakers, whose rigorous celibacy was in other respects the antithesis of complex marriage.[49]

While still at Putney, Noyes was anxious to differentiate "Bible communism" from other communal ventures that encouraged greater withdrawal from the larger society. His journal, *The Perfectionist*, took simultaneous aim at both Shakers and Fourierists in July 1843: "We do not believe that any of the schemes of seceding communism, which at present abound, are the representative executors of [the spirit of the Gospel]."[50] After the Putney Community was well established, the Shakers continued to be attacked as sinister and doctrinally impure proselytizers. In a metaphor heavy with menace Noyes noted: "Shakerism is silently spreading wide its nets."[51] The failure of Shakerism to abjure its own peculiar doctrine of the Second Coming continued to gall Noyes. No matter how heterodox it was in other respects, for Noyes Shakerism was at one with mainline Christian denominations in perpetuating "the heaven-daring falsehood... that Christ did not come... within the generation in which he lived."[52]

Yet Noyes could also see the virtues of the Shakers, particularly when in doing so he might play the Shakers off against the Fourierists. Thus sandwiched among the pejorative comments were oddly charitable remarks, suggesting the Shakers possessed at least relative superiority over their competitors: "In our view, the Shakers' plan of communism has far better claims to public interest and confidence than any of the recent schemes; and Ann Lee better deserves the name of a 'benefactor of the human family' than Fourier, or Henshaw, Ripley or Collins."[53] This otherwise unpredictable rapprochement with Shakerism may owe less to new-found ideological compatibility than to new fears of organizational competition. The Shakers had been the most active proselytizer among communitarians. By 1843–44, however, Fourierism was undergoing spectacular growth, particularly in the Burned-over District, impelled by the organizational and propagandistic skills of Albert Brisbane.

Perfectionist perceptions of associationism were almost as ambivalent as its views of Shakerism. Less than half a year after comparing Fourier unfavorably to Ann Lee, Noyes published a lengthy essay on Fourierism that was notably more balanced. Associationism was portrayed as "refreshing" in its "conservative moderation," "yet we are not converted to its principles." The problem lay in the Fourierist emphasis upon the creation of proper social and economic institutions, as opposed to Noyes's view that the fundamental problem was the creation of noble characters: "good men" precede, rather than follow, "good institutions."[54] Where the spirit is "vitally diseased," it must be cured by an "internal process."[55] Fourierism was

The patriarchal John Humphrey Noyes, shown here on the Oneida Community's grounds in about 1863. He is the figure in the right foreground, standing astride, with top-hat in hand, the extended Community "family" behind him—164 men, women, and children, about three-quarters of its membership at that time. *Courtesy Oneida Historical Committee*

fundamentally misguided, since it concentrated only upon the outward manifestations, the symptomatology, rather than the root cause.

By the spring of 1846, on the eve of the transfer to Oneida, Noyes had grown even more mellow in his views on Associationism, in part no doubt because the Fourierist agitation of earlier years had receded. Noyes now portrayed the Putney group as the true communitarians, moving forward in the knowledge that they alone possessed the true doctrine. At the same time, he indulged in some curious historical revisionism: "We have been Associationists theoretically for more than ten years [i.e., since before 1836], and practically in a small experimental way, for six years [since 1840]."[56]

Neither estimate accords well with the known facts, although both may represent Noyes's subsequent recollection. There was always a measure of *de facto* communalism at Putney, the natural product of group living in a hostile environment. In no sense, however, was the Putney group a formally organized utopian venture before, at the earliest, 1844. *De facto* communalism, accordingly, is what Noyes apparently meant when he observed that "about six years ago we began the experiment of external union of interests." But ever mindful of the need to differentiate pure from impure communitarians, he was careful to add: "This experiment has always been a secondary matter with us. Our primary project has been to publish the gospel of salvation from sin, and to form a SPIRITUAL PHALANX."[57]

The audacious appropriation of the central Fourierist metaphor marked both the symbolic ascendancy of Perfectionism over Associationism and Noyes's irrevocable self-identification as a utopian. Having a dozen years earlier proclaimed his desire to "live or die for [the millennium]," Noyes had now scaled down his dreams from world transformation to the creation of a perfect world in miniature.

THE FOURIERIST COMMUNITIES

The Fourierist phalanxes were the single most numerous class of communities founded in the 1840s. Bestor identifies twenty-five begun between 1841 and 1846, while Okugawa counts twenty-three.[58] Neither the Perfectionists nor the Shakers at the peak of their vitality approached this level of activity. Since Fourierism never achieved complete cohesion as a social movement, communities were often distantly related local ventures, but all sprang ultimately from the mind of Fourier—or rather what his American disciples chose to think was in his mind.

Albert Brisbane provided whatever central focus Fourierism had. Born and raised in the Burned-over District, he was strikingly atypical of its population. His father's family, with roots in the Philadelphia area rather than in New England, moved to Batavia, between Rochester and Buffalo.[59] In a region of evangelical Protestants, his father was the town skeptic.[60] Brisbane was thus largely insulated from revival religion, the more so since he was sent to New York City for his education at seventeen and spent his young manhood in Europe.

His intellectual "grand tour" was the stuff of legend. He sat at the feet of Goethe, Heine, and Hegel, but it was the reclusive, irascible Fourier who set his mind ablaze in 1832.[61] The dour prophet could scarcely have given his young follower much encouragement; Brisbane later recalled that "in the three years of my association with Fourier, I never saw him smile."[62]

Nonetheless, Brisbane, the searching son of a skeptical father, was drawn to Fourier's curious theism, which superimposed upon the God of the philosophers the belief that that remote deity had fashioned a code for social life, discovered by Fourier himself.

Brisbane resolved to bring this code, which purported to explain society as Newton's physics had explained the material world, to America. The task was made far more feasible with the conversion of Horace Greeley to Associationism in 1841. Brisbane wrote a Fourierist column on the New York *Tribune*'s front page, from March 1842 until September 1843, possibly the first regular column of signed opinion in any American newspaper.[63] On October 5, 1843, Brisbane founded *The Phalanx*, a periodical devoted to the growing band of American Fourierists, which he edited until he returned to Europe in the spring of 1844.

Not content with journalistic efforts alone, Brisbane agitated for the formation of Fourierist societies to advance the master's ideas and to insure their implementation in self-sufficient rural communities. By mid-1844 a thousand people had actually moved into the four largest communities, and Bestor estimates fifteen to twenty non-resident supporters for every community member.[64] If so, that suggests a movement roughly half the size of Millerism. Fourierism's decline, however, was as dramatic as its rise. Undercapitalized, dependent upon the generosity of their non-resident patrons, the communities struggled unsuccessfully through the depression years that followed the Panic of 1837. By the time Brisbane returned from his European trip at the end of 1844, the communities were dissolving, and once sympathetic newspapers other than the *Tribune* grew suddenly skeptical.[65] The $400,000 capitalization that Fourier had recommended for a single community was not to be had in an economy where, as Brisbane later recalled, "between Albany and Buffalo there were, I should say, scarcely a dozen men who had escaped bankruptcy."[66]

THE VITALITY OF THE SHAKERS

Despite the general shift away from sectarian communities, the Shakers remained highly visible. In part, this was the result of their active proselytizing among revival Protestants. It was also no doubt due to their reputation for meticulously organized, prosperous communities, which drew a steady stream of visitors. It is more difficult to know, however, whether perceived Shaker vitality was matched by increases in size. Foster identifies three phases of Shaker growth: an initial period between Mother Ann Lee's death in 1784 and the turn of the nineteenth century; a second phase up to 1820; and a third expansion between 1837 and about 1855.[67] The second and third phases in particular were associated with movement into new regions of the country, especially the Midwest and the Ohio Valley. Yet it remains difficult to clearly link missionary activities and the development of new Shaker communities, on the one hand, with actual growth in membership on the other.

The Shakers' uncompromising insistence upon celibacy required a continuous infusion of new members through the conversion of adults, with or without children, and the acceptance of orphan children who could be kept until their majority. The absence of natural increase as a recruiting mechanism produced an inherently precarious situation, since it was never clear that the existing generation of members would be replaced.[68] While Shaker population figures exist, they are most often estimates, sometimes contradict one another, and make it extremely difficult to determine whether the movement was growing, contracting, or just maintaining itself. A 1799 Shaker estimate placed the membership at more than 1,600.[69] Stephen Marini's estimate for 1815 is 4,000, while an 1823 Shaker estimate placed their numbers at 4,000–4,300.[70] Edward Deming Andrews places the peak size at 6,000 in the mid-1850s.[71] While these somewhat contradictory figures still suggest impressively steady growth, this long-accepted picture has been at least partially called into question by William Sims Bainbridge's research with census records.[72]

Bainbridge utilized the manuscript enumerations for religious censuses. Unfortunately, Census records do not reliably identify individuals for religious purposes prior to 1840, which makes it impossible to substantiate early claims of Shaker size. The religious censuses were also separated by twenty-year intervals. Nonetheless, they present a picture of size and directionality that significantly differs from those cited earlier.

Census figures show total Shaker community populations of 3,608 for 1840; 3,489 for 1860; and 1,849 for 1880.[73] Although all communities suffered decreases in memberships between 1860 and 1880, a mixed picture emerges between 1840 and 1860, when some communities expanded while others declined. Without comparable figures for 1800 and 1820, it is difficult to make reliable inferences, yet Bainbridge's data permit some provisional observations: First, the movement appears to have been significantly smaller than previously thought, although still large for a network of communal settlements. Second, unless the twenty years between the censuses of 1840 and 1860 contain a very large but transient population gain, the Shakers were merely holding their own during the 1840s. Their missionary activities were vigorous because they had to be in order to replace losses through death and defection.

THE TEMPORAL AND SPATIAL DISTRIBUTION OF UTOPIAS

Utopian communities did not emerge in an even stream, nor were they evenly distributed over the country. They were concentrated in a few relatively brief periods and were located in rural settings, near the urban centers where their supporters clustered.

Identifying the universe of American utopian movements has always been hindered by the brief life spans of many communities, which often did not permit the accumulation of documentary evidence for later investigators. Nonetheless, 270 communities have been reliably identified for the 132 years between 1787 and 1919.[74] The foundings of these communities exhibit a wavelike pattern.

Fully one-third of the communities—91—were begun in two seven-year periods:

1842–48	55 founded
1894–1900	36 founded

Although no comparably rigorous utopian census yet exists for the years after 1919,[75] the period after World War I holds two other utopian waves, the first during the Great Depression and the second during the 1960s.[76] The first wave in the 1840s reveals its magnitude when compared to the adjacent decades:[77]

1820–29	15 founded
1830–39	11 founded
1840–49	60 founded
1850–59	22 founded

Put somewhat differently, the communities of the 1840s accounted for almost 60 percent of all the communities begun between 1820 and 1859. Indeed, notwithstanding substantial communitarian activity in the 1890s and 1930s, this magnitude of experimentation was not equaled until the communes of the 1960s.

"Utopia" may be "no-place" etymologically, but the communities themselves had precise spatial locations. These locations were as interesting for where they were not as for where they were. Arthur Bestor pointed out in 1951 that although they were rural, they were not sited on the frontier. Despite often primitive living conditions, sometimes approximating the rigors of frontier life, utopian experimentation did not take place along the advancing edge of western settlement. Of the ninety-nine nineteenth-century communities Bestor studied, forty-five were located in the Northwest Territory of Ohio, Indiana, Wisconsin, Illinois, and Michigan. Another twenty-eight lay in western New York, sections of the Ohio Valley outside the Territory, and adjoining areas of the upper Mississippi Valley. More complete data for the pre-Civil War decades yields the distributions by state found on Table 4.1.[78] "In point of fact," Bestor wrote, "Communitarianism developed in a fairly normal environment of settled agricultural and commercial life."[79] Communitarians might have wanted to escape from the perceived evils of the society at large, but they rarely leap-frogged settled areas to do so. Given their need for large and inexpensive parcels of land, a partial explanation lies in the continued availability of such blocs east of the Mississippi and north of the Ohio throughout the period.[80] It was not necessary to move very far in order to satisfy the need for separateness and self-sufficiency; indeed, moving too far risked economic disaster. The Harmony Society—known also as "Rappites" after their leader, Father George Rapp—had been the first German communitarian group to cross the Appalachians, having come from southern Germany first to Beaver County, Pennsylvania, and then to their settlement of Harmonie, Indiana, on the banks of the Wabash River. They sold the settlement to Robert Owen, however, and moved back East to Economy, Pennsylvania, because in the early 1820s, Indiana was simply too far from the markets upon which the Rappites relied.

While the establishment of communities generally moved from east to west, the process lagged behind settlement, so that communities appeared in available pockets of land within already settled areas.[81] Up until 1800, twelve of the fifteen communities founded by then lay in eastern Pennsylvania or New England. By 1860, however, communities had been established throughout the Ohio Valley, the upper Mississippi Valley, and as far west as Texas and Oregon.[82]

This westward flow, lagging slightly behind settlement itself, exhibits one major anomaly—the sudden growth of communitarianism in New York State during the 1840s, at a time when the logic of population movement dictated greater activity in the Middle West. Communities had, after all, developed in Ohio and Indiana by the 1820s; Louisiana and Missouri by the 1830s; and Illinois, Iowa, and Wisconsin by the 1840s. Nonetheless, the 1840s became a period of extraordinary utopian proliferation not only in Ohio, northern Indiana, Illinois, and Wisconsin, but in upstate New York, where utopian energies might well have been considered spent.

Until 1840, according to Bestor's data, only eight out of fifty-three communities had been founded in New York. In any given decade after 1663, no more than three communities had been established in New York, and in some (the 1810s, for example), none at all. But of fifty-four begun during the 1840s, ten were in New York State, excluding the Oneida branches and the non–New York communities organized by New Yorkers.

Okugawa's date is again very similar: fifty-two communities begun nationally in the 1840s, of which ten were in New York. Much of the spurt was accounted for by the Fourierist wave in the first half of the decade, which accounted for seven of the ten communities. At the end of 1843, Albert Brisbane reported to his fellow Fourierists: "I have visited lately the central and Western part of [New York State], and have been surprised to see that the principles of a Reform, based upon Association and unity of interests, have found their way into almost every part of the country."[83] The other communities included one that was strongly indebted to Owen's ideas (Skaneateles), a German-speaking sectarian group far better known after its move to Iowa, where it became Amana (first called Ebenezar), and the Perfectionists (Oneida).

THE COMPOSITION OF UTOPIAN COMMUNITIES

Communitarian populations were noteworthy only in their very ordinariness. The conception of the utopian community as a smug haven for intellectuals is wide of the mark, for they often imposed an arduous physical existence on their members which effectively discouraged dilettantes.[84] Brook Farm, the retreat favored by Boston Transcendentalists, passed its first years (1841–44) heavily laden with ministers and writers, but when the community took a clearly Fourierist path in 1844, the membership shifted to professionals, business persons, and workers.[85] New Harmony possessed much the same reputation for supercharged intellectuality, based upon Owen's famous keelboat journey down the Ohio bearing Philadelphia's scientific and intellectual elite to his new community. The "boatload of knowledge" brought an unprecedented body of notables westward, but it was neither the usual mode of utopian recruitment nor did it do anything to strengthen New Harmony's cohesiveness.[86]

The communities differed greatly in recruiting practices. New Harmony alternated between the introduction of scholar-celebrities who quickly left and an open door to others who came out of questionable motives. Longer-lived communities, such as the Shakers and Oneida, demanded acts of personal renunciation, which included the signing over of assets through contracts enforceable in the courts of the larger society.[87] The greater the personal investment, the greater the propensity to remain through difficult times. Acts of renunciation were reinforced on a regular basis by such internal behavioral controls as rituals of group confession to abase the backslider and the systematic elimination of opportunities for per-

TABLE 4.1

Number of Utopian Experiments by State

1800–09

Kentucky	2
New York	1
Ohio	2
Pennsylvania	1

1810–19

Indiana	2
Massachusetts	1
Ohio	1
Vermont	1

1820–29

Indiana	4
New York	3
Ohio	5
Pennsylvania	2
Tennessee	1

1830–39

Indiana	1
Louisiana	2
Missouri	1
New York	2
Ohio	4
Pennsylvania	1

1840–49

Illinois	5
Indiana	6
Iowa	2
Massachusetts	4
Michigan	2
Missouri	2
New Jersey	1
New York	10
Ohio	11
Pennsylvania	7
Texas	3
Vermont	1
Wisconsin	6

Table 4.1 *(continued)* 1850–59

Connecticut	1
Indiana	2
Iowa	3
Minnesota	1
Missouri	1
New Jersey	1
New York	2
Ohio	3
Oregon	1
Pennsylvania	1
Texas	1
West Virginia	1
Wisconsin	4

sonal privacy. Not surprisingly, the more extensive the renunciation and control, the longer the community lasted.[88]

The social background of utopians was broadly representative of the geographical areas from which they came. The New York State experiments drew, predictably, from New York and New England. The Shakers were among the most numerous utopians, with their regional network of communities and aggressive recruiting. The wide range of Shaker agricultural and craft enterprises contributed to self-sufficiency at the same time that it provided scope for individuals with similar pre-conversion backgrounds: barrel-making, the preparation of medicinal herbs, broom-making, and so on.[89] The Shaker efforts to secure converts from among disillusioned participants in revivals insured that mainstream denominations, such as Baptists and Methodists, were well represented. Only in two respects was Shaker membership unusual: age and sex composition. A high proportion of Shakers came in childhood, adolescence, or young adulthood. This may have been a response to the uncertainties of youth which found temporary surcease in the highly structured Shaker "families" and almost certainly owes something to the relative paucity of public social welfare institutions. In any case, the influx of the young appears to have been greatest around mid-century. In 1840, Shakers were not conspicuously younger than the general population. The number of the very old among them was, however, unusually high throughout much of the movement's history, perhaps because of the security the communities offered the elderly, perhaps because Shakers were more fit, or simply that the rapid defection of those who had come as children left the aged behind.[90] Just as the age distribution became skewed after the census of 1840, so too did sex ratios. The image of Shakers as predominantly female is based upon the composition of the movement after the Civil War. Communities always contained more women than men, but the imbalance was modest in the early decades of the century, and may simply have been due to the greater longevity of women. Thus, in 1819 the New Lebanon and Watervliet societies contained 312 males and 421 females. Between 1840 and 1849 an equal number of men and women—fifteen—entered one "family" at New Lebanon.[91] In 1840, the first year for which census figures are available, all Shakers communities were 57.7 percent female, as against 48.8 percent of the population. However, the imbalance became dramatic with the passage of time: 59.1 percent in 1860; 64.5 percent in 1880; and 72.2 percent in 1900.[92] In short, the demographic peculiarities of the Shakers were a product of the post–Civil War era. In the 1840s they appear to have been far more typical of the general population.

Fourierist communities drew a varied, not to say plebeian, membership. Of the sixty-seven individuals who joined Brook Farm in its first Fourierist year (1844), there were seven professionals, six business people, and forty-three workers. The latter included shoemakers, farmers, carpenters, and printers.[93] The largest Fourierist community of all was the North American Phalanx, founded in 1843 in Monmouth County, New Jersey. Its roots, however, lay in the Albany area from which sixty of its members had come.

> Among them were a morocco manufacturer, an agent for the Erie Canal, a homeopathic doctor, grocer, a shoe store proprietor, a druggist, a coachmaker, a coal dealer, a stove dealer, a lawyer, a painter, the owner of a small steamship line, the part-owner of a tobacco company, a blacksmith, a carpenter, a wood turner, a silver plater, a mason, a hatmaker, and their families.[94]

In the Burned-over District itself, Fourierist communities ran heavily to farmers and laborers.[95] The Fourierist society in Rochester was dominated by propertied professionals and shopkeepers, but the community which the society founded at Sodus Bay was another matter; two-thirds to three-quarters of the 256 who resided at one time or another came from outside Rochester. Their rural origins strongly suggest that they were farmers. The relatively small number of urban artisans who did affiliate quickly left.[96] Urbanites might sympathize with Fourierist aims but were unable or unwilling to effect the necessary break with their accustomed way of life.

Occupational variety was also evident among the Oneida members. "The men who joined the society were neither poets nor political anarchists, but farmers and mechanics who knew how to run a mill, plow a field and lay a foundation."[97] The majority were farmers, with a heavy admixture of artisan occupations. Eventually, there was a sprinkling of professionals (a lawyer, a Methodist minister), but the community retained its association with occupations that involved manual labor and manufacturing.[98]

The former livelihoods of utopians were those customarily found in a society composed of farms and small towns, and in roughly the same proportions. The members do not appear to have been primarily intellectuals in search of an arcadian sanctuary. Their religious affiliations, too, appear to have been typical, where such information is available. Congregationalists predominated among the Oneida Perfectionists, but then 85 percent of the first members came from New York, Vermont, and Massachusetts.[99] Whatever factors of self-selection were operating, they did not function to give the communities a makeup significantly different from what prevailed in the world outside. However unusual the social arrangements of the utopias, their members were unexceptional. Whatever the reasons may have been for the swift failure of some ventures, it was not because utopians were "unworldly," because they lacked survival skills, or because they were unused to wresting a living from a harsh landscape.

MILLERISM AND THE UTOPIANS

THE LOCATION of communal groups within well-settled areas suggests the uneasy balance the utopians tried to maintain between separation and engagement. On the one hand, the corruption and imperfection of the world demanded separation and the opportunity to begin anew. On the other, the larger significance of such an endeavor was lost if it remained the preserve only of a committed elite, for then it lost its power to influence the behavior of others. Hence communities were constantly pulled between the need to create a microcosmic millennium within an unredeemed society and the desire to draw that society towards their vision of a perfect future. These contradictory forces manifested themselves in the physical design of communities, their patterns of behavior, and their place in the movement of people and ideas.

The insularity of utopian communities was physically and metaphorically confirmed by the systematic employment of gates and fences, for territorial boundaries could not be left in doubt.[1] High levels of self-sufficiency made frequent contact with the outside unnecessary for most residents in any case. Notwithstanding the commitment to a physically separate existence, however, spatial boundaries were semipermeable, permitting transactions in both directions. Some of the contacts must have been unwelcome, as the existence of post-contact cleansing rituals at Oneida and the Shaker communities suggests. Often they were the result of economic necessity, where, as in the case of Oneida, commerce in manufactured goods underwrote the group's standard of living.

Utopian groups were well aware of one another's existence, as well as of the Millerites'. The likelihood of mutual knowledge increased when in the 1840s communitarianism retrogressed from an emphasis on Middle Western locations to upstate New York. A return to the east, with its superior transportation and communications networks, increased the opportunities for mutual awareness. Indeed, Arthur Bestor suggests that the siting of later colonies may even have been influenced by knowledge that earlier groups had chosen the same area:

At the height of the movement, between 1840 and 1849, . . . twenty-four experimental communities of all types were founded in the three states of Massachusetts, New York, and Ohio, and exactly half were within thirty miles of a pre-existing colony of Shakers or German sectarians. Only two were more than sixty miles distance from such a center of communitive example and influence, and none was as far away as seventy-five miles.[2]

Whether deliberate or fortuitous, the overlapping pattern of location facilitated information transfer.

Neither physical separateness nor sectarian exclusivity blocked the movement of persons and ideas. Occasionally, indeed, systematic efforts were made to reach out to those with related but differentiable beliefs. Three types of evidence argue for the existence of a millenarian-utopian network that drew together those who yearned for a perfect future: First, there were attempts to systematically recruit members of similar groups through formal proselytizing, including the use of itinerant missionaries. This was vigorously employed by both the Shakers and Millerites. Much more numerous were cases of individual or small-group migration from one community or movement to another. Virtually every group received members from or sent members to other groups. It is difficult to know the proportion of utopians and millenarians who entered without prior affiliation in similar ventures, but a sizable number appear to have been "seekers," individuals in quest of levels of fulfillment that had eluded them in the past.[3] Finally, many reports testify to groups' mutual knowledge, sometimes expressed as conscious imitation of others' practices. Most groups printed and circulated books, newspapers, pamphlets, and periodicals for themselves and for sympathizers, which were exchanged for the publications of others. The relatively recent mass circulation newspapers, eager to build readerships, gave prominent play to articles on religious enthusiasm and social experimentation, accentuating or even inventing sensational details. The curious often traveled to revivals and communitarian experiments to satisfy their hunger for information. These varying modes of contact suggest that all groups could glean at least some knowledge about likeminded predecessors and contemporaries as they experienced the contradictory forces of separatism and mutual awareness.

INTERGROUP KNOWLEDGE AND IMITATION

Exchange of information among millenarians and utopians in the Burned-over District was facilitated by a growing and sophisticated communications network within a geographically compact area. The Erie Canal reached Little Falls, east of Utica, by 1820 and was completed to Lake Erie in 1825. Tributary canals extending north and south of the main "ditch" were constructed well into the 1830s, supplemented by a growing network of tollroads.[4] The circulation of ideas rested not only upon this infrastructure but upon a national literacy rate that had reached 75 percent by 1840,[5] conceivably higher among the New England-bred population of upstate New York. Sectarians were prolific writers and publishers, and the internal evidence of Perfectionist and Fourierist periodicals suggests that elaborate systems for the exchange of publications kept groups abreast of one another's activities.

The vigorous religious press of New York and New England diffused sectarian positions that might otherwise have achieved purely local notice. The significance of publication as a precondition for growth was nowhere more evident than in the dissemination of William Miller's views. They first appeared in a Baptist paper, the *Vermont Telegraph*, of Brandon, a short distance from Miller's home. The paper later issued these articles as a pamphlet. By 1839 Miller's views had been accepted by the editors of the *Christian Palladium*, published in New York Mills, New York, and thereafter it became an organ for the systematic propagation of Adventist ideas. Joshua Himes oversaw two major publications, the *Signs of the Times* in Boston and the *Midnight Cry* in New York. At least one copy went to every clergyman in New York State. By 1843–44, these publications were aided by book rooms in Buffalo and Syracuse.[6]

Utopians proved equally adept if somewhat more restrained publicists. Although the most ambitious Owenite publication program was in England, more than a dozen periodicals were issued in the United States, most of them in New York State. They continued to appear through 1844, long after most of the Owenite communities had disbanded.[7] By 1843–44

Noyes had developed a farsighted conception of print media. Already active as an anti-Millerite writer, he planned a preaching campaign in New York City against Second Adventism for the spring of 1843, but the mysterious throat ailment that began in 1842 forced him to cease all public speaking by the beginning of the following year.[8] The cancellation forced him into still greater reliance on the printed word, and he wrote George Cragin: "I am more and more persuaded that our strength is to lie in publishing rather than in preaching. The invention of printing has changed everything, . . . we must devote ourselves to training a regiment of writers."[9] By the following year, he had formulated a grandiose plan for government by plebiscite, in which ballots would be distributed and collected by rail: "Let a periodical paper be established at the seat of government, as the sole method of proposing, discussing, enacting and recording the laws. Let the whole people, with their papers for their gathering point, resolve themselves into a permanent legislative convention."[10]

Albert Brisbane was not an ideologist of the media, but he was a consummately gifted practitioner. His propagandistic efforts proceeded along two fronts simultaneously. The column in Greeley's *Tribune* adroitly reached out to the unattached and curious. The frequent and insistent articles asserting the compatibility of Fourierism and religion argue the desire to reach a new and skeptical audience. The column overlapped on the lifespan of the "house organ" of American Fourierism, *The Phalanx*, which after a few false starts, appeared irregularly between 1843 and 1845. It was succeeded by *The Harbinger* from 1845 to 1849. By then, Fourierist efforts were in others' hands, and indeed *The Harbinger* was moved from New York City to Brook Farm in 1847.[11]

More than anything else, the mutual knowledge acquired by millenarians and utopians suggests both an underlying community of belief and an ability to separate means from ends. There was a high level of agreement about ends. Thus, there was general commitment to a future state of affairs in which unhappiness would not exist and in which people would feel bound together in a fulfilling common enterprise. The precise manner in which this utopia/millennium was to be achieved, however, and the actions appropriate for the period prior to its achievement, remained in vigorous dispute. Agreement about the end permitted selective borrowing of techniques by groups otherwise unsympathetic toward one another.

The Shakers were reasonably well acquainted with the German-speaking communal groups that settled early in Pennsylvania and Ohio and later established such outposts as Amana west of the Mississippi. Personal visits were the principal medium, facilitated by the Shakers' far-flung missionary expeditions. Nonetheless the language barrier made a full interchange of ideas difficult, and occasional suggestions of federation between Shaker and German pietist groups were never implemented.[12]

A week after Robert Owen arrived in America in 1824, he visited the Shaker community at Niskeyuna near Albany, and the following year purchased the Rappites' land and buildings in Indiana. Owen's negative views on religion notwithstanding, his reactions to both groups were notably positive. For their part, the Shakers were well-informed about Owen's reforms at New Lanark. Prior to the purchase of Harmonie, Indiana, from the Rappites, and its rechristening as New Harmony, Owen had corresponded with George Rapp and exchanged publications with him. When he visited Harmonie, he met not only with Rappites but with Shaker emissaries from Ohio and Kentucky.[13]

By the 1840s, Owenite community building had spent itself. Notwithstanding the somber state of the communities themselves, Owen's personal prestige remained high. In 1844, he returned to the United States after an absence of seventeen years in order to visit his sons in New Harmony. On the way, he stopped at the Ohio Phalanx in Belmont County, an enterprise of Pittsburgh Fourierists in which the millenarian writer H. H. van Amringe played a major role.[14] His visit to the Ohio Phalanx symbolized his growing sympathy for American Fourierism, then at the brief pinnacle of its influence, and until his departure for England in October 1845, he tried to engineer a fusion of Fourierism and the remnants of Owenism, a venture that foundered on the ideological objections of Brisbane, John Collins, and others. Despite Owen's pleas that his American disciples join the phalanxes, few did.[15]

The Oneidans exhibited perhaps the greatest catholicity of view concerning other groups, attributable to their own growing prosperity, Noyes's intellectual syncretism, and the longevity of their enterprise, which encouraged them to see themselves as the culmination of others' less successful efforts. The Perfectionists drew heavily upon Owenite and Fourierist ideas in the physical organization and expansion of Oneida.[16] Noyes, occasionally fulsome in his praise for Owen and Fourier, acknowledged a special debt to the Fourierist experiment at Brook Farm, which ended just as Oneida began.[17] The Oneidans possessed at least two written accounts of visitors to the North American Phalanx, from which they may have adopted principles of economic organization, building design, and sexual practice.[18]

The world the utopians inhabited was consequently far less insular than the form of their communities suggested. The fact that a group organized its common life on the basis of separation and self-sufficiency did not imply ignorance or disinterest about the world beyond its gates. Pressed as most were economically and prone to factionalism, they understood that one's crisis was often another's boon as the disaffected moved from group to group. The most extreme manifestation of this competitiveness was conscious, systematic proselytizing.

SYSTEMATIC RECRUITMENT FROM OTHER GROUPS

Millerites and utopians competed for the same members. To the extent that eschatological hopes were periodically raised by religious revivals, the reservoir of potential members was occasionally expanded as the previously uninvolved experienced intense upswings of emotional religiousity. Curiously, however, there was relatively little formal "raiding" of other groups. Millenarians and utopians only occasionally systematically recruited from one another, and more often tacitly respected each other's boundaries. While happy to receive those who voluntarily changed affiliation, they did not often seek to disengage those already attached.

Millerite recruitment benefited from widespread religious revivalism. Their adroit use of revivals made it difficult for the casual observer to separate them from more conventional evangelical Protestants. Particularly in Second Adventism's early phase—prior to 1840—its spokespersons gained access to revivals on the presumption that they differed little from Finney and his followers, and clergy who extended lecture invitations to Miller may well have been expecting simply another revivalist.[19] Miller's access to pulpits was particularly significant in the days before his writings were widely disseminated, and before he benefited from Joshua Himes' formidable organizational talents. As the millennial predictions of 1843–44 approached, Millerism was spread by a dogged force of self-appointed itinerant preachers.

The Shakers, persecuted in England and cut off from normal social life by celibacy and the community of goods, were far more realistic about the need to battle for souls. Since they asked far more of their members than mere personal assent to Ann Lee's teachings, and since celibacy required the constant replenishment of their numbers from the outside, they began early to send out missionaries. Their most fertile fields were the revivals themselves, which often raised expectations that the churches could not satisfy. Beginning in the 1780s, while Mother Ann was still alive, Shaker missionaries followed the revivals through New England, New York, and Kentucky, offering a stable way of life rather than a quick psychological "fix."[20]

When the Shakers and the Millerites confronted one another after the Great Disappointment, it is difficult to determine where Millerite searching ended and Shaker proselytizing began. In the past the Shakers had plucked up those on the fringes of emotional revivalism, but Millerism was a movement that, to all appearances, had utterly failed, leaving thousands of adherents stunned and bewildered. The Shakers did not have to labor in order to convince Millerites that they had unmet spiritual needs; they had merely to open themselves to the yearnings of people suddenly deprived of their sense of meaning. Hence the interactions between Shakers and Millerite Second Adventists belongs not to the history of proselytizing but to the more complex saga of intergroup migration.

INTERGROUP MIGRATION

The millenarian-utopian network consisted not merely of the exchange of publications and visits in order to satisfy intellectual curiosity; it often involved the movement of persons from one group affiliation to another. These transfers occurred for many reasons: in some instances, a group ceased to have a continued corporate existence, as in the case of utopian communities that dissolved. In other instances, a group no longer met the needs of all its members. An unknown proportion of the disaffected may well have returned to such mainstream organizations as recognized religious denominations, major political parties, and middle-class social reform associations. However, the weight of evidence strongly suggests that many defectors moved to groups only marginally different from those they had left. The sheer number of millenarian and utopian groups in the 1820s, 30s, and 40s accounts for the complexity of voluntary transfers. Bestor infers from it the existence of an overarching ideology:

> The most striking evidence of the reality, the unity and the strength of the communitive tradition is furnished by the men and women whose loyalty to it impelled them from one community to another. The social idealism it inspired was often powerful enough to override religious preconceptions permitting many adherents lightly to cross the line dividing theocratic communities from free-thinking secular ones.[21]

The pattern of intercommunal migration appears to have been set early and maintained throughout the history of American communal experimentation. Otohiko Okugawa reports that of the 270 communities he identified between 1787 and 1919, migration can be established in most of the cases. Migration sometimes occurred when a community was established, drawing members with earlier community experiences. This was the case for three-fourths of the communities. During the community's existence, it often received members from other groups, a situation which occurred in 64 percent of the cases. In 62 percent of the cases, when communities dissolved, at least some of their members migrated to other utopian experiments. More frequently, sectarians moved to other religious groups, while those in nonreligious groups tended to move to likeminded communities. Nonsectarian communities in general experienced more migration, but this may have been a result of the shorter life span of secular utopias.[22]

Crossgroup transfers were already evident by the 1820s. Despite Robert Owen's well-publicized aversion to religion, two Kentucky Shakers joined New Harmony.[23] When the Owenite communities failed, the Shakers in turn more than recouped earlier losses. Several refugees from New Harmony became Shakers, including Frederick Evans, who was to become the leading figure in Shakerism. Other Owenite adherents to Shakerism made up in numbers what they may have lacked in individual distinction. When the Valley Forge, Pennsylvania, Community broke up in September 1826, after a life of only nine months, emissaries from it entered negotiations with the Mount Lebanon Shakers. The result was fifty or more conversions.[24]

The Great Disappointment provided an unprecedented opportunity for millenarian-utopian migration, for few among the disappointed Second Adventists were prepared to risk further failures. Whether or not this produced, as Whitney Cross suggests, "the largest [Shaker increase] since the early days," it must have been considerable, for in 1846, two hundred Millerites are known to have joined Shaker groups in western New York and Ohio.[25] In at least one case, a Millerite group requested a Shaker missionary.[26]

A major link between the two groups was Enoch Jacob, who edited the Cincinnati Millerite paper, The Western Midnight Cry. In 1845, the title was changed to The Day-Star, and in 1846, after Jacob's conversion to Shakerism, it became a major organ for communicating the Shaker message to Millerites.[27] One of Jacob's readers was an anguished Second Adventist, Henry Bear, who left a detailed account of his journey to Shakerism. Bear was impressed not only with the Shakers' ideas but with the manner in which they had realized their egalitarian beliefs: "The principle of a united consecration convinced me of their superior love, for while the Shakers lived in common in their houses, the adventists were living, some in fine houses, and others in poor rented hovels. Some could, and would, ride in fine carriages while others had to walk."[28] Bear reports attending a "convention" at the Whitewater, Ohio, Shaker community together with "not far short of a hundred" Millerites, including Jacob, and shortly thereafter converted.

The demise of Millerism was not the only event of the decade from which the Shakers benefited. When the Fourierist phalanxes collapsed, at least a few Associationists transferred allegiance. Despite the small numbers, these must have been particularly welcome converts, in view of the disdain in which Fourierists had held Ann Lee's followers.[29] It also stands as an exception to the reluctance of secularists to join sectarian communities.

The end of the decade brought Millerites into the Oneida Community. Earlier, while Noyes was still at Putney, he had suffered defections to Millerism. By 1843–44, nine adults and five children had left Putney, and almost surely some had switched to Second Adventism, for Noyes had written of it as early as 1842 that "it has found some weathercocks among our nominal brethren."[30] Within five years, the situation was reversed. "The Oneida Family Register," in which were inscribed the Community's members at the beginning of 1849, identifies eight as former Millerites. Noyes continued to attract Second Adventists as late as the mid-1860s. D. Edson Smith and his wife, early members of the ill-fated Millerite community of Celesta in Sullivan County, Pennsylvania, subsequently joined Oneida. Recalling the Celesta connection decades later, Smith remembered: "It was the *socialistic* or communistic idea that imprest [sic] me. I was born with very strong communistic proclivities. And at that time [about 1864] I was deeply interested in the 'Second Coming' idea."[31] By 1900 the Smiths were living in Santa Ana, California, which suggests that they had become Townerites, a faction which formed within the Oneida Community in the 1870s and migrated West shortly after the Community became a joint-stock company in 1881.

As long as Millerism remained a vital force, however, utopians eyed it warily, for Second Adventism shared their desire for perfection even as it rejected all hope of significantly improving human institutions. While communitarians viewed with dismay the thousands marching behind Miller's banner, they cherished the hope that they would be the beneficiaries of Miller's error—an expectation which, as we have seen, proved to be more than mere wishful thinking.

UTOPIANS' PERCEPTION OF MILLERISM: A Study in Ambivalence

John Humphrey Noyes remarked of the Millerites that they "hear the same voice we have heard, that God is coming into the world and the day of judgment is at hand; but to them the voice is not clear enough to save them from the delusions of their own imagination."[32] The utopians could never fully grasp the reasons for the misunderstanding, especially since the voice sounded eminently clear to them. The utopians' antipathy was dictated by doctrinal disagreements, competition for members, and the belief that Mill-erism was irrational and fanatic. In this they reflected the attitudes of many non-communitarians: clerics citing theological and exegetical errors, re-formers bemoaning the loss of members to their causes, and newspapers revelling in descriptions of alleged irrationality.

To Noyes's Perfectionists, then still in Putney, Millerism had produced an "excitement ... throughout the land."[33] It was, indeed, a "wind ... sweeping over the country."[34] John Collins, founder of the Skaneateles Community, in Mottville, New York, reported inquiries about Millerites "from every part of the country."[35] William Lloyd Garrison, neither a uto-pian nor an Adventist (indeed unsympathetic to both), found himself an in-voluntary witness to their rise, since the social and intellectual circles of New England abolitionism were also reservoirs for communitarian and Millerite recruitment. From this vantage point, Garrison saw a veritable Millerite onrush: "Thousands have been converted to this strange faith."[36] He professed to see in Millerism's rise "an event scarcely paralleled in the history of popular excitements. Multitudes, who were formerly engaged in the various moral enterprises of the age, have lost all interest in works of practical righteousness and think and talk of nothing else but the burning up of the world."[37]

The seriousness with which Millerism was taken is evident from the energy consumed in its refutation. Noyes's periodicals, *The Witness* and *The Perfectionist*, published eighteen articles on Millerism between 1840 and 1845. The centerpiece was a five-part series, "The Second Coming of Christ," in 1842 and 1843 numbers of *The Witness*.[38] Like Charles Finney, Horace Greeley, and others, Noyes concentrated upon demonstrating that the internal logic of Miller's argument was flawed, and that he had incor-rectly understood the sacred texts that provided the necessary warrant for his conclusions.

Noyes saw in Miller's ideas the penultimate expression of "that old desparate [sic] delusion of Christendom,—the denial that [Christ] *has al-ready come,*" for the Second Coming had taken place "within the lifetime of some of his [Christ's] followers."[39] Like many others, he was impressed by the appearance of internal consistency in Miller's scheme of Biblical in-terpretation. Hence Miller could only be defeated by breaching the logical bastions of his argument. The closed system of traditional millenarian thought within which Miller worked would only yield "by demonstrating that his calculations ... are false."[40] Thus considerations of both principle and practicality argued for rebuttal of Miller in the very terms of Biblical theology that he himself employed. The need to breach a logical system ac-counted for the space anti-Miller articles consumed in Perfectionist publi-

cations, for it was difficult to engage one part of Miller's argument without
dealing with all of it.

Significantly, the need to address Miller's doctrine was shared even by
critics of a more secular turn of mind. John Collins of the Skaneateles Community had little use for religion. Noyes had seen in Miller Christianity's
false views concerning the Second Advent; Collins also professed to see
much that was typical of Christianity. Miller was not an unrepresentative
fringe figure, but in fact stood upon the same foundation as his orthodox
Christian opponents. By implication, to defeat Miller was to defeat Christianity, although of course by 1843–44 Miller's opponents among orthodox Christians were numerous and vocal. Yet Collins was convinced that
the defeat of Miller would aid the cause of secularism rather than of mainstream Protestantism: "When men can rise to a clearer insight into the internal springs of nature, into the character and motives of their own minds,
they will need no revelation beyond nature to instruct them what to obey."[41]

Communitarians generally eschewed the more sensational charges
about Millerites retailed in the penny press. On the other hand, their patience wore thin when Adventists retained their following after the initial
disappointment in 1843. Anticipating that failure would cause immediate
collapse, utopians became testy when Millerites persevered. Noyes's *Perfectionist* began in 1844 to reprint lurid accounts from the general press about
irrational Millerite economic behavior.[42] "Its pretences, and its failure have
come within our immediate observation," wrote John Collins, referring apparently to Millerites in Central New York.[43] The Fourierist *Tribune*, which
largely rejected the sensationalism of such competitors as James Gordon
Bennett's *Herald*, published an account of Millerites disposing of their
wealth in anticipation of the great day.[44] William Lloyd Garrison was not
alone in his view, expressed in March 1843, that "the delusion has not long
to run, and let us rejoice,"[45] but he and others like him had to contend with
more than a year and a half of continued chiliastic expectation.

Although sympathy for Millerism was distinctly muted, it was not absent. Three factors predisposed utopians to view Miller as less than the
complete embodiment of evil—as, at worst, a sincere if misguided individual. In the first place, Miller's social views, while not closely linked to his
theology, were nonetheless clear and well known. They were not drastically
different from those of his communitarian critics. His reformist credentials
commanded a grudging respect. Second, as the anti-religious John Collins
recognized, Miller's doctrines were an exaggerated version of teachings
long current in the Christian churches. Hence indiscriminate attacks on
Miller could easily pass into attacks on Christian orthodoxy; conversely, a
respectful attitude toward religion in general inhibited critics. Finally, hope

remained that the excitement over adventism would lead individuals to reflect on the meaning of history. They might begin in error, but once that error was exposed, they might then move forward to a higher stage of knowledge and spiritual growth.

Although Miller did not dwell on his social views, particularly in his
later life, there was no question of his fidelity to reform causes. Garrison
observed that "the cause of temperance, of anti-slavery, of moral reform, of
non-resistance finds in him an outspoken friend."[46] Francis Nichol, Millerism's foremost modern apologist, portrays Miller as an anti-abolitionist,
but David Rowe has demonstrated that Nichol treated literally a letter that
was intended sarcastically.[47] Much of Second Adventism's leadership was
conspicuously abolitionist as well, including Himes, Charles Fitch, and
Elon Galusha.[48] Since so many prominent utopians were vigorous opponents of slavery—Noyes, Collins, and Brisbane among them—they clearly
found it difficult to publicly flay a fellow reformer.

Similarly, Miller's claim to stand in the Christian mainstream was
compelling enough to deflect some of the hostility directed by religionists.
Miller himself opposed sectarianism, even when by 1844 the momentum of
his doctrine caused uncontrollable defections of Adventists from the existing churches. Noyes's *Perfectionist* approvingly reprinted Miller's un-
heeded December 3, 1844, warning against sectarian ventures.[49] Clearly,
the religious issue placed utopians in a situation of conflicting pressures. On
the one hand, they wished to deflate Millerite claims. On the other, most of
them did not wish to portray themselves as opponents of religion. In some
cases, like Noyes's, they were in fact deeply committed to religious beliefs,
heterodox though they were in some respects. Others, like Albert Brisbane,
were not formally religious, but wished to present themselves as sympathetic to religion in general. As Millerism moved toward its climax, Brisbane's newspaper column was increasingly concerned with demonstrating
the harmony between Fourierism and religion. He devoted three columns to
it in the fall of 1842 and five in the first four months of 1843.[50] He was at
pains to demonstrate that adherence to the Associationist cause was compatible with, and indeed the logical result of, religious commitment.

The hope was, of course, that Millerism might stimulate a process of
inquiry, which would bring new members to the utopians' doors. It is difficult to determine how much of this hope represented considered judgment
and how much the fantasizing of individuals confronted with a temporarily
formidable opponent. When Noyes observed that "we have reason to rejoice
that this delusion makes occasion for many to examine honestly the subject
of the Second Coming," he may well have been alluding to the proto-Mil-
lerite vision he himself experienced during his 1834 breakdown.[51] John Col-

lins, perhaps less burdened by a tortured psyche, shared the hope that "the inquiries we have [concerning Millerism], coming from every part of the country may eventuate in moral instruction."[52]

The Fourierists were invariably less forthright, referring unmistakably to Millerism yet never permitting the name itself to flow from their pens. Notwithstanding their indirection, they too professed to see in the movement a hopeful sign, an imperfect indicator of a broader millennial expectation. This view appears most clearly in a lengthy review in *The Phalanx* of January 5, 1844, of *Nature and Revelation*, by H. H. van Amringe. Van Amringe, unlike Miller, saw the Second Advent as a spiritual rather than a physical event. Clearly referring to Miller, the anonymous reviewer remarked:

> It is almost universally believed that Christianity, at the present day, enjoys a high state of prosperity, and that the Millennial reign, which is now shortly expected, will be an enlargement, and a happy fruitfulness of the religious principles which form the fundamentals of the established creeds of Christendom. Some persons, indeed, look for an actual coming of Christ in the *Body*, while others interpret the promises of the Second Advent *spiritually*.

After noting van Amringe's spirituality with approval, the essay concludes in fine millenarian fashion: "Old things are now to pass away, and all things are become new."[53] So far as *The Phalanx* was concerned, Miller's errors lay in details rather than in broad outlines.

The utopians' fascination with and ambivalence toward Millerism may have resulted from their seeing much of Miller in themselves. At one level, the distinction between the communitarian and the chiliast seems obvious—the former retreating to a self-contained community, the latter awaiting divine intervention in history—but the communitarians shared Miller's hope for a great overturning. They simply drew a different set of inferences from it. The burgeoning of communities in the 1840s was a response to both the widespread yearning for a transformed world and the phenomenon of Millerism itself. The utopians believed they had discovered a third route to the millennium, neither the gradualism of the postmillennialists nor the catastrophism of the premillennialists. This third way emphasized the perfection of one small area at a time to form, as it were, millennial islands in a turbulent sea.

NATURAL DISASTERS AND THE MILLENNIUM

 THE ERUPTION of millennialism during the 1840s came in the wake of two waves of disasters between about 1810 and 1844. The first, early in the century, consisted of natural calamities. While several fell equally upon New England and New York, their greatest impact was felt by the rural population of western and northern New England. The floods, epidemics, and crop failures described in this chapter acted as goads that pushed an increasingly impoverished farming population westward into the Burned-over District.

A second series of disasters—the subject of the following chapter—occurred in the 1830s and 40s, overlapping upon the final shocks of the first wave. The second group differed in both its causes and its impact. Where the earlier stresses resulted from uncontrollable natural forces, the later ones resulted from the structure of society and the economy. Where the first had pushed hill-country farmers into the fertile valleys of upstate New York, the second hit soon after they had settled into what they believed would be a more secure existence. These sequential calamities turned hopes for the millennium from a distant dream into an imminent reality. What was once conventional piety became an event that was anticipated daily.

This was so because the catastrophic events of three and a half decades had had two profound effects on the inner lives of their victims: First, the disasters had to be given meaning. Why were sufferings visited upon a population of conspicuous religious devotion? Disasters must not only be survived; they must be fitted into a picture of the world as an ordered place, where moral purpose informs even apparently arbitrary events. Second, the more forcefully the question of moral order was posed, the greater the tendency to question orthodox positions; and the greater the suspicions about orthodoxies, the greater the receptivity to other ways of thinking about the world.

THE SETTLEMENT OF THE BURNED-OVER DISTRICT

The growth of Burned-over District millennialism in the 1840s cannot be understood apart from the people who settled it. Settlement is rarely a random process. The proximity of populations, available transportation routes, incentives and disincentives for migration, the security and promise of adjoining, sparsely populated areas—all may dictate the size, dynamics, and composition of new populations.

In the case of the Burned-over District, the most significant reservoir of potential settlers lay in New England. As they entered New York, they brought with them the values, cultural patterns, even the very architecture, of the towns they had left. In the absence of large numbers of persons from other areas, the New England migrants effectively placed the stamp of their origins upon all non-urban sections of the district; even early cities such as Rochester, destined to eventually receive foreign immigration, remained heavily Yankee. Between 1790 and 1820 a New England society of church, state, and family had been transferred to the "Second New England" of Upstate New York. Just as its farm families replicated the corporate households of New England, so its developing towns "were little more than a paternalistic update of the New England village."[1] Millennialism was part of the same legacy. The inhabitants of the district brought with them religious patterns in which millennial themes and emotional excitation were already present. They had grown accustomed to view the world as an arena in which God's plan unfolded in history and, in consequence, a locus for confrontations between the holy and the mundane.

No less important were their motives for moving in the first place. While New York was not without its attractions, notably the availability of fertile land, the migration at its most massive was also a movement of escape. However glowing the reports from the west, major population movements, particularly in the period that directly preceded the most intense millenarian activity, were in response to the rapidly declining quality of rural life in New England. The stresses to which many rural Yankees were subjected in the early nineteenth century did much to push them out. The period, particularly from about 1810 through 1832, was a time of massive, multiple natural calamities. In the rugged back country of western and northern New England the rocky soil and primitive transportation required heroic expenditures of labor to sustain even a modest standard of living. Given their meager resources, farmers could count on little in the way of a margin of safety for bad times: "the hill country remained in the best of times a marginal subsistence economy, in the worst of times an agricultural disaster."[2] Often only the supplemental income provided by home handicraft occupations permitted farm families to survive at all.[3] The extraordinary combination of natural hazards during the approximately twenty years up until about 1832 went far beyond the recuperative powers of many of these communities.

The ravages of nature were not, to be sure, focused exclusively on New England. Climatic disturbances and epidemic disease, for example, were of international scope in the early nineteenth century. The significance of natural disasters lay in the inability of a marginal agricultural population to effectively withstand them, and in their predisposition to interpret their fate in religious terms. Natural calamities lent themselves to an understanding as divine chastisement for sins, which in turn required further efforts at religious rejuvenation. In this circular process, the ethos of religious enthusiasm facilitated a religious interpretation of disaster victimization, which in turn increased the likelihood of further religious revivals. Migration patterns drew this victim-population, with its attendant religious attitudes, into New York.

The Revolution had opened Upstate New York for settlement when, through the vicissitudes of war and the inevitable white pressure for land, the Iroquois had been compelled to relinquish most of their territorial rights, a process complete by the late 1780s.[4] Subsequent settlement was sufficiently rapid so that by 1800 what was later to be the Burned-over District was a settled rather than a frontier area, and by 1825 "all of the territory in New York had come into the private or public possession of the white man, and expansion of settlement had reached the boundary limits."[5]

The majority of these settlers were New Englanders, with smaller streams coming up from Pennsylvania and New Jersey.[6] Although Rhode Island and New Hampshire were represented among the initial settlers, the majority came from western Connecticut, western Massachusetts, and western Vermont—and roughly in that order.[7] With the exception of extreme western and southern New York, almost all parts of the upstate area were settled by 1810. New York land opened up after the Revolution, often tied to large-scale speculation, provided the most accessible outlet for excess population in the New England hill country.[8] The tendency of New Englanders to move in clusters of families from the same town made it easy to reproduce New England society in the new settlements, and where migration did not occur *en masse,* relatives soon joined the original settlers to produce culturally homogeneous communities.[9] As early as 1799–1800, revivals began to appear in western New York. They peaked again noticeably in 1807–1808, suggesting that the penchant for emotional religiousity had been transplanted along with other cultural patterns.[10]

Between 1810 and 1830, significant population drops occurred in towns in western and northern New England.[11] While leapfrogging emigration to Illinois, Ohio, and Wisconsin was now a factor, significant numbers continued to move into New York State. By this time, however, the consequence of migration was rarely settlement, except in occasional pockets around which earlier migrants had moved; rather, the result was the consolidation and increase of already existing communities.

In this process of filling-in, Vermonters were particularly conspicuous. The first Vermont migrants had simply moved across Lake Champlain to adjacent areas of New York State. Although Vermont settlers also moved into central and western New York prior to 1810, when they did so, they intermixed with persons from Connecticut and Massachusetts. By 1820, however, land in northern New York near Lake Champlain had either entered private hands or been worked to exhaustion. The Vermont migration, consequently, was diverted to central and western New York where fertile land was still available, and in such numbers that recognizably "Vermonter" communities began to appear.[12]

The significance of this migratory shift lay in the religious culture of Vermont, subtly distinguishing it even from neighboring areas of New England. This distinctiveness resulted from the mountain barriers that isolated Vermont from the rest of New England and preserved its frontier character into the early 1800s. Broken up internally by mountain barriers as well, it was a society where social controls were weak and political, social, and religious dissent was difficult to suppress. Indeed, Vermont's reputation for ideological *laissez-faire* may well have attracted dissidents who felt threatened in areas to the south, making it a sanctuary for points of view out of favor elsewhere.[13]

Vermont, like most of the New England hill country, was itself populated during a series of migrations between 1770 and about 1810.[14] The rudimentary society established there owed much to supporters of the Great Awakening revivals. When the religious climate in Connecticut and Massachusetts became hostile to the Congregationalist supporters of Jonathan Edwards, they sought the freer atmosphere to the North.[15] A full generation or more prior to the migrations into New York, the Great Awakening had institutionalized postmillennialism among the "New Lights," as the Awakening's theological reformers were known. The Second Coming was deferred until the completion of a process of spiritual renewal on earth. The apocalyptic moment now depended upon the spread of personal and communal piety for which the stimulant was clergy-led campaigns of self-examination and prayer.[16] Vermont preserved and concentrated the Great Awakening heritage, and even those who had not themselves lived through it knew it at vivid second hand through the tales of participants.

These and similarly devout but insular populations were also the most vulnerable, for they lived in the least materially advantaged circumstances. Their movement into the Burned-over District between 1810 and 1830 resulted less from the pressure of people upon land than from the magnification of this pressure through a series of traumatic events.

NATURAL CALAMITIES 1810–1832

Attempting to establish a baseline against which to measure natural disturbances is an extraordinarily difficult task. In the absence of a continuing inventory of natural stresses that might identify normal periods, judgments concerning periods of intense stress are bound to appear subjective. Clearly, no such systematically established baseline exists for the early nineteenth century. Nonetheless, some judgments are possible that go beyond pure subjectivity. Thus, we may take account of the self-understanding of contemporaries, manifested in newspaper reports, sermons, and other indicators of opinion. Reasonably safe inferences may also be drawn from the proximity in time of reported stresses and out-migration. These considerations seem particularly appropriate for the Jacksonian period, which in general has been characterized by such terms as "optimism," "expansion," and "progress." Consequently, evidence of despair, pessimism, and danger must be taken seriously, precisely because they contradict the general impression of sunny improvement.

The other major consideration concerns the different abilities of communities to absorb stress. Clearly, hill country New England was relatively more vulnerable than fertile flatlands to the west and south. All other things being equal, a subsistence population may experience as a disaster events accepted by more prosperous groups with some equanimity. The calamities of the period in fact divide into those of broad extent, encompassing the whole northeastern United States, and those limited to smaller areas such as clusters of counties. The former included such national, indeed international, events as epidemics and climatic changes, the latter such localized calamities as floods. In both cases, however, the destructive capacity of the events depends upon the interaction of natural forces with the stress tolerance and recuperative capacities of the affected populations.

Vermont in particular was struck by a large number of spatially circumscribed but intense natural stresses, including flood, disease, and food shortages. Two-thirds of the mills in Rutland and Windsor counties were destroyed by flash floods in 1811, which also drowned livestock, washed away soil, and carried off bridges.[17] In 1813–14, cerebro-spinal meningitis, known popularly as "spotted fever," spread from the Burlington military garrison throughout the state. Estimated fatalities exceeded 6,000, a mortality rate of about 3 percent, given the 1810 population of 217,000.[18] Major floods hit the southeastern section of the state in 1826 and the Champlain valley in the west in 1830. The valley floods were particularly destructive at this time because food production was moving from the exhausted hilltop farms to lower-lying areas and because the deforestation of hillsides increased the already heavy runoff. Agricultural productivity and the local availability of food were not only compromised by the floods; farmers used to planting without fertilizer found their soil exhausted. What could be grown was prey to the blights that occurred after 1824 and to the grasshoppers in 1826. The once plentiful fish and game began to disappear from streams and forests and "were all but extinct by the mid-1830s."[19]

These events were bracketed by much larger catastrophes at either end of the period—the climatic disturbance of 1816, with its sudden and devastating freezes, and the cholera epidemic of 1832. Both were among the most significant natural disasters of the period. "The spring and summer months of 1816 registered mean seasonal temperatures which were among the lowest in the recorded meterological history of the Western world." Unlike abnormally cold winters, the 1816 phenomenon was made especially dramatic by the injection of winter cold into what would normally be high summer, so that snow and ice remained present in parts of New England for twelve consecutive months.[20] The outbreak of cholera sixteen years later confronted the Western world with an international medical problem. "Cholera was the classic epidemic disease of the nineteenth century, as plague had been of the fourteenth."[21]

The weather of 1816 became enshrined in folklore as "Eighteen-hundred and froze to death" and "the year without a summer." The reasons are not far to seek. Abnormally cold temperatures, especially during June, July, and August, occurred all over western Europe, eastern Canada, and the northeastern United States. A cold wave covered all of New England from June 6 until June 11, accompanied in northern areas by up to six inches of snow. The snow line ran from a point just north of Troy, New York, diagonally northeastward to Brunswick, Maine, encompassing almost all of Vermont and New Hampshire and most of Maine. More frosts were to come, on July 9 and on August 21 and 30.[22] As a result, attempts to replant crops by farmers with access to additional seeds failed.

The bizarre cold waves had a devastating effect upon Indian corn, New England's staple crop. Already planted near the northern limits of its climatic zone, it was virtually destroyed by the frosts. The hill farms on which it grew were, as has already been seen, far too fragile to absorb the losses, unlike the more southerly areas where abnormal cold left the fruit and vegetable crops relatively intact.[23] Failure of corn and hay crops deprived farmers of feed for their stock, which now had to be sent to market at depressed prices.[24] At the same time, grain prices rose sharply, not simply because of the reduced supplies, but because western Europe, also hard hit, imported unusually large quantities.[25]

The cause of the climatic anomalies was as baffling as the effects were damaging. It was attributed variously to lightening rods and other disrupters of the flow of natural electricity and to sunspots so prominent they could be seen with the naked eye.[26] None of the speculation appears to have identified the true cause: the extraordinary quantity of volcanic dust thrown into the upper atmosphere by the eruption of Mount Tambora in Indonesia that began April 5, 1815. The volume of debris, some 25 cubic miles, was sufficient to reduce incoming sunlight over some areas.[27] Failure to guess the cause is perplexing in light of Benjamin Franklin's earlier suggestion of a volcanic hypothesis as an explanation of temperature fluctuations.[28] Thus, the freezes of 1816 combined attributes of destructiveness, surprise, and incomprehensibility. The sunspot explanation, while it appeared to offer some understanding, was itself a source of anxiety, since the conspicuous solar disturbance suggested a fundamental instability in the universe.

The severity of the suffering that accompanied the crop failures is difficult to determine with any exactitude. There is consensus that the most serious consequences occurred in northern New England, both because it lay above the snow line and because its farmers were already struggling to stay above the subsistence level. Stephen Marini calls the situation a "famine," while Henry and Elizabeth Stommel suggest that the ability of America to maintain large-scale exports to Europe argues for at least minimally adequate food supplies.[29] America certainly did not experience the hunger-induced civil violence that occurred in Europe,[30] perhaps because by 1817 crops had returned to normal levels.

However, by the growing season of 1817 many New Englanders had already left their hardscrabble farms. "When this cold season piled itself on top of all the preceding afflictions, a good many Vermonters were ready to quit. And who could blame them?"[31] Between 1810 and 1820 Vermont alone lost 10–15,000 people, many because of the summer of 1816, and many to the Burned-over District.[32] Ironically, upstate New York's weather had been almost as bad. It does not figure in most accounts only because regular reliable temperature readings were limited to a few New England colleges. However, newspapers and travellers' reports suggest that frost also covered much of New York, Pennsylvania, and Ohio.[33] In any case, in a time when information flows were partial and inefficient, it is not at all clear that persons sitting dejectedly in freezing farmhouses had reliable information about conditions elsewhere.

The same irony reappeared in the case of cholera, which struck both New York and New England almost simultaneously, yet does not seem to have reduced the westward migratory flow. The arrival of cholera in 1832 was a shock, but it was not a surprise. The epidemic began in India in 1817, then moved slowly westward, principally carried by British troops and ships and Muslim pilgrims. It reached Europe by 1831 and England by 1832. Irish immigrants who landed at Grosse Ile on the St. Lawrence, near Quebec City, brought it to North America the same year. Cholera reached Plattsburgh, New York, on June 11, Burlington, Vermont, June 13, and New York City on June 26. Thence the disease moved along the Erie Canal, reaching Rochester July 12 and Buffalo on July 15. Although data is fragmentary, existing reports suggest the disease was of epidemic proportions through the eastern seaboard, interior New England, and interior New York.[34] The relatively leisurely transit of the disease across the Middle East, Europe, and the Atlantic made its appearance in America predictable; indeed, elaborate though unsuccessful measures were taken to establish quarantine points on the U.S.–Canadian border. However, the forewarning, coupled with lurid reports of the disease elsewhere, heightened rather than reduced alarm. The dramatic onset of symptoms, their frightening character, and the rapidity with which death often followed seemed to magnify the threat. Death occurred in about half of those who contracted the disease.

The total failure of physicians to either adequately treat or understand it amplified public apprehension.[35] As late as 1849, when cholera struck again, physicians remained convinced that it was not a contagious disease. Most identified its cause as some ill-understood peculiarity of the atmosphere in areas of its occurrence, although some suggested electrical or magnetic origins, as had been done with climatic disturbances.[36] Thus one contributor to a serious medical journal suggested that "the electric fluid, within the crust of the earth, alter(s) and affect(s) the exhalants forming the atmosphere in the routes." This led him to the novel hypothesis that the

Asiatic cholera and the Irish potato blight stemmed from the same causes, and that therefore "the cholera has existed as a disease in the potato."[37] Although this surely stands as one of the more bizarre attempts to identify the origins of either disease, it indicates the depth of incomprehension with which physicians greeted the cholera outbreaks.

In the absence of secular remedies, resort was made to religion. Although Andrew Jackson refused to sanction a day of public fasting in 1832, many clergymen viewed the epidemic as punishment for human sins. As evidence, they pointed to the disproportionate death rate among blacks and immigrants, assumed to be among the least worthy elements of the population.[38] Richard Carwardine, paraphrasing Dr. Johnson, observes that "the very real fear of death ... concentrated the mind wonderfully on the evangelical message of repentance and escape from sin," resulting in the so-called cholera revivals to purge sin and appease an angry God.[39]

The epidemic dealt its heaviest blows in urban areas, where poor sanitation and population density allowed the disease to spread rapidly. Since cholera was carried from place to place along transportation arteries, and since those arteries (such as the Erie Canal) generally connected the larger and more commercially active centers, the disease moved naturally from one city to another.[40] Although cities bore the brunt, the epidemic had serious effects in the countryside as well. The immediate rural hinterland of cities was vulnerable. Moreover, cholera first made its appearance in the Champlain Valley astride the New York–Vermont border, whence it moved down the Hudson Valley toward New York. Hence Northern New England lay almost directly along its route from Canada into the United States.

The consequences of the manifold natural hazards between about 1810 and 1832 were threefold: First, the precariously situated hill farms became even less tenable than they had previously been. Second, the rural population was pushed westward, and in the process a substantial number were deposited in the Burned-over District, this despite the fact that some of the same hazards had extended into the District as well. By the 1850s, scarcely any self-sufficient farms remained in interior New England.[41] Third, the disasters produced a disquieting impression about the spiritual state of the world. People schooled to view nature as God's slate found it difficult to believe the disasters were random events or the outcome of impersonal processes for which naturalistic explanations could be given. The conception of suffering as divine punishment died hard, particularly in rural areas, and among people who took their religion seriously, suffering had to be understood in religious terms, for the less merited it appeared, the more it called into question conceptions of moral order. If one function of disasters was to punish wrongdoing, another was to prepare the way for the millennium.

The greater the tumult in the natural world, the less persuasive postmillenarian optimism seemed, and the more plausible the premillenarian argument became. Since the "latter days" had traditionally been viewed as a time of tribulation, the worse conditions became, the more imminent the millennial time.

Consequently, these natural calamities created conditions highly favorable to the rise of a movement such as Millerism. The natural hazards dislodged a devout population from the precarious and physically isolated farms and settlements of the New England hills. From there, already well-defined routes funneled them into the Burned-over District, an area which was at once compact but equipped with excellent internal communications. In addition, the stresses of the twenty-year period of natural disasters fitted the premillenarian model far better than it fitted postmillenarian explanations. The adequacy of postmillennialism was called into question, since incremental improvement was now less evident, and at the same time, the unfashionable premillenial view of history now appeared more compatible with events.

Postmillennialism might have survived this encounter with calamity if the displaced Yankee populations could have resumed their lives in a more secure environment. New York State appeared to offer precisely such security with its fertile, rock-free soil and its absence of internal communications barriers. Nonetheless, the tranquility of this "Second New England" was to be abruptly shaken, and by causes very different from the earlier catastrophes.

7

SOCIOECONOMIC DISASTERS
AND THE MILLENNIUM

THE POPULATION of the Burned-over District was significantly augmented by western and northern New Englanders
driven from marginal farmland by a series of natural disasters in the early decades of the century. Having arrived in upstate New York
as victims, they assumed that their troubles were behind them, and they
quickly became integrated into the clone of New England society already
established in the region. The fertility of such areas as the Genesee Valley
and the stimulation given commerce by the completion of the Erie Canal
suggested a locale that was prosperous and buffered against natural hazards. Storms, epidemics, and the like had always drawn from premillennialists a delicious apprehension, fear mingled with the quiet satisfaction that
one knew the direction of God's plan. They thus survived earlier calamity
confident of its meaning but hopeful that rich land in New York would protect them from recurrence.

By the late 1830s, however, the national economy suffered a major collapse. The depression which followed the Panic of 1837 and lasted until
about 1844 was no less devastating in its own way than the natural disasters
of earlier years. It was also even more puzzling, for it could not be easily fitted into traditional religious explanations of suffering. The boom and bust
economy was set against an increasingly troubled social background. Old
verities about the stability of family life did not survive the transplantation
of New England society. The economy that produced depression also produced changes in the relationships between men and women and between
parents and children. The promise of the Burned-over District proved to be
a bitter illusion.

113

CALAMITY RETURNS: Panic and Depression, 1837–44

The period preceding 1837 was "an era of economic growth unparalleled before that time."[1] The boom was especially evident in the towns and farmlands of the Burned-over District. The commerce of New York State increased tenfold between 1791 and 1831, and the population quadrupled between 1790 and 1820. In Ontario County, it more than doubled between 1810 and 1820 alone. Mills sprang up along the downward rushing streams, and land-poor New Englanders turned the fertile soil of the Genesee Valley to wheat production. The completion of the Erie Canal in 1825 dropped Great Lakes-to-the-Atlantic freight rates from $100 a ton to $25 or even $15.[2]

The onrushing prosperity of the Jacksonian years suffered an abrupt interruption in the Panic of 1837. Although the banking upheaval appeared temporary, a second, more fundamental economic contraction in 1839 began a four-year depression, continuing, with only brief interruption, until 1843–44. The murky origins of the panic lay in massive speculation permitted by the unbridled extension of credit and in the vicissitudes of the Anglo-American cotton trade. Speculation in cotton and public land peaked in November 1836. Questionable banking practices had been used to finance internal improvements, notably the expansion of transportation arteries, and in any case, many banks had catered to a clientele with neither credit nor capital.[3] In July 1836, the national government sought to curb western land speculation by requiring that public lands be purchased only for specie (gold or silver coins) rather than with banknotes. In early 1837, the Bank of England refused to accept paper from American banks in cotton transactions. Peter Temin challenges the belief that the requirement for specie to buy western land contributed significantly to the panic by draining specie from the East. While acknowledging the psychological role played by the change in land purchasing, he places greater economic weight on the fall in prices paid in England for American cotton, which resulted in defaults on American debts secured by cotton.[4] Whatever the balance among causal factors, credit contracted with shuddering abruptness, with only specie accepted in payment for both domestic and international debts. As confidence in banknotes fell, a run on the limited supply of specie became inevitable.[5]

Cotton firms in coastal cities began to collapse. Holders of banknotes quickly found that banks first limited and then suspended the exchange of notes for specie. The suspensions began in the south in May 1837, reflecting the depressed price of cotton. However, the overextension of credit domestically and the change in land purchase policy were sufficient to spread alarm in the north and west. Specie conversions ceased in New York City on

May 10. The panic then spread up the Hudson River and along the Erie Canal in a manner not unlike the diffusion of cholera five years before, until by May 12 the Burned-over District was well encompassed. Most of the country east of the Mississippi had experienced the suspensions by May 22.[6]

The panic had mixed effects. The suspension of specie payments did not cause a total halt in banking. Rather, individuals reverted to the previous practice of utilizing banknotes and checks, since neither silver nor gold coins were available.[7] On the other hand, the withdrawal of credit in a credit-hungry economy was not without consequences, and descriptions of the panic's effect on business run to the hyperbolic—whether in Albert Brisbane's assertion cited earlier that only a dozen men between Albany and Buffalo avoided bankruptcy, or in the observation that "in the fall of 1837, nine-tenths of the factories in the Eastern states were said to be closed."[8] Since the early casualties were overextended businessmen, their financial collapse led to high urban unemployment.

The stagnation of 1837 initially appeared to be a transient phenomenon, for specie payments were resumed in 1838. The recovery, however, was shortlived. The price of cotton once again fell in late 1839, producing a partial specie suspension. While temporary, its end did not signal a return to prosperity. Rather, it introduced four years of skidding prices. It is perhaps a moot point whether the period from 1839 to 1844 was a contraction comparable in magnitude to the Great Depression of the 1930s, or merely a deflation in which prices fell but production did not. Prices fell farther between 1839 and 1843 than between 1929 and 1933—42 percent as against 31 percent. Temin infers from consumption data that production in all likelihood was little changed, and that agricultural production in particular was not greatly affected, if only because the large rural population had little alternative but to continue growing crops while selling them for less.[9]

Although production may have been sustained, depressed prices were not a trivial concern. This was particularly so because of contemporaneous changes in the character of agriculture and the vulnerability of farmers to market conditions. The period 1800–40 was marked by a transition from an agriculture of local self-sufficiency, insulated from larger economic fluctuations, to commercial agriculture, in which crops were raised for distant sale. The farm improvements necessitated by market competition in turn produced a need for capital. Additional cash was required to pay store bills and to speculate in land. Consequently, by 1830 a substantial number of eastern farms had been mortgaged.[10] The opening of transportation arteries such as the Erie Canal brought formerly distant markets within reach and stimulated more specialized production. In central and western New York

State, this meant the cultivation of wheat for western markets, although by 1840–60, the same transportation system permitted large amounts of competing western wheat to move east as well.[11]

Wholesale agricultural prices fell sharply from late 1841, through 1842, into 1843. They reached bottom in March of that year. At the 1843 trough, prices were lower than at any other point in the pre-Civil War period.[12] Although prices were generally higher in eastern than in western markets, prices dropped in Cincinnati as well as in New York City. The drop, however, was proportionately greater in the east, exacerbated perhaps by the appearance of grain from the midwest.[13] In short, a major agricultural depression was in progress. The economic promise of upstate New York, symbolized by the Canal, had with relative suddenness turned to ashes. Already overextended, farmers found themselves unable to generate the cash they required.

The depression that struck the Burned-over District was part of a much larger economic decline throughout the Western world. The depression of the early 1840s occurred at the trough of the economic cycle commonly referred to as the "Kondratieff wave" or "long wave." This forty-to-sixty-year periodicity is linked to the name of N. D. Kondratieff, the Soviet economist whose writings in the 1920s asserted that capitalist economies exhibit rhythmic expansions and contractions.[14] Kondratieff's work received its first substantial attention in the United States during the Great Depression, which it appeared uncannily to foresee.[15]

Kondratieff examined numerous statistical series for France, England, and the United States between about 1780 and 1920. This period of 140 years yielded two and a half cycles, most clearly evident in price data. He was far better able to describe the cycles, however, than to account for their occurrence. His critics charged him with advancing a deterministic scheme rather than an explanation of economic behavior.[16] The debate about causality between long-wave theorists and their adversaries is less germane to present purposes than the regularities Kondratieff and those who followed him discerned, for the Kondratieff wave closely parallels well-known periods of economic vigor and slackness. Of particular interest here is the relationship between the Kondratieff cycle and the events of the early 1840s.

Kondratieff argued that the cycle rose from a trough in the late 1780s and early 1790s to a peak from 1810 to 1817, and fell to a trough in 1844–51. This first Kondratieff downswing corresponds closely to turning points in wholesale prices, which bottomed out in 1851 in France, 1849 in England, but as early as 1843 in the United States.[17] W. W. Rostow, re-examining Kondratieff's formulation, places the bottom of the downturn at 1848.[18] In any case, there remains agreement that the economic decline neared or touched bottom in the mid-to-late 1840s.[19]

Thus in ways that remain to be fully explained, the decline of the American economy after 1837 seems to have been a particularly serious manifestation of a larger economic crisis. In an era before the full development of industrial production, the drop in wholesale commodity prices fell with particular force on the population of agricultural districts. In the past such market fluctuations had been buffered by the subsistence character of many farms. As long as production had been oriented to local consumption, larger economic forces were of limited importance. By the 1840s, however, farming had lost its subsistence character and was now directed at production for distant markets, which made it hostage to forces farmers could not control.

Loss of control was exacerbated by the mysterious character of a boom and bust economy, for one's fate now seemed determined by incomprehensible forces. National economies made distant localities both the beneficiaries and the victims of uncounted anonymous decisions taken in distant commercial centers. Economic decisions were peculiarly impersonal and invisible; they could neither be seen nor identified, yet they had the power to determine the quality of individual and community life.[20] Thus, like natural calamities, economic disasters had to be confronted on two levels. Their effects had to be mastered, and their position in the moral order had to be understood.

THE INSTABILITY OF FAMILY LIFE

The effects of economic stress were exacerbated by the perceived instability of the central social unit, the family. This paralleled the situation in the earlier period of natural disasters when vulnerability increased because the central economic unit, the family farm, was too precariously situated to shield individuals from natural hazards. Now that the hazards were non-natural, their weight fell upon the web of interpersonal relationships, but the family and the structure of social roles within it were themselves undergoing stress.

Family crisis was, ironically, the child of prosperity. The boom years of the Second New England, instead of strengthening family ties, weakened them by creating incentives for behavioral change. A traditional agricultural way of life could not be sustained under the multiple influences of population growth, orientation to market demands, and the growth of opportunities in commerce and industry. The sense of family instability rose through the 1820s and by the 1830s had engendered a feeling of crisis. The rise after 1830 of a practical literature for the guidance of family life serves as an unobtrusive measure of loss of confidence.[21]

By the time the second generation in the Burned-over District came of age, population was beginning to press against the supply of cheap, fertile land. While a falling birthrate provided partial adjustment to resource limitations, the more immediate consequence was the drift of male children away from the farm family. Some moved to the towns with their growing commercial and industrial employment opportunities, while still others moved toward the frontier.[22] In either case, the consequence was the loss of parental control. Sons in distant places, their future no longer directly tied to the family farm, necessarily made their own way. At the same time, the family unit ceased to be as formidable a concentration of common labor. Daughters, far less free to choose alternative styles of life, remained to produce a surplus of females over males.[23]

More remote economic forces also compelled changes in family structure. As we have already seen, farmers had ceased to produce for their own and their neighbors' use and were instead growing for distant markets. The demise of the self-sufficient farm had two significant consequences. First, it made rural families dependent rather than independent. They needed others for what they themselves could not produce, and they required customers to purchase what they grew. Second, the end of self-sufficiency drastically diminished the economic significance of women, whose labor was no longer required to make at home what now had to be bought. The reduced economic role for women resulted in the division of life into a male sphere of work outside the home and a female sphere of domesticity within it. Foster suggests that because of the division of economic functions, "the gap between the worlds of men and women became wider than possibly at any other time in American history."[24]

As a result of the division between male and female spheres, the prevailing surplus of females, and the growing independence of older children, women became progressively more isolated from the world around them.[25] Deprived of productive economic activities and no longer intimately sharing in the work roles of their spouses, women found compensations in revival religion. Women assumed disproportionately important roles both as converts during revivals and as workers in the benevolent societies the revivals spawned.[26] Millenarian movements held particular appeal for women who already centered their lives around emotional religion.

The economic upheavals after 1837 thus fell upon families straining to redefine male and female roles, the proper relationship between parents and children, and the extent to which the family should be linked to the external world. Neither the resources families could command nor their sense of cohesiveness prepared them for the strains of economic depression.

THE MILLENARIAN RESPONSE TO DISASTER

The timing of millenarian activity suggests the potential significance of the economic tumult. The most important period of Shaker revivalism began August 16, 1837, a few months after the panic.[27] John Humphrey Noyes began the organization of the Putney community in the early 1840s, and it reached a formal state of organization by 1844. Although revivalism had been at a low ebb in 1837, it surged after the panic and reached a peak of activity in 1843. Millerism itself crested as the economy hit bottom.[28]

These may appear to be parallel responses, but in fact Second Adventists and utopians understood economic collapse in very different terms. Further, there is little direct evidence that the actions of any single group reflected personal deprivations suffered by its members, although given the scope of the depression and the population from which the movements drew, many who joined may have been victims. The movements are best understood not as instances of relative deprivation—the poor organizing against the rich—but as attempts to introduce alternative conceptions of moral order. For whether or not conditions adversely affected a particular individual, the pervasiveness of stress and suffering raised fundamental questions concerning the nature of good and evil. Individuals reared in a culture that had made the religious revival into an institution could scarcely ignore these questions regardless of their personal situations. Events suggested a world unhinged, while orthodox beliefs continued to proclaim a dogma of progressive improvement.

Millerism revived a traditional premillennialism of signs and portents. According to it, the condition of earthly life varied inversely with the nearness of the Second Coming: the worse the state of the world, the closer the millennium. In this "the worse, the better" perspective, the accumulating misery of the early 1840s merely added to natural calamities of prior decades. Yet Second Adventists could not easily bridge the gap between natural disasters and economic breakdown, for in addition to the general requirement that the millennium be preceded by escalating tumult, premillennialists were locked into the traditional vocabulary of signs and portents. As we have seen, not all events fitted equally well within this structure, designed to accommodate wars and acts of nature.

The Millerites were trapped within this analytic framework. On the one hand, the economic dislocations contributed to the general decline expected of the "latter days," with its sense of the world running down like a faltering machine. The experience of everyday life appeared to validate the predictions of an imminent end. However, while Second Adventism could accommodate the general characteristics of growing misery, it could not readily deal with the details. For unlike the natural disasters in the early years of the century, the depression was difficult to incorporate within the stylized language of portent analysis. The abrupt fluctuations of boom and bust were too novel to have found their way into the vocabulary of signs. Consequently, the Millerites were beneficiaries of the pervasive sense of unease but had nothing specific to say about the state of the economy and its consequences. The Millerite press, it will be recalled, exhaustively reported the wars of the Ottoman Empire and the Dorr Rebellion, yet failed to address the deteriorating economic conditions. Since this resulted from the rigidity of their categories rather than callousness or ignorance, it gave to Second Adventist literature a peculiarly detached, almost surreal character. Trapped by the limitations of their rhetoric, Millerites were never able to directly discuss the malaise around them. The peculiar shape of pre-Civil War calamities, mixing the natural and artificial, provided Millerism with its opportunities but also established limits to its growth, since Second Adventism was unable to encompass more than a part of it.

The utopian communities were in a more favorable position, for in two respects they spoke to issues of economic inequality and insecurity. First, their very ways of life exemplified values of equality and security. The provision of basic needs—food, clothing and shelter—was a community function. The individual did not have to rely upon personal resources; indeed, those resources were often forfeited to the community as a condition of membership. Requirements for the redistribution of property acted as a social leveller, since the elimination of differences in personal wealth greatly reduced distinctions of rank. Second, some of the communities explicitly sought to eliminate poverty forever. Their efforts took the form of both institutional innovations and the development of belief systems directed at explaining and preventing social and economic problems.

The emphasis on the communal provision of basic needs theoretically freed the individual from the quest for the necessities of life. In practice, however, not all communities exhibited the well-organized prosperity of the Shakers or the growing bourgeois comforts of Oneida. Frequently undercapitalized, sometimes lacking members with the necessary agricultural skills, communities often provided a standard of living inferior to that enjoyed outside, yet even in these cases the principle of joint responsibility for material well-being differentiated utopias from the *laissez-faire* world around them.

Communitarians were self-consciously aware of economic evils and of the need to recast conceptions of work and property. Their ideas rationalized social arrangements entered into spontaneously and pragmatically, while at the same time providing guidelines for the further redesign of institutions. Economic innovation was as much a part of religious as of secular communities. The Shakers rejected the belief that work was part of the curse of Adam, and imbued it with a special dignity. At the same time, they rejected the prevailing ethic of individual self-seeking in favor of communal effort.[29]

Utopians' interest in economic forces often predated their communal ventures. Throughout his life Albert Brisbane had a quasi-Populist fascination with the mysteries of finance. As a young man of twenty-six, he may already have been an implacable foe of bankers, and a monetary reformer who advocated a national currency and the demonetization of gold and silver.[30] If so, he returned to it in later life as a supporter of the Greenback cause in the 1870s.[31] As early as 1835, John Humphrey Noyes had attacked the uncontrolled pursuit of economic gain which two years later produced the panic: "speculation, after devouring its rations, is made to prey upon itself."[32] He subsequently saw the panic as an example of the dangers of reform, which separated social problems from one another. The temperance movement, he argued, had unknowingly contributed to economic collapse by holding out financial gain as the reward for sobriety. The result was "the raving madness of a MONEY-MANIA, produced in a great measure by the conversion of drunkards into a nation of swindlers."[33]

Fourierists' analyses tended to be more restrained. Their agenda centered on the sufferings of the working poor, "ground to death by the oppressiveness of ... society."[34] Profits needed to be redistributed to benefit those whose labor had produced the goods. These were not people among whom depressions passed unnoticed. Brisbane himself attributed the successes of Associationism to the bad times of the early 1840s, "well calculated to awaken the poor farmers to the hardships of their condition and to lead them to catch eagerly at any scheme for their relief."[35]

The split among utopians was over the proper response to the social crisis. John Collins, an Owenite, differed significantly with Fourierism over remedies, yet "I cannot but rejoice in the able expositions of the rottenness and inhumanity of our present social condition."[36] For Noyes, the Fourierist diagnosis did not go far enough. The elements of the social organism were not simply "dislocated"; they were *"vitally diseased"* and consequently required the most fundamental of remedies.[37]

What, then, was the proper response? Brisbane, like Noyes, had little use for conventional politics: "Politicians and legislators are engaged in superficial controversies and quarrels, which lead to no practical results."[38] Fourierism offered a deeper understanding, which its partisans sought to demonstrate was identical to Christianity. If that were the case, then creating social and economic change became a religious duty. They attacked Owen for his efforts to sever social improvements from a Christian basis,[39] but it was precisely Brisbane's identification of the two that Noyes found unpalatable. Fourierism was directed toward the praiseworthy goal of "perfecting social machinery," but neglected the cardinal necessity of producing "good men" as a vital precondition for good institutions.[40] In this, Noyes returned to a theme he had enunciated in his youth, when in a letter to William Lloyd Garrison he flirted with revolution against a government that protected slaveholding ("Is it not high time for abolitionists to abandon a government whose President has declared war upon them?"), only to transcend "mere" social improvement:

> All the abhorrence which now falls upon slavery, intemperance, lewdness, and every other specific vice, will in due time be gathered in one volume of victorious wrath against *unbelief*. I wait for that time as for the day of battle, regarding all the previous movements as only fencing-schools and manoevres of military discipline—or at best as the preliminary skirmishes which precede a general engagement.[41]

Thus the utopians, whether in religious or secular garb, maintained a lively curiosity about the workings of the economy. They were equally repelled by the injustices inflicted on the poor and by the selfishness exhibited by the rich and ambitious. Their preoccupation with family structure flowed directly from this revulsion. They saw the nuclear family as an agency for encouraging and legitimating selfishness. The instability of the family did not so much signal its collapse as it indicated its contraction, from an extended family that reached out to others, to the minimal unit necessary to acquire wealth. They were not so much anti-familial as they were advocates of radical family expansion, creating environments where the family and the community would be coterminous.[42]

The message of the decade was garbled to the Millerites, filled with the appropriate foreboding, yet made confusing by unfamiliar signs. They tried to clarify the message by emphasizing the occasional comet or troubles in the Levant, yet they did so at the expense of more far-reaching turmoil in American society. The intellectual system of Millerite millennialism dis-

played formidable internal cohesion but sacrificed empirical relevance. The utopians, whose belief systems were rarely so tight-knit, were far more atuned to the new anxieties. They looked to the portents of a modern age— financial panics rather than earthquakes and disrupted family structure in-
· stead of far-off battles. Thus the 1840s did not take utopians unaware. In- deed, it stimulated their most impassioned outbursts. The depression, far from constituting an embarrassing exception to their view of society and history, seemed the most convincing validation of their efforts.

ORGANIZING FOR THE MILLENNIUM

SECOND ADVENTISM was at least as much the victim of its rhetoric as it was of disconfirmed predictions. Its apparatus of Biblical interpretation forced it to ignore precisely those social issues on which the utopians were free to concentrate.

If one part of Millerism's dilemma was intellectual, another was organizational. Commitment to an imminent millennium demands more of individuals than adherence to more limited causes. If the belief is not shared by most members of the society, which is particularly the case in western chiliasm, then millenarians must be able to defend themselves against the taunts, ridicule, and even physical hostility of their more orthodox fellow-citizens. If the end-time is only a few years, months, or weeks away, then conventional obligations seem trivial and eschatological yearnings begin to preempt the ordinary business of life. Millenarians consequently live in suspension between the mundane world which is about to be destroyed and the sacred world about to be revealed. Normally accepted routines of work, leisure, and domesticity seem ill-adapted for the frustrations of anticipation. In short, the organizational attachments of normal life appear inappropriate to an abnormal time. Family, political party, church, and business enterprise depend upon the indefinite continuity of life, while the millennium demands discontinuity. How, then, ought chiliasts organize themselves in the awkward interlude between imperfection and redemption?

The 1840s provided a striking juxtaposition of two organizational models. The Millerites employed a strategy of confrontation. Utilizing the most sophisticated forms of mass communication available, they took their message into the most densely populated urban centers. The utopians adopted an almost diametrically opposed approach. While eager to propagandize, they were equally anxious to avoid unnecessary physical contact with others. Instead of confronting non-believers, they withdrew into their communal enclaves. Instead of moving aggressively into the cities, they elaborated miniature societies in the countryside.

THE ORGANIZATION OF TRADITIONAL MILLENNIALISM

Millerism inherited the beliefs of a millenarian tradition that extended into the Middle Ages. Hence it may be useful to begin by examining the structure of pre-modern chiliastic groups.

Before the nineteenth century, millenarian movements can scarcely be called "organized" at all in the sense of possessing role specialization, chain of command, and the delegation of authority. They were customarily small, cohesive, and grouped about a prophetic leader. Indeed, millennialists were if anything *anti*-organizational, contrasting their own intimacy with the coldness of orthodox religion. Christian groups often consciously sought a return to the practices of the early church, which they regarded as more authentic than the bureaucratization of ecclesiastical institutions.

The romanticization of spontaneous behavior and the rejection of institutionalized authority manifested themselves in the deliberate rule-breaking of antinomianism and in charismatic leadership. The tendency of millennialists to see themselves as perfect and the rest of the world as sinful implied that behavioral restraints appropriate to others were not binding upon them. Indeed, among some groups such as the Jewish followers of the false messiah Sabbatai Zevi and (more arguably) the Brethren of the Free Spirit in the Low Countries, breaking religious taboos demonstrated the violators' sense of special virtue.[1] "Law" was for others—the evil, the unredeemed, the imperfect. Those who already felt themselves to be living in the new time had no need for these expedients and felt compelled to manifest their superior virtue by dabbling in the forbidden.

The antipathy toward law was integrally related to the dependence upon charismatic authority. Most millenarian groups were led by individuals whose followers believed them to be endowed with extraordinary capacities. The attribution of special talents had the effect of superceding more mundane forms of authority. The pronouncements of governmental officials or conventional religious leaders could not match the quasi-revelational authority of charisma. Just as charismatic leaders are not bound by the norms of past or present, so they are not obliged to remain consistent. The line between the forbidden and the permitted may be redrawn as the whims and intuitions of the leader dictate.

Both antinomianism and charisma worked against complex organization by emphasizing change over continuity. The past lost its normative legitimacy. No rule was inherently unbreakable, both because rule-breaking validated spiritual superiority and because charismatically generated pronouncements superceded other norms. Such groups produced an anti-organizational milieu, making it difficult to delegate authority, draw up long-range plans, or divide different functions among specialized office-holders.

The major difficulty for millenarian groups has always been growth, since commitment tends to decline with distance from the leader and from the reinforcement that fellow members could offer. Personalistic leadership might change goals so rapidly that systematic recruiting became difficult. Even where the group appears to spread, the danger is that it may do so by drawing upon persons who affiliate for opportunistic reasons. Open recruitment of untested outsiders implies a dilution of the group's elite character.

In practice, these dangers were not often apparent, for the environment of pre-modern millenarianism reinforced the bias toward smallness and compactness. Movements usually occurred in relatively remote rural areas. Eruptions in urban areas, such as late–fifteenth-century Münster, while widely reported, were in fact uncommon until modern times.[2] Given their back-country locales, opportunities for expansion were often limited by rudimentary transportation and communication. The typical pattern was for a group to expand within a well-defined region until challenged by religious or civil authorities, to be defeated, and to retreat into a clandestine and even smaller form. Premodern groups were hardly ever able to control large territories, and even when able to fully invest the region of their origin, were highly vulnerable to outside pressure.

The agrarian character of premodern movements was reinforced by the vulnerability of rural life. Subject to the recurrent stress of natural disasters, remote regions held disproportionately victimized populations, for whom the promised millennium appeared both plausible and inviting. Additionally, governmental and religious authority moved slowly and inefficiently in such areas. Neglect arising from administrative inefficiency permitted movements to grow and solidify, as they could not have in regions adjacent to urban centers. This pattern survived in the politically unintegrated parts of southern Europe into the early twentieth century and in the non-Western world into the present.

The Millerites departed from this pattern in several respects. In the first place, they were politically quiescent, offering neither overt nor rhetorical opposition to civil authority. Millerism recruited successfully from among social and political reformers, but once affiliated, they abandoned their former causes. Miller himself advocated scrupulous attentiveness to the requirements of the existing order even as he anticipated its demise. There is no reason to doubt his post-Disappointment insistence that "I have never taught a neglect of any of the duties of life, which make us good parents, children, neighbors, or citizens. . . . Those who have taught the neglect of these . . . acted in opposition to my uniform teachings."[3]

Miller's insistence upon fidelity to duty suggests that in a second respect he differed from other millenarian leaders: he was not charismatic. His autobiographical writings appraise his own efforts with a modesty wholly untypical of charismatic authority: "That I have been mistaken in the time [of the Second Advent], I freely confess; and I have no desire to defend my course any further than I have been actuated by pure motives."[4] The major thrust of his enterprise lay in the construction of an apparatus of Biblical interpretation, pursued with a zeal that verged on pedantry. Perhaps because of this plodding quality, and because Miller insisted upon the absolute authority of Biblical texts, Adventists rarely engaged in antinomian acts.[5]

Finally, Millerism proselytized on a massive scale. Under Joshua Himes's shrewd direction, the Adventists imitated and elaborated upon the already impressive propagandistic techniques developed by the revivalists of the Second Great Awakening. As Ernest Sandeen observes, "the one distinctive feature of Millerite Adventism was its uniquely successfully system of popularization, comprising a network of fugitive newspapers, adman's posters, and the moveable tent."[6] The movement thrust outward with an expansionism that set it apart from the purely local millennialism of previous times. These behavioral and organizational departures from conventional millenarian practice contrast dramatically with the Millerites' ideological traditionalism. Millerism was among the first chiliastic movements to move aggressively into highly urbanized areas and to seek converts by systematically employing a combination of face-to-face persuasion techniques borrowed from revivalism and printed propaganda appropriate to an era of mass literacy. Thus, any explanation of Millerism's failure must account not only for its ideological archaism but for its organizational modernity.

THE GROWTH OF URBAN AMERICA

In 1840, America was still primarily an agricultural society whose population was 89.2 percent rural, but at the threshold of urban growth. The smallness of the urban sector reflected two factors—the non-urban location of early industry and the absence of large pre-industrial cities. Self-sustaining industrial growth began simultaneously with the burgeoning of Millerism,[7] but much of the early industrial activity occurred at waterpower sites in rural or semi-rural settings. Much early factory production thus occurred where energy sources could be tapped, rather than in already densely populated regions.[8] Although many mill sites became nuclei for later urban growth, the initial effect was to disperse rather than concentrate industrialization. In the second place, no American city possessed a substantial premodern history, not even Boston. In the early 1700s, New York, Philadelphia, and Boston were scarcely more than large villages and remained small by English standards for decades thereafter. The mid—eighteenth-century population of Philadelphia was about 20,000, while such seaports as Boston, New York, Newport, and Charleston held fewer than 15,000 each— this at a time when "one Englishman in every six had at some time lived in [London]."[9] By 1775, Philadelphia had grown, but only to 40,000; London was well in excess of half a million. Since half of all American city dwellers were divided among Boston, New York, Philadelphia, and Baltimore, no community seized a dominant administrative or cultural position.

The growth of cities was severely retarded by the Revolutionary War, even if one employs the census' relatively permissive definition of a city as any community in excess of 8,000. Since the existing cities were mainly ports, they bore the brunt of the conflict, and many inhabitants fled. In the early 1800s, moreover, westward migration was a further drain. Consequently, in the late 1700s urban areas had to make good the deficit caused by wartime population shifts and the outflow that would be caused by western expansion. Notwithstanding these factors, the share of total population in cities did indeed rise, whether in the census' figures or the more conservative statistics collected by Adna Weber, as shown in Table 8.1. The magnitude of urban increase is clearly evident in the growth rates in the decades between censuses. The decade of the 1840s manifested an unusually high rate of urban growth, closely followed by the decade 1820–30, during which the Burned-over District absorbed its new population.[13]

With its historic roots in agrarian areas, millennialism now sought to penetrate the novel yet alluring territory of the city. In a general way, the problem was that of establishing intense but unorthodox commitments among a large, diverse population, in which every point of view was subject

TABLE 8.1

Urbanization Before the Civil War

% Share of population in cities		Decennial percentage rates of increase in proportion of population living in communities over 8000[12]
Census[10]	Weber[11]	
1790 5.13	3.35	—
1800 6.07	3.97	60
1810 7.26	4.93	69
1820 7.19	4.93	33
1830 8.76	6.72	82
1840 10.76	8.52	68
1850 —	12.49	99

to critical examination. The dilemma of commitment in an urban setting was notably acute in the pre-Civil War period, for the urban population was itself constantly on the move. Cities gained population by in-migration from rural areas, but also through city-to-city movement. The work of Stephen Thernstrom and Peter R. Knights demonstrates that many residents of any given city lived there briefly, only to leave when economic opportunity beckoned. That meant not only neighborhood to neighborhood moves within cities but often leap-frogging to distant towns. The most mobile were not the middle-class, possessed of the means to go elsewhere, but rather the poor, who instead of being anchored to their place of residence, shifted from city to city in search of the main chance.[14] Thus the more deprived contributed not only their poverty to the urban environment but their rootlessness and lack of established social affiliations.

Urban population movement was a function not only of the desire for new opportunities but of the availability of movement itself. In this respect, the circulation of persons and ideas were joined, for in an era in which all messages were of necessity physically carried by human beings from place to place, "the movement of news and information was synonymous with human spatial interaction."[15] Just as Millerism stood at the threshold of explosive urban growth, so it stood at the boundary separating distinct eras in communication, defined by the opening of the first telegraph line between Baltimore and Washington on May 24, 1844. The telegraph destroyed the spatial bias of communication, the differential speed at which information could be carried over given areas.[16]

While a qualitative change occurred with telegraphy, communication and transportation had advanced considerably in the two decades that preceded it. These advances included both increases in speed, by which the spatial bias was reduced, and increases in channel capacity, increasing the number of persons and the quantity of information diffused. These changes were particularly pronounced in the northeast, where railroad construction, canal building, the exploitation of natural waterways, and the capacity to exploit new printing technology could all be found.

The Burned-over District was a particular beneficiary of these changes. The opening of the Erie Canal connected western New York with New York City via Hudson River steamships and with Boston through stagecoach to Albany. The link to New England was further strengthened with the completion of a Boston-Albany rail link in 1841.[17] The New York City–Albany ships had carried nearly 200,000 passengers by the early 1830s, many of whom connected to or from the Erie Canal. William Miller himself traveled by this means to New York City in the Spring of 1833. Although extremely early in his public career, his identity became known, and he delivered an impromptu lecture and distributed pamphlets (presumably the Brandon, Vermont, articles) to the passengers.[18] In the winter, when the river froze and canals were closed to navigation, stagecoaches allowed at least a fraction of the traffic—perhaps 8 or 10 percent—to continue. Given the competitive advantages of canals, railroads did not significantly penetrate the district until the 1850s, but fifteen years earlier were already an important element in coastal New England and the Middle Atlantic states. Similarly, coastal shipping, a consequence of economic expansion, moved commodities, persons, and information among the Atlantic and Gulf ports.[19]

The position of New York City became central, for stagecoaches, relay express riders, and rivers and canals connected it with the interior, while merchant shipping and railroads tied it to other coastal cities. This network of personal, postal, journalistic, and commercial contacts had by the early 1840s made New York the dominant point for the transmission of public information.[20] Information on religious enthusiasms in the Burned-over District became rapidly available in other parts of the country as information passing through New York was relayed over land or water. The informational centrality of New York was also a partial consequence of and an important stimulus to a new type of popular journalism.

News of Millerite activities was especially widely reported in the popular press, a function of Himes's campaigns on the outskirts of large cities, and of the fact that Millerism made good copy at a time when newspaper circulation wars were beginning. The centrality of New York in inter-city communications meant that news from elsewhere found its way into New York papers, and the anti-Millerite campaigns mounted by the New York press diffused along transportation arteries.

THE FATE OF URBAN MILLERISM

The decision to appeal to city dwellers seemed at first well founded. Cheap printing techniques were as available to the Millerites as to their adversaries. During a four-year period, the Second Adventists distributed an estimated four million pieces of literature—nearly one for every five men, women, and children in the United States. The Millerites developed their own mass press, although the distribution figures may be inflated: 50,000 copies of *Signs of the Times* during 1840, not a peak Adventist year; 600,000 copies of *Midnight Cry* during five months in 1842.[21] The famous tent meetings drew as many as 10,000 people. These meetings created temporary communities in which controlled information was received by an audience already predisposed toward it.

The difficulty did not lie in the meetings *per se* but in what happened once the audience left. Its members returned to principally urban places of residence in which the message of Millerism was diluted and challenged by other doctrines; in which the social support received from co-religionists had to compete with the apathy, not to say the hostility, of the general population; and in which the ultimate concerns of a millennial vision were contradicted by the mundane and often frivolous activities of daily life. The Millerites could draw a social boundary around themselves for the period of a revival meeting but could not sustain that separation once the revival ended. The result was a sequence of spectacular but short-lived successes.

The problems inherent in the maintenance of high commitment in an urban environment had already been grasped by more conventional revivalists who had begun to penetrate urban areas by the early 1830s. They quickly found that the rapidly growing cities lacked those conditions that had contributed to the early growth of the Second Great Awakening in small towns:

> Of crucial importance in producing revivals of this kind was the cultural and ethnic homogeneity of a relatively tightly knit community such as a New England township, with its common religious traditions, its experience and expectation of periodic revivals, and a population small enough for all the families to be acquainted. In this environment,

once a revival had broken out in the churches themselves ... and had
soon become common knowledge, it was often possible to bring the rest
of the community into the revival's embrace.[22]

Effective urban revivalism depended upon the creation of a stable network
of support organizations—Sunday schools, Bible and tract societies, and
missions. It soon became clear that pressures to maintain regular business
hours and the competition of new, specifically urban leisure-time activities
(taverns, theatres, and political rallies, for example) made protracted religious activities far more difficult. Day-long and even week-long religious
services, which had been a staple of rural and small-town evangelism, met
strong resistance in most cities.[23] Millerism occurred at a time when cities
were entering an era of high growth, in which their already diverse composition was being further intensified by high rates of intra- and inter-city
mobility.

In retrospect, it is easy to understand why Millerism was drawn to the
city: Improvement in transportation made access easier. Cities were growing rapidly and hence held the prospect for mass proselytizing. The cultural
cliché of the city as a place of vice and debauchery perversely reinforced its
religious attractiveness; these were people in dire need of salvation. Finally,
well-developed techniques for itinerant revivalism suggested a way of reaching this tempting reservoir. Himes and his colleagues made fundamentally
erroneous judgments, however. While they correctly assessed the ability of
new transportation and communications channels to spread their message,
they failed to foresee the ability of these same channels to carry the messages
of their opponents with equal or greater effectiveness. Similarly, they accurately perceived in the camp meeting a potent social invention, but they did
not accurately perceive its limitations. In rural and small-town settings,
camp meetings and similarly structured revivals could directly reach nearly
the entire community population. Thus, the social boundaries of the revival
and the boundaries of the natural community were virtually coextensive.
But no tent, however enormous, could enclose more than a fraction of an
urban population, so that all urban revivals had to confront populations the
majority of which were not directly involved in it.

The freedom to desist from normal economic behavior and to adopt a
theocentric style of life were severely circumscribed in the cities. Significantly, the extant stories of Millerite abstention from routine activities in
fact come from rural areas, rather than from cities where they would be expected to draw greater notice.[24] In the presence of a population that was either disinterested or scoffing, Millerites quickly backslid. In the absence of
an institutional apparatus to provide social support for believers, Millerism

had difficulty competing in an urban environment. Not until early 1844 did large numbers of Millerites systematically break with the churches, and then the lateness of the hour and Miller's own ambivalence about organizational separation prevented the establishment of an effective organizational network.[25]

In the end, Millerism remained strongest in those upstate areas where the insularity of village life prevailed. The westward shift of the movement in 1843 returned it to an environment in which entire communities might effectively be proselytized and in which self-contained coteries of believers were better protected against outside hostility. These populations, drawn by adversity from western New England, strongly resembled the communities in which the First and Second Great Awakenings had originated.

It is questionable whether any mass millenarian movement could have consolidated its membership under these conditions. The organizational problems of the Millerites were paralleled by those which confronted secular millenarians such as Socialists in Europe and America. The history of radical political organization in the 1800s suggests that at least until midcentury the unpalatable choice lay between secret societies so small as to be political innocuous and mass organizations whose beliefs were so diluted as to be trivial.[26] Like them, the Second Adventists found it impossible to combine large numbers with high commitment to a deviant ideology.

UTOPIAN COMMUNITIES AS AN ORGANIZATIONAL ALTERNATIVE

One of Millerism's major difficulties was its failure to maintain boundaries in urban areas and thus separate itself from non-believers. The better defined the boundary, the less the opportunities to convert others. Since spreading the Adventist message was the overriding goal, Millerism was forced into the uncomfortable trade-off of gaining access to potential members at the cost of jeopardizing the following it already had.

The utopian communities foreswore the goal of mass followerships. The creation of a largely self-sufficient rural community precluded a group of more than several hundred. The land-population ratio ranged from slightly more than five acres per capita to somewhat more than eleven.[27] Taking the midpoint of eight acres per inhabitant, a community of 200 would have required 1,600 acres of land, at a time when the average farm size was only 200 acres. Even taking account of the generous supply of land at the time, these requirements placed a relatively low ceiling upon the population of individual communities. This, rather than ideology, may explain the tendency of some of the more successful communities such as the Shakers and Oneida to hive off new communities rather than simply to expand the original settlement. Thus the segmentation of utopian communities was at least as much an ecological response as it was the result of introspection on the nature of the ideal community.

Utopians recognized the link between loyalty and physical separation, which perhaps explains why there were virtually no urban communities until the 1960s. The utopians' problem, however, was in identifying how much separation was required.

Rosabeth Moss Kanter, working with a modified version of Bestor's inventory of communities, measured the longevity of ninety groups founded between 1790 and 1860. Only eleven lasted twenty-five years or more, while seventy-nine dissolved before they had been in existence a quarter of a century. Indeed, when she intensively studied a third of the original set, she found that most lasted fewer than two years, including all the Fourierist experiments.[28] Longevity was closely related to the members' commitment to the enterprise, and commitment in turn was the product of two processes. Communitarians had to be detached from their pre-communal life and simultaneously provided with a new sense of identity. Groups that allowed ties with old lives to persist were destined to dissolve quickly, while those that demanded renunciation of former status, wealth, family connections, and beliefs fared much better, provided that the inner vacuum created by the acts of renunciation was filled by a new identity deemed more precious than the old.[29]

Fourierists, who awkwardly straddled the external world of social reform and the internal world of their separate communities, could not resolve factional struggles any more than the Owenites twenty years earlier. The Sodus Bay Phalanx, near Rochester, N.Y., for example, experienced in addition to its economic problems an unresolvable dispute about Sabbath observance.[30] The Shaker communities and Oneida, by contrast, required the full investment of members' energies and resources. The psychological pressures systematically exerted on members who deviated from communal norms were usually sufficient to either drive out the unadaptable or modify their behavior.[31]

Most communities were independent ventures. They were influenced by one another, with individuals migrating among them, but most were separate corporate entities. This principle of segmentation partially insulated them from each other's failures. Marginal differentiation in beliefs and practices meant that one group's misfortunes did not necessarily presage disaster for others. The closer the organizational links among communities, the greater the interdependence of their fates. The results of intercommunal linkage were sometimes positive, as in the Shakers' case. Often, however, the result was negative, as it was for the Fourierists. Albert Brisbane's tireless organizational work gave Fourierism a federative structure that ironically contributed to communal vulnerability. In 1844, for example, four upstate New York communities, including Sodus Bay, formed the American Industrial Union "for the purpose of counteracting inducements to competitive rivalry among themselves, as individuals or institutions; and to the end that the advantages of location, climate and facilities of production peculiar to one shall enure to the benefit of all."[32] Instead of contributing to the "benefit of all," this and other efforts to make Associationism a cohesive movement implicated all in the difficulties of some.

Fourierist leaders tried to immunize surviving communities by publicly dissociating themselves from the failures. However, the Fourierist penchant for federation made it impossible to fully abandon sinking ships, for in the public mind all Associationist ventures were linked together.

Apart from such cases, American utopians were sufficiently segmented so that the damage caused by any single community's demise could often be contained. Segmentation was reinforced by the spatial location of the communities. All were rural. Most were at least five miles from a town and were not on a waterway or railroad.[33] Settlement and social organization did not exhaust or even unduly restrict the availability of cheap land prior to the Civil War, so that compact blocs were available for purchase throughout the period. Given the tendency of utopians to work land somewhat more intensively than their neighbors, recourse to the frontier was unnecessary.[34]

The locational pattern confronted utopians with an organizational dilemma. On the one hand, there was little incentive to establish communities in remote areas. Considerations of practicality hence led utopians to generally remain where they were, forsaking towns and cities for the immediate rural hinterland. On the other hand, the avoidance of frontier treks carried its own risk, for if one remained in settled regions, old life-patterns might never be broken and the new society that was envisioned might remain contaminated by the environment. The tension between engagement and separation was greater than it might have been had the communities been established in unpopulated areas.

Most communities wanted both separation and engagement, the separation to ensure a different way of life and the engagement in order to influence the behavior of others. Where separation predominated, as in the German-language communities, long-term survival was possible but with minimal impact upon the larger society. Where engagement predominated, as at Brook Farm, quick dissolution was predictable, for members never fully detached themselves from old patterns of behavior. The Shakers and the Oneida Community were far more successful in achieving a balance, as the result of highly developed systems of internal social control to detect and purge the ways of the world.

Physical boundaries were insufficient unless they also marked social boundaries. A community's landholding was significant to the extent that behavior changed within it. Social boundaries were more easily maintained when they coincided with physical boundaries. When spatial location was a metaphor for social difference, the transactions that occurred across the physical boundary provided a precise indicator of the distinctiveness within. Utopians recognized that the possession of territory is the most effective way of maintaining social difference. But utopians did not always recognize that territory confers autonomy only if there is the will and capacity to control cross-boundary transactions—who comes and goes and for what purposes, what is read and heard and how much trade is required.

At a less-conscious level, utopian experimentation manifested long-standing American cultural bias against urban life. The Jeffersonian anti-urban tradition identified the city with selfishness and immorality. This tradition assumed increasing relevance during the rapid urban growth of the 1830s and 40s, with its rising problems of urban poverty and disorder.[35] Those committed to beginning society on a new foundation could only have seen in the city a peculiarly unhealthy and unpropitious setting for their efforts. Rather than become trapped in the morass of urban problems, the utopians chose to begin in the putatively unspoiled and positively valued countryside. In this respect, utopians and Millerites were mirror images of one another, for the Millerites were attracted to the city precisely because its inhabitants were wretched; their souls were more in need of saving.

COMPARING MILLERITE AND UTOPIAN ORGANIZATION

Neither the Millerite proselytizers nor the utopian community-builders could resolve the organizational question of the nineteenth century: How could high commitment to a deviant belief system be maintained in cities? Proselytizing could marshal numbers, but it could not keep them. Communities could maintain high commitment, but only among small groups. Second Adventism, however, was inherently unstable, while utopian communities could potentially, and in many cases actually, stabilize themselves for significant periods.

Millerism's instability was as much a consequence of its organizational aspirations as of its failed predictions. Since it did not supply adequate social reinforcement to its urban followers, they quickly fell away. In the absence of membership data, one can only speculate that in addition to the sharp drop that followed predictive failures, significant numbers also left during the period of most conspicuous growth. Thus the size of the followership—accepting Miller's own figure of 50,000 highly committed adherents—may have masked significant movement in and out. The movement's contraction appears closely related to a retreat out of large cities, back to small towns, principally in the Burned-over District. There, much diminished in size, it could stabilize sufficiently to preserve a core of Adventists against the day when the movement took conventional denominational form. Its days as a mass movement over, Adventism could retain the loyalty of the small numbers able to provide one another with social support.

Utopian communities required no such metamorphosis, since most were small, bounded, and intimate by design. Stabilization required effective boundary maintenance and a recruiting system sufficiently rigorous to weed out the frivolous. Stabilization, however, meant reduced expectations of world transformation. Except insofar as communities remained exemplars, they directly touched relatively few lives.

These organizational considerations may appear irrelevant to the concerns of people who desperately desired the imminent perfection of life on earth. A stable organization, after all, presumes the continuation of the status quo. Yet for several reasons organizational requirements were important even for chiliasts whose eyes were set on the last days. The most evident reason is that the provision of a stable social framework permits more successful adjustment to prophetic failure. We cannot know how long Millerism might have persisted or how large it would have been if its members could have endured their disappointments within a more formal structure. Although the millennium can be thought of as an absolute, the concept is malleable enough to fit a number of forms of rationalization. The postmillennialists had already installed one such form, in which the millennium came in increments over a long period of time. Adventists who soldiered on experimented with other rationalizations, such as recalculations of the date or the spiritualization of physical events. When events became invisible, predictions became nonfalsifiable. The utopians were rationalizers as well, for they believed something very like the millennium could be attained within their own spatial limits. The utopian way of life consequently became a surrogate for the more far-reaching transformations which were beyond the capacities of the communities. Life in the communities thus prefigured changes which at some distant time would encompass the world. In the meantime it provided compensatory satisfactions to the communities' members, who could, as it were, live the millennium in advance of its arrival.

9

THE MILLENARIAN PROCESS

EXPECTATIONS for a transformed future in the 1840s were expressed in two distinct styles. Millerism stayed within the stylized framework of portent analysis, even as it adopted the most modern forms of mass communications. Utopian communities displayed greater sensitivity to social and economic issues even as they withdrew from the public arena. The curious character of the decade lies not simply in the intensity of its eschatological longings but in the diverse forms they took. The stresses that played upon the inhabitants of the Burned-over District account for the millenarian hopes, but one must probe deeper to account for the dispersion of energies into such different forms—one avoiding all association with social and economic issues despite its intense pursuit of urban support, the other cultivating an acute sensitivity to the anxieties produced by social and economic upheaval, yet content to remain within its communal settlements.

This bifurcation of the millenarian impulse was in large part attributable to changes that had occurred in the nature of disaster itself.

DISASTER IN HISTORY

The survival of human life has always depended upon a balance between the severity of collective stress and the vulnerability of populations. Premillennialism developed in the traditional societies of western and central Europe beginning in about the eleventh century. In this agrarian social order, disaster came principally from nature. The low level of technological development limited the capacity of human beings to inflict suffering and injury upon one another. The limits lay neither in human virtue nor self-restraint but in the restrictions inherent in an age of animal and human energy, primitive transportation, and face-to-face personal combat.

Traditional millennialism was, like most of the rest of life, an affair of the countryside. Norman Cohn, in his influential work, *The Pursuit of the Millennium*, argued a very different position, that millennialism in the Middle Ages (and by extension subsequently) was quintessentially urban, the result of the interplay among unemployment, anomie, and overcrowding in the expanding textile towns of western Europe.[1] The anxieties of their urban proletariats were discharged through the demagogic chiliasm of unscrupulous charismatic prophets. The initial plausibility of this urban thesis lies in its reinforcement of two strong cultural predispositions, the belief in the corruption and disorderliness of cities, and the presumption that urban crowds are necessarily irrational.[2] Since neither is self-evidently true, any argument premised upon them must be examined with care.

Although a fuller critique appears elsewhere,[3] four points suggest that Cohn's thesis requires substantial reservations. First, documentary evidence almost invariably overrepresents events in urban areas, the location of most institutions that compile retrievable records. Second, the preindustrial city was far smaller and structurally different than those of the nineteenth and twentieth centuries; the Münster of the Anabaptist millenarians held fewer than 20,000. All such cities combined contained only a fraction of the total population, which remained overwhelmingly rural through the eighteenth century. Third, the cyclical unemployment affecting small numbers of textile workers was a far less important threat than epidemic disease or famine, each of which was capable of rapidly reducing population by as much as one-third. Finally, even taking account of the urban bias in the historical record, there is ample evidence of significant rural millennialism. Peasant uprisings, often tinged with messianic hopes, accounted for a far higher proportion of collective unrest than the conspicuous but atypical urban movements.[4]

It seems reasonable to conclude, therefore, that millenarian movements were not notably urban phenomena, and that stresses to which traditional societies were most likely to respond were those enshrined in portent analysis, natural aberrations, and, to a lesser extent, wars. Indeed, the tenacity of traditional premillennialism resulted from the close match between its categories and the significant forms of harmdoing. Since these categories included most sources of collective suffering, they and their related millenarian ideas might be effectively deployed in order to give moral significance to otherwise inexplicable events.

However, this fit between millenarian conceptualizations and sources of human misfortune became decidedly less harmonious by the late eighteenth century.[5] Their growing incongruity was the result of two developments: the declining perceived significance of traditional forms of harmdoing and the rising perceived significance of novel forms. The decline of traditional modes resulted from both intellectual and material causes. Keith Thomas points out, for example, that magic began to decline in seventeenth-century England even before there was any objective increase in the degree of physical security: "The change ... was thus not so much technological as mental."[6] This growing feeling of human mastery reduced the sense of impotence in the face of natural perils. These sentiments were initially more evident among elites than among masses, and in cities more than in rural areas. Even where the commitment to mastery over nature existed, its practical exercise was often constrained. The constraints were in part technological, but they were also social, for relatively rigid social stratification, with its implied duties that inferiors owed to superiors, necessarily limited opportunities to manipulate the physical world.

The social fragmentation in America that was so prominent a part of the period between 1830 and the Civil War played a dual role in the process of asserting mastery. On the one hand, as social controls weakened and opportunities for social mobility grew, chances for unfettered inventive and entrepreneurial activity increased as well.[7] The release of productive energies and the liberation of individual ambition required the taming of the natural world. If its forces could not always be controlled, human impotence was at worst temporary, a deficit of knowledge and technical skill rather than a limitation in principle. A thoroughly manipulative attitude toward nature necessarily eroded the older link between natural phenomena and divine providence. Given the confidence in human enterprise, it was more difficult to view natural anomalies and disasters as divine messages for the edification of an errant humanity.

Social change, however, was not simply a liberator of energies, for social transformations could themselves be disasters. The same developments that liberated some profoundly unnerved others. Disaster was no longer a condition inflicted by nature or the prerogative of warmaking rulers. A culture newly imbued with belief in the efficacy of human action created conditions that rewarded some but victimized others. The new victims were associated with these new, anthropogenic stresses[8] that arose out of industrial production, with its emphasis upon repetitive unskilled work; out of the nationalization of the economy that both reduced local self-sufficiency and

imposed the perceived tyranny of supply and demand; and, finally, out of
the wrenching fluctuations of boom-and-bust that made each economic improvement hostage to mysterious, ill-understood forces.

The early and mid-nineteenth century was the watershed dividing a
time of traditional calamities from a period of qualitatively different catastrophes.[9] In the past lay the disasters identified as apocalyptic portents—
earthquakes, floods, famines, epidemics, and traditional warfare. Such calamities were becoming rarer because they could be controlled and predicted, as in the case of floods and diseases, or because general mastery over
nature made them appear less threatening, as in the case of earthquakes. But
the time ahead was in fact not necessarily more peaceful or secure, for new
disasters that had been inconceivable before in time became commonplace—mechanized warfare, economic depression, and genocide among
them. By and large, the waning destructive capacity of nature was more than
matched by the rising destructive capacity of human beings.

Since there are no definitive boundary lines in history, it belabors the
obvious to say that the two eras merged into one another. One can assign
no precise date to the shift in the balance. Clearly, appalling acts of human
cruelty preceded the nineteenth century, just as devastating natural catastrophes have followed it. Nonetheless, one may generally discern a shift
around the pivot of the first five or six decades of the 1800s. Events in New
England and New York between 1810 and about 1844 constitute a striking
microcosm of the process, with their dramatic grouping of natural disasters
at the beginning and humanly caused catastrophes at the close.

As so often occurs at times of fundamental change, the ideas available
to organize experience lagged seriously behind the experience that needed
to be understood. In a condition of perceived disorder, however, old ideas
seemed better than none. The initial appeal of Millerism lay in its claim to
narrow the gap between beliefs in justice and an apparently capricious reality. The vulnerability of Millerism lay in the fact that it failed to directly address the most novel and disturbing aspects of experience, and hence offered
only generalized solace. At the same time, the utopians groped toward a
new understanding of the conditions for moral order. Their barely disguised
millenarian speculations, because they were not constrained by traditional
scriptural interpretations, could take account of events the Millerites were
compelled to minimize. The changes in the sources and types of collective
stress engendered a search for ways to reconcile these stresses with beliefs
about a benign and ordered universe. Although Millerites and utopians utilized different resources in attempting to effect this reconciliation, both
sought routes to moral order that distinguished them from the accepted be-

lief systems of their times. Second Adventism and utopian community-building may be conceived as the end stage of a process through which human groups seek to accommodate collective stress.

A MODEL OF THE MILLENARIAN PROCESS

When the environment prevents individuals from readily meeting their needs and satisfying their desires, they are said to be "under stress." Small amounts of environmental resistance have a tonic effect, stimulating the senses and drawing forth reserves of energy. As levels of environmental resistance rise, however, the effects become unpleasant to more and more people, who attempt to eliminate the stress or escape from the stressful situation. Except for a minority of stress-seekers attracted by challenges and obstacles, "stress, anxiety, and fear are considered unwanted states imposed by a cruel environment—by our corrupt fellows, by a harsh natural world, and by a devilish internal legacy of our formative years."[10]

High stress may not only be unpleasant, it may endanger survival itself, as when disease exceeds our ability to provide effective therapies. The result may not only be individual suffering but death.

Just as stress varies in intensity—producing stimulation, discomfort, or death—so it afflicts groups as well as individuals. A human community exists to meet the needs of its members, and when it can no longer do so for substantial numbers, the result is collective rather than individual stress. When segments of a community cannot sustain their conditions of life, the consequence is more than multiplied instances of individual suffering and frustration, for the failure of a social system to sustain its members may make the very existence of a community problematic. An ongoing social system must provide minimum levels of food, shelter, security, and health.[11]

Every community consequently must develop social coping mechanisms for the management of collective stress. Since the vicissitudes of nature, human aggressiveness, disease, and economic instabilities can all jeopardize group survival, collective ingenuity has historically been devoted to keeping stress at bay, preventing it where possible and limiting it when prevention is impossible. Social coping mechanisms handle stress at three levels. The levels are commonly activated in sequence, later mechanisms coming into full play only as predecessors fail. The three levels, to which we shall shortly turn, are: damage control systems, which attempt to prevent stress or repair its consequences; theories of mistakes, which seek to explain those instances in which damage control systems fail to operate effectively; and, finally, alternative worldviews, which may take hold when theories of mistakes are perceived to be insufficiently persuasive.

When a community undergoes traumatic stress, the restoration of stable social life depends upon more than merely making good the material losses. If the community is to survive in anything like its prior form, the community's beliefs must be interpreted in ways that are compatible with the disaster. At the individual level, victims attempt to make sense out of what has happened and confront the inability of existing institutions to protect them. At the collective level, the society's institutions respond by offering a theory of mistakes[12]—a set of propositions that explain the inability of the community to fully meet its members' needs.

Stresses are sometimes so intense and prolonged that theories of mistakes become discredited, hollow rationalizations that no longer convince. As adjuncts to the community's fundamental values, they are implicated in the failure of communal institutions. When theories of mistakes have been discredited, the world is perceived as a moral anarchy which can be neither controlled nor understood. Since perceptions of moral disorder are incompatible with stable group life, the only alternative to demoralization and disintegration is an alternative world view.[13] In this manner, heterodox conceptions of reality stigmatized in normal times are sometimes adopted willingly in times of crisis.

Thus the coping mechanisms stand in a hierarchical relationship. Damage control systems usually function well enough to maintain stress at levels which, if not tolerable for all individuals, at least permit the community to maintain itself. When damage control temporarily fails, theories of mistakes seek to explain the failure, and when they can no longer do so persuasively, the way lies open for competitive conceptions of reality.

All ongoing communities devise techniques that insulate their members from harmful stress. This array can include elements as diverse as law enforcement and military defense; weather prediction; medicine and sanitation; and food production, storage, and distribution. These elements of damage control are fundamentally protective, for they strive to erect a wall between the individual and uncontrolled human passions or natural disasters.

However, even societies at high levels of technological and social complexity can only partially attain this goal. They must therefore be capable of handling the effects of unpreventable stress. When preventive damage control fails, resort is made to compensatory damage control. In order to restore the status quo, remaining resources are directed to the survivors. The mechanisms for doing so include traditional forms of self-help, by families, neighborhoods, or villages, together with such complex institutional forms of compensation as private insurance and public and private social welfare organizations.

The sense of vulnerability felt by Americans of the 1830s and 40s reflected fundamental social and economic changes which were altering the ethnic and class composition of the population, the deference inferiors had habitually paid to superiors, and the stability of family life. The transition from social rigidity to at least relative mobility implied invigorating opportunity, but also bespoke the fragility of familiar social arrangements. As a result, "the theme of decline and doom remained a constant one throughout the first half of the nineteenth century," both despite and because of proliferating opportunities.[14] One expression of this anxiety was the growth of protective and compensatory institutions. The asylum, almshouse, penitentiary, and orphanage attempted to isolate and rehabilitate the ominous social deviants thrown up by immigration, internal migration, and a boom-and-bust economy.[15] In much the same manner, evangelical Protestants translated their postmillennial aspirations into organizations directed at social betterment. Temperance, abolition, and poor relief associations sought ultimate goals of spiritual growth, but they were also barricades thrown up against forces of danger and evil.

The growing system of damage control was primarily urban, for in the urban centers poverty, crime, and immorality were most visible and feared.[16] The smaller the community, the less likely that it could support or have ready access to the new institutions of vigilance and good works. This web woven of alternate strands of fear and benevolence addressed concerns that appeared endemic—alcoholism, crime, poverty—the stigmata of what later periods would refer to as the "underclass." Consequently, significant numbers of people lay outside the protective embrace of pre-Civil War damage control systems, even though those systems had greatly expanded. Rural inhabitants especially could not expect to enjoy the same measure of security afforded city dwellers.

Given the limited capabilities of all systems of damage control, events can occur for which these systems offer little or no protection. Failures of protection and compensation have obvious material consequences, in the form of deaths, injuries, property destruction, and lost productivity. Significant as these may be, however, there are intangible losses of comparable significance. We wish not only to be physically protected from sickness, poverty, and like afflictions; we also wish to live in a morally ordered universe free of what we perceive as unmerited suffering. The suffering may be unavoidable but it should at least not appear to be capricious. As Melvin Lerner has expressed it: "We want to believe we live in a [just] world where people get what they deserve, or, rather deserve what they get."[17] Events that cannot be directly controlled can appear indirectly controllable if they can be assimilated to a conception of moral purpose.

Damage control systems may not be able to prevent first-order effects of collective stress, such as death and injury. If failures occur, it becomes critical to preserve conceptions of moral order, for if the universe is conceived to be purposeful, life may gradually resume its course following calamitous events. Since every instance of human suffering implicitly calls moral order into question, it falls to theories of mistakes to meet these challenges by rationalizing the failure of damage control.

Traditionally, religion has been the principal custodian of theories of mistakes. These theories have assumed some of their most complex forms in theological speculation on sin and suffering interpreted or justified as punishment for misdeeds, testing of faith, or preparation for life after death. These beliefs have often been intermingled with strictures concerning the inscrutability of God's purposes and the expectation of a heavenly reward for earthly misery.

Since the late eighteenth century, however, theories of mistakes have also included prominent secular elements. They have incorporated folk ideas about chance, luck, or fate, seeking to make intelligible the intrusion of uncertainty into human life. There are also conceptions of risk-taking implicit in ideas about economic competition and entrepreneurship, which both justify success and rationalize failure. Like their religious predecessors and counterparts, secular theories of mistakes often include a strong emphasis upon a benign future. Confidence in the inevitability of progress enables current unpleasantness to be endured in the expectation of its eventual extinction. Closely allied to this has been faith in science as the instrument for the future alleviation of present ills.

The 1830s and 40s constituted a period in which religious theories of mistakes remained extremely strong even as these new, secular theories were on the rise. It was thus not uncommon to express general confidence in the existence of a providential design while simultaneously accepting *laissez-faire* economics. Individuals sometimes subscribed to elements of more than one theory; different social groups were sometimes exposed or receptive to particular kinds of explanations. Thus religiously derived theories generally retained prestige in rural areas at times when secular theories were making inroads among urbanites.

The inconsistent application of religious theories reflected their metamorphoses over the previous two centuries. Seventeenth-century theologians, as well as most believers, assumed that all events, whether in nature or human affairs, constituted a moral unity, such that the resulting advantages and deprivations constituted a providential judgment on individuals. "Behind such ideas lay the universal reluctance to recognize that the rewards and punishments of this world did not always go to those who deserved them. The doctrine of providences was a conscientious attempt to impose order on the apparent randomness of the human fortunes by proving that, in the long run, virtue was rewarded and vice did not go unpunished."[18]

The disposition to regard worldly events in providential terms began to wane in the late seventeenth century, but continued to exert influence as late as the nineteenth, particularly in evangelical Protestant circles. Despite the rising prestige of science, "nineteenth-century Evangelicals and sectarians had as literal a faith in the doctrine of divine providence as any to be found in the age of Cromwell or Baxter."[19]

Nonetheless, the ascription of moral meanings to events became more difficult as those events came to be understood as the outcome of natural processes, and as techniques developed, in medicine for example, for more effective human intervention. If the afflictions of the natural order could be controlled or manipulated by human beings, they could not as readily be regarded as divine judgments. A tension consequently developed between providentialism and a more manipulative and naturalistic outlook. The survival of providentialism into the nineteenth century resulted both from the fact that not all social groups were equally acquainted with natural science and also from the fact that a naturalistic position only incompletely addressed the anxieties and guilt of victims. The desire to live in a just world, characterized by deservingness and moral order, was not adequately met by the view that suffering was the result of accident.

Postmillennialism, which was rapidly achieving the status of an orthodoxy, insisted upon the primacy of the human will, working in harmony with divine grace. If there were problems, injustices, and suffering, then they would be solved, rectified, and alleviated by renewed human exertions. Individuals could change themselves, and people acting in concert could change society. While God was presumed to be the ultimate source from which these energies were drawn, initiative and implementation now lay in the hands of human beings. With its robust confidence and optimism, postmillennialism flourished when success begat success, each new advance building on past achievements and pointing toward future triumphs. Revivals and organizations for social and religious reform rolled forward in a seemingly unstoppable wave. As a theory of mistakes, postmillennialism had the advantage of being a partially self-fulfilling prophecy. Where premillennialism lingered over evidence of destruction and decline, postmillennialism looked to more optimistic signs: the numbers of converts, the frequency of revivals, and the spread of organizations dedicated to moral edification and uplift. All of the postmillennialist indicators could in fact be created, assuming that there was a will to do so, and inasmuch as the millennium was to arrive bit by bit instead of all at once, partial fulfillment was all that was required at any given moment.

The incremental view of millennial attainment supported a powerful conception of moral order, for if suffering was still the human lot, it was also given to human beings to progressively end it. However difficult to bear, the ills of the moment could be tolerated in the realization that at some future time, they would be dissolved. The vulnerability of the conception lay in the fact that it was hostage to events. Although postmillennialism was partially self-fulfilling, incomplete control over external forces limited the degree to which its goals might be willed into existence.

Consequently, the disasters of 1810–44 created conditions in which theories of mistakes were required. The more intense the stress, the more those subjected to it required confirmation that events followed a meaningful pattern. Initially, postmillennialism seemed to provide this assurance. The conviction of inevitable improvement made the unpleasantness of the moment appear merely a temporary setback. Postmillennialism provided a viable theory of mistakes when applied to intermittent calamities, but faltered under the added stress of the post-1837 depression.

A theory of mistakes can withstand profound contradictions while retaining the loyalties of those socialized to it, but there may be stresses for which it cannot offer convincing explanations. Such sweeping catastrophes occur infrequently, but when neither damage control systems nor theories of mistakes shield against them, there may be recourse to the third level of social coping mechanisms, the formation of alternative worldviews.

Few societies are in fact so homogeneous that all their members perceive the world similarly. Theories of mistakes do not command universal assent, even in the most stable times. While such theories offer "official" explanations for misfortune, they coexist uneasily with a substratum of deviant beliefs. This subterranean realm of deviant ideas may include religious heterodoxy, political radicalism, or magic and the occult. In any case, it is likely to be publicly stigmatized and may be officially repressed, for it offers ways of organizing experience that challenge normative conceptions. Although deviant belief systems often have little public visibility—indeed, visibility may mean ridicule or worse—they have a stubborn survival capacity within popular culture. In periods when stress can be readily accommodated, they persist among small coteries of believers.

In times of high collective stress, deviant belief systems confront a markedly more sympathetic audience. Their official adversaries having been at least partially discredited, these maverick ideologies benefit from a temporarily open marketplace of ideas. Once ignored, scorned, or suppressed, they now may be perceived in a new and favorable light, not only because of an insupportable vacuum that develops when theories of mistakes are invalidated, but also because the alternatives appear to possess a greater ability to address the crisis of meaning. They assert moral order where none may appear to exist, typically by claiming access to previously untapped sources of power, identified with some body of hidden knowledge, and often promulgated by a charismatic figure. This knowledge purports to contain principles for the classification of phenomena into good and evil, pure and impure. The world becomes a Manichean battleground upon which cosmic forces contend. The outcome of the struggle is to be a millennium, in which the corrupt existing order will be replaced by a new and flawless form of social organization.

During the 1840s, alternative world views were available in abundance, from the Millerites through secular and religious utopians. The attention they received was out of proportion to the numbers of their followers, suggesting intense interest even among skeptics. They were perceived as part of the general societal tendency toward extreme or deviant beliefs, to which contemporaries attached the label "ultraism." While a suggestion of irrationality still clung to the term (linked, perhaps, to the English abhorrence for religious "enthusiasm"), the tendency to group these movements together indicates an awareness that they presented a competing version of reality. Irrespective of their numerous doctrinal differences, from the standpoint of nominally orthodox onlookers they represented a concerted challenge to received ideas about justice and morality.

The conspicuous attention paid ultraism was in part a tribute to the organizational and propagandistic talents of such men as Himes and Brisbane. But it also suggested the presence of an audience large enough to support sectarian publications, attend meetings, and read the equally voluminous attacks in more mainstream newspapers and periodicals. The visibility of millenarians was a product of their own commitment, the curiosity of some non-members, and the hostility of others. The tension among them typifies an era when the upholders of orthodoxy lack the self-confidence to ignore challenges at the intellectual margins, and where skepticism has grown to the point where even highly deviant belief systems might be heard by a mass audience.

Millerites and utopians advanced different world views. The Second Adventists argued that disasters should be thought of as intimations of divine judgment. Since the greatest cataclysms were still to come, the task was not to protect against the comparatively minor dangers of flood and earthquake but to gather the righteous remnant that would outlast the "burning up of the world." By this measure, contemporary ills could be both given a function in a divine plan and reduced to the status of warnings. In any case, direct divine judgment would quickly replace the ambiguities of communication by natural disaster. The utopians offered a very different account. They located the causes of suffering in the human will and institutions rather than in the wildness of nature. These institutions were so far beyond repair that they had to be abandoned in favor of a new society constructed on moral principles. The principles invoked generally included equality of wealth, equality of social position (although not necessarily of spiritual attainment), and relative equality between the sexes. These might best be realized by making it impossible for any individuals or select groups to place their own interests above those of the community.

Millerites and utopians had different capacities for expressing their alternative world views in social forms. Second Adventism was disdainful of the need for cohesive organization. Its absence could be rationalized by insisting that the imminence of the Second Coming made human organization superfluous. Nonetheless, as we have seen, Millerism's organizational diffuseness contributed to its rapid contraction. Utopians not only judged existing institutions to have failed, they insisted as an organizational corollary that substitute institutions be created. Communalists' sensitivity to economic disasters gave them an advantage over Millerism in confronting the fragmented society of the 1840s. Their insistence upon organizational reconstruction gave concrete form to this ideological advantage. Not only could they provide a more incisive critique of social problems; they could also offer a way of life in which those problems would presumably disappear. The communities were thus supposed to functioned as counter-societies with more effective damage control than the larger society beyond their boundaries. (In fact, this goal was not always attainable, because communities were insufficiently insulated from their environment and because internal fractures reduced their cohesion.)

The factors that created this open marketplace in world views were transient. The economic difficulties passed. Organizational failures among Millerites and some utopians increased public skepticism. The festering issue of slavery and union pre-empted all others. It was no longer possible, as it had been earlier for Miller and Noyes, to set abolition aside in favor of allegedly more fundamental spiritual issues. Millenarian energies were either redirected into the sectional battle[20] or drained away.

Yet if the history of millennialism teaches any lesson, it is that the chiliastic expectations of one era erupt in another. Eschatological themes lie dormant but do not disappear. Although the post–Civil War period lies outside the immediate confines of our discussion, it may be useful to conclude by sketching the directions millennialism took in the century that followed the Civil War.

MILLENNIALISM 1865–1940

Post-bellum millennialism was episodic and diverse. It ebbed and flowed in three wavelike movements. Its diversity lay in the increasingly dramatic contrasts between the religious and secular. After the 1840s, millennialism reached notable peaks in the 1890s, 1930s, 1960s, and 1970s. In each era, utopian communities coexisted with mass movements, but the mass movements were as likely to advance political and economic ideologies as religious creeds. Not until the 1970s did traditional religious millennialism regain some of the lost ground, a phenomenon to which attention will be directed later.

By the end of the nineteenth century, millennialism was dominated by secularizing tendencies. This occurred despite the partial recovery of religious chiliasm after the Millerite debacle. Adventist theologians, together with other evangelical Protestants touched by millenarian speculation from England, exerted increasing influence within the Baptist and Presbyterian churches. Yet notwithstanding chiliasm's renewed legitimacy, its supporters were primarily urban clergy, without the upsurge of popular interest shown in the 1840s.[21] Fin-de-siècle millennialism belonged to secularists who conceptualized salvation in terms of economic panaceas. The dominant millennialism at the turn of the century was Populist, with its associated varieties of radical economic reform.

Populism, Richard Hofstadter wrote, "looked backward with longing to the lost agrarian Eden." At the same time, it saw the road to redemption blocked by "a sustained conspiracy of the international money power."[22] This emotionally charged Manichean vision, although not held by all who called themselves Populists,[23] brought an essentially millenarian vision into the national political arena by the time of the election of 1892. Cognate themes of a millennium achieved through economic restructuring appear in the writings and public careers of Henry George and Edward Bellamy. George's *Progress and Poverty* (1879) became the largest-selling economic tract of all time, promising to eliminate social ills at one stroke by deriving all public revenue from the taxation of land. Although George narrowly lost the New York mayoral election of 1886, he remained a major focus of radical social change until his death in 1897.[24] Bellamy's 1886 utopian novel

Looking Backward, with its call for the nationalization of industry, became the basis for a network of Nationalist Clubs, which, if not as large or vocal as George's single tax movement, nonetheless constituted a mass movement in its own right. In addition, between 1894 and 1900, thirty-six new utopian communities were founded (including two single tax and two Bellamyite communities), the largest number since the foundings of the 1840s.

The next major peak occurred in the 1930s. In this case, too, secular themes predominated, although the influence of militant fundamentalism, notable since the 20s, could also be felt. Like the Populists of thirty years earlier, figures such as Huey Long, Father Coughlin, and Dr. Frances Townsend projected a millennium brought into being by some uniquely efficacious economic nostrum.[25] Long's share-the-wealth plan, Coughlin's monetary proposals, and Dr. Townsend's revolving-old-age-pension plan elevated economic tinkering to the position of master-lever in the attainment of a virtuous society. In addition, all evoked potent images of a rural arcadia from which humanity had been expelled by conspiratorial greed, but to which Americans could now return.

The New Deal itself became the vehicle through which others launched sweeping communitarian experiments. Between 1933 and 1937, a variety of government agencies established ninety-nine new communities, with almost 11,000 units of housing, at a cost exceeding $100,000,000.[26] Convinced that full industrial employment would never return, advocates of subsistence homesteads, such as M. L. Wilson and Rexford Guy Tugwell, sought to build a new society in the countryside. Other as yet uninventoried private utopian initiatives attempted to return urbanites to the land.[27]

Both the millenarian wave of the 1890s and that of the 1930s occurred during depressions comparable to the downturn of the 1840s. Although space does not permit an examination of these cases as detailed as that already provided for the 1840s, the dynamics appear strikingly similar: Severe collective stress called forth millenarianism in the form of both mass movements and utopian communities. Ideas previously dismissed as crank found eager followings after traditional conceptions of moral order appeared to lose validity. *Laissez-faire* economics had sanctified as part of the natural order a condition in which individuals were expected to reap the gains and bear the burdens of economic decisions, yet as the ratio of winners and losers shifted, this no longer provided solace. The losers' fundamental problem was less their material interests (although this was surely important) than their perceptions of injustice. Hence the emerging visions of the millennium not only promised immediate future benefits; they incorporated the victims' suffering within a vision of moral order.

THE APOCALYPTIC MOOD 1960–85

No period in recent American history has seen as rich a growth of eschatological groups and writings as the quarter-century since 1960. One national magazine has characterized it as "apocalypse chic," while another devoted a cover story to explaining millenarian theology to a sophisticated and secularized readership.[28] The range of millenarian activity possesses a breadth that invites comparison with the 1840s—urban and rural communes, cults (many of a millenarian character), intellectual and academic considerations of the end of the world, radical political groups of both rebellious and revolutionary varieties, and expansive fundamentalist religious organizations encouraging millenarian interpretations of political events.

The complexity of the period does not lie simply in the variety of ideas and organizations. In at least three significant respects, the chiliasm of the post-1960 period overturned conventional expectations: It was not a period of pronounced economic stress. Indeed, it was for the most part a period of prosperity, and many of those associated with the apocalyptic mood were members of favored groups, such as college students and fundamentalists in the high-growth areas of the southeast. Second, the political millennialism of radicals in the 1960s came only a few years after the apparent triumph of political consensus in the 1950s. Finally, for the first time since the pre-Civil War period, religious millenarianism was sufficiently vigorous to compete effectively with its secular counterparts. A resurgent fundamentalism brought a heightened anticipation of the last days.

This most recent period of millenarian ferment—William McLoughlin calls it a new Great Awakening[29]—was not an era of natural disasters or of economic depression, yet neither was it a time of stability. Indeed, Americans perceived it as a period of almost unprecedented political and social turbulence. The decade between the assassination of John Kennedy and the resignation of Richard Nixon threatened symbols of political legitimacy and order more directly than any period since the 1930s. Political assassinations, racial and political rioting, the most unpopular war in American history, and perceived misuse of government power implied to many that political institutions were undeserving of support, morally tainted, or incapable of governing effectively. At the center of that decade of disorder lay the events of 1968, including the riots at the Democratic National Convention and the assassinations of Robert Kennedy and Dr. Martin Luther King, Jr.

The traumatic character of these years was measured not only in the magnitude of civil unrest but in the sense of anxiety, malaise, and loss of confidence. Such events suggest that "disaster" functions as a mental construct which can be linked not only to observable death and destruction but to events that symbolize loss of control and meaning. Highly destructive events are not always classified as disasters. World War I overshadowed the simultaneous world influenza epidemic, even though more lives were lost in the epidemic. Relatively non-destructive events can be characterized as disasters when onlookers regard them as confirming the existence of far greater future dangers. The Haymarket Riot (1886) resulted in few deaths, yet was "apparent evidence of impending disasters" to Americans already apprehensive about political radicalism and urban immigrants.[30] In like manner, Americans in the 1960s grew to expect calamity, seeing in each new act of violence further indications of its imminence.

The ten years that followed John Kennedy's assassination were experienced as a sequence of disasters, even though the routines of daily life and the other forms of institutions remained intact. "Disaster" became a construction placed upon ambiguous events. The more frequent such untoward events became, the greater the disposition to view them as defining American experience rather than as aberrations. As the subjective experience of disorder grew, theories of mistakes functioned less well. The psychopathology of assassins, the relative deprivation of ghetto rioters, and the ineptitude of officials were less convincing explanations than suggestions of conspiracy, a comforting if inaccurate way of reintroducing moral order. An evil cabal, whose minions must be defeated by the forces of righteousness, must surely lie at the center of such disorder.[31]

The unexpected growth of political radicalism was both a cause of the anxiety and a response to it. In 1960, Daniel Bell had offered his "end of ideology" thesis, asserting that the traumatic economic and political events between 1930 and 1950 had left ideologies of both Left and Right exhausted: "For the radical intellectual who had articulated the revolutionary impulses of the past century and a half, all this had meant an end to chiliastic hopes, to millenarianism, to apocalyptic thinking—and to ideology. For ideology, which once was a road to action, has come to a dead end."[32]

The exhaustion was compounded by disillusionment over ideologies in power abroad and the rise of a political consensus in the United States. On the one hand, European totalitarianism had demonstrated the consequences of millenarians in power, while, on the other, the prosperous welfare state of the 1950s seemed to command almost unanimous assent. The old struggles, with their quest for "a new utopia of social harmony," appeared neither desirable nor necessary.

Bell's essay reflected the political blandness of the 50s, yet Bell saw in the interrupted polemic the potential for a climactic new discharge of millenarian energies: "The new generation, with no meaningful memory of the old debates, and no secure tradition to build upon, finds itself seeking new purposes within a framework of a political society that has rejected, intellectually speaking, the old apocalyptic and chiliastic visions. In the search for a 'cause,' there is a deep, desperate, almost pathetic anger."[33] *The End of Ideology* described the muted political discourse of the 1950s but its detection of "deep, desperate ... anger" pointed forward to the New Left eruption in the 1960s. The New Left appeared to contradict the argument that ideology was moribund; ideological rhetoric reached an intensity unseen since the 1930s. But in fact the existence of the New Left confirmed the end of ideology thesis. For the New Left was to post–Civil War secular millennialism as Millerism had been to traditional religious millennialism— the final, dramatic burst that precedes senescence, the penultimate attempt to extract meaning from a belief system at the end of its capacity to speak to present circumstances.

This terminal ideological exhaustion was confirmed by the tendency of many in the New Left to migrate into non-political activities.

> The journey out of politics was gradual. First came collectives as a base for conventional radical political activity. Then came collectives as laboratories where radicals could learn about how people interacted so that the lessons might be used for the revolution. Then, finally, came the commune purely for self-discovery. In the end, it seems, many radicals totally surrendered to the dropout, subjective ethic that they had professed to despise.[34]

Where the utopian communities of the 1840s, 1890s, and 1930s offered economic equality, those of the 1960s offered personal growth, a dematerialized and psychologized millennium.[35] A millennium of revolutionary liberation was swallowed up in a millennium of Maslowian self-fulfillment. The communes grew rapidly beginning about 1965 and went into equally rapid decline by the early and mid-1970s.[36] Their decline coincided with the return of traditional premillennialism, a development as unforeseen in religion as the New Left had been in politics.

The heady days of countercultural radicalism had profoundly unsettled traditionalists, threatened by what they regarded as assaults upon patriotism, family structure, and the work ethic. Quite apart from the more dramatic events of the 60s, a number of social and legal changes helped prepare the way for a new millenarian ambiance: the women's movement, with its challenge to traditional gender roles; the increasing frequency of sex before and outside of marriage; the visibility and activism of the gay community; and Supreme Court decisions banning school prayer and permitting abortion. While many viewed these developments as long overdue, others saw them as the march of sin and immorality that validated a Manichean view of the world: just as the U.S.–Soviet rivalry was the international expression of the battle between light and darkness, so the confrontation between traditional and innovative conceptions of right behavior was the domestic expression of the struggle.

The premillennialism of modern fundamentalists, such as the Reverend Jerry Falwell, arose out of a system of Biblical interpretation developed by the English evangelical, John Nelson Darby. Darby, a contemporary of William Miller's, taught a different approach to unlocking scriptural secrets, "dispensationalism." Dispensationalism was a complex system for dividing world history into religiously significant periods or "dispensations." The effect of these new historical divisions was to push the fulfillment of Biblical prophecies into the future. Where Miller and those like him insisted that prophecies had been progressively fulfilled throughout history, the dispensationalists placed most prophetic fulfillment in the future. The attractiveness of dispensationalism became immediately evident following the Great Disappointment, for such traumas were far less likely where few promises were made concerning immediate events. Dispensationalists were able to combine Biblical literalism with deferred prophecies largely because of their insistence the prophecies concerned the Jewish people rather than the church.[37]

Dispensationalism was modestly influential until the post–World War II period. Then, with the founding of Israel in 1948, and more particularly with Israeli consolidation of control over Jerusalem in 1967, the influence of dispensationalism rose dramatically, for its adherents could now argue that prophecies were in process of fulfillment and that the millennial clock was running. The New Apocalypticism, grounded in dispensationalist theology, has produced a literature of its own, epitomized by Hal Lindsey's *The Late Great Planet Earth*, which sold 7,500,000 copies, to make it the largest selling non-fiction book of the decade.[38] It was only the most conspicuous of a mass-market genre which saw eschatological signs in the vicissitudes of world politics. As we have already seen, mastery over nature made the search for natural portents less productive. However, the new political constellation made it possible to salvage part of portent analysis by concentrating upon the other major category of premonitory events, wars and the overturning of nations. Events in the Middle East occurred within the context of conflict between the United States and the Soviet Union. Protracted political tension without the promise of early resolution also made the use of political portents attractive. The seemingly unending East-West crises increased the likelihood that at least some dire predictions would be confirmed. At the same time, fear of nuclear weapons cast doubt on the inevitability of progress through scientific discoveries.[39]

The prominence of eschatological speculation is novel, but its visibility may not reflect increased numbers of millenarians. The battle between fundamentalists and liberals, so often noted in the 1920s, may have led academic observers to misjudge fundamentalist numbers, assuming that the side with the less compelling argument must necessarily be smaller. In fact, the size of fundamentalism may well have remained constant, even in periods when it was subjected to the harshest ridicule.[40]

Whether or not there are more fundamentalists, apocalyptic arguments have an enhanced ability to be heard. Five factors appear to account for this. First, church memberships (as distinct from numbers believing particular doctrines) have changed dramatically since the 1950s. Liberal denominations, inhospitable to premillennialism, have shrunk or barely maintained themselves, while more doctrinally conservative groups, such as the Southern Baptists, have achieved notable membership increases. While the expanding denominations have not necessarily been overtly millenarian, their emphasis on Biblical literalism makes them more receptive to premillennial arguments.

Second, the change in denominational growth patterns, with greater resources available to evangelical Protestants, has given millenarians access to a broad range of communications media. The systematic use of publications and television has diffused millenarianism beyond its core of committed adherents. This new communications capability has often fused with a third factor, the shift in political attitudes toward the right. If the New Right's membership is disproportionately fundamentalist, taking apocalyptic ideas seriously may be politically prudent.

Fourth, the region most often identified as the fundamentalist heartland—the South from Texas and Oklahoma eastward—has experienced a dramatic increase in population and economic productivity. This too has indirectly increased the prestige attaching to fundamentalist views by identifying their followers with an area of growth and wealth rather than with economic backwardness and cultural marginality. The "Bible Belt," in H. L. Mencken's derisive phrase, loosely referred to rural areas of the South and Middle West in which individuals read the Bible in literal terms.[41] If the criterion is denominational membership, Mencken's identification remains valid. Counties in which 25 percent or more of the population belong to fundamentalist denominations lie overwhelmingly in the nonurban South, with a scattering in the upper Middle West and north central states. Because denominational identification only imperfectly measures belief, however, it is useful to apply less formal measures. Thus Stephen Tweedie's analysis of viewing patterns for fundamentalist television programs indicates that in addition to the traditional Bible Belt, fundamentalism is also important in the urban South (with the exception of Miami and Washington), as well as in small cities in Pennsylvania, New York, Ohio, lower Michigan, Indiana, Iowa, Nebraska, and the Dakotas.[42]

The immediate audience for the New Apocalypticism is consequently more diverse than stereotypes of fundamentalism suggest. Migration from rural to urban areas, together with aggressive religious broadcasting and publications programs, has established a potentially millenarian audience outside farms and small towns, almost certainly larger than church membership data might suggest.

The fifth and final factor is perhaps the most complex, but it may well be the most potent. At virtually the same time that the literature of the New Apocalypticism was achieving popularity, a parallel secular literature was rising to a position of influence among intellectuals, government officials, and business leaders. This secular apocalyptic literature contended that because of the failure of individuals and nations to act wisely, decisions were being taken or were about to be taken which would destroy "civilization as we know it." The genre began with Barry Commoner's *The Closing Circle* (1971) and the report for the Club of Rome, *The Limits to Growth* (1972). A string of likeminded books followed, among them Robert Heilbroner's *An Inquiry into the Human Prospect* (1974), L. S. Stavrianos' *The Promise of the Coming Dark Age* (1976), and Jonathan Schell's *The Fate of the Earth* (1982).

The secular literature, divorced from religious traditions of portent identification, attribute the future calamity to a wide range of causes: nuclear war, spiritual exhaustion, environmental degradation, overpopulation, and the depletion of basic resources. The secular apocalypticists insist upon the interrelatedness of the human and natural worlds; events in one produce consequences in the other, such as the nuclear winter predicted as the result of an exchange of missiles or the greenhouse effect produced by the burning of fossil fuels. This link between the human and natural recalls the unity presumed by the premillennialists. Premillennialists, however, expected events in the natural world to occur first, as warnings of what was in store for humanity. Recent secular writers insist that human actions are more significant, for they can drastically effect the quality and even the survival of the natural world.

The emphasis in this literature upon the imminence of destruction conceals a more optimistic millenarian component, just as premillennial cataclysms were intended to usher in a period of peace and plenty. Stavrianos regards crises as the birthpangs that announce a new epoch of "the transcendence of Homo sapiens to Homo humanus."[43] Alexander Solzhenitsyn, although writing out of the Russian Orthodox tradition, was perceived as a political dissident when he told a Harvard audience that the crisis of the West "will demand from us a new spiritual blaze; we shall have to rise to a new height of vision, to a new level of life."[44] Even the most pessimistic claim to discern grounds for other than total despair. The Limits to Growth was followed by a second report to the Club of Rome which promised that it was still possible to turn from the "path of cancerous undifferentiated growth ... to ... the path of organic growth."[45] The nuclear threat that preoccupies Jonathan Schell may well produce "a republic of insects and grass," but "if it is possible to speak of a benefit of the nuclear peril, it would be that it invites us to become more deeply aware of the miracle of birth, and of the world's renewal. 'For unto us a child is born.' This is indeed 'good news.'"[46]

Notwithstanding these expressions of hope, nowhere can one detect the robust confidence of the Millerites, for whom the consummation was inevitable rather than merely probable or likely. Nor is there the more measured optimism of utopians, who had profound doubts about the world's capacities for improvement but did not doubt their own ability to redeem small segments of it. The micro-millennial alternative is clearly not available under conditions in which the coming calamity permits neither defense nor escape. Only Robert Heilbroner approaches the utopian option, and only if it is adopted by entire nations. Whole societies, he suggests, must choose quasimonastic ways of life, with diminished emphasis on material goods and the compensatory cultivation of ritual and aesthetic pleasures. "The struggle for individual achievement, especially for material ends, is likely to give way to the acceptance of communally organized and ordained roles,"[47] sentiments of which Noyes or Brisbane would have approved, yet which here can be effective only if adopted by millions rather than hundreds.

Although this literature can clearly be distinguished from the religious, its seriousness of purpose and the intellectual audience to which it is directed have legitimized apocalyptic themes. These ideas of sudden transformation are no longer dismissed as the product of a regional religious subculture. Thus the secular writers have inadvertently buttressed the authority of their less sophisticated premillennial counterparts. The two groups are divided by matters of style and nuance rather than by fundamentally different views of the world. Indeed, the religious and secular apocalyptic writers have far more in common than pre- and postmillennialists did in the nineteenth century. They identify different agents of disaster but both predict a final conflagration.

Yet one must be careful not to overdraw the parallels with the 1840s. While millennial themes grow in profusion, they possess as yet no dominant organizational expression. The New Left radical politics of the 60s is moribund. The countercultural communes have withered away. Cult movements have stabilized and show no evidence of further expansion. The New Apocalypticism continues in fundamentalist circles, but its followers do not seem disposed to the acts of withdrawal and renunciation that distinguished Millerism. Secular doom-sayers, although they claim an influential audience, concentrate on propagandizing rather than organization. Only the small groups of survivalists, living in wilderness areas with their stores of food, have actually organized for Armageddon.

Larger movements may yet appear. Just as ideas sometimes are after the fact rationalizations of behavior, so behavior often follows ideas. The movements of the 1840s followed a decade when millennialists and utopians spoke primarily to those already convinced. This phenomenon of speaking to the converted often precedes an expansionist phase, for it provides an opportunity for ideas to incubate and develop, for a core of committed followers to gradually assemble, and for ideas to slowly diffuse. As long as damage-control systems and theories of mistakes can manage the effects of stress, alternative world views will not take hold beyond these small followings. However, they lie prepared, waiting only for damage control to fail and for theories of mistakes to be discredited. Then, as they touch a newly receptive audience, fringe millennialist ideas suddenly acquire the capacity to drive people to action. The catalyzing effect of disaster transforms speculative ideas into militant creeds, and disaster, unfortunately, is usually only a matter of time.

The immediate future provides an additional cultural trigger in the proximity of the millennial year, 2000. Once the symbol of a technological consummation, where human ills would yield to scientific solutions, the year 2000 is certain to revert to its ancient chiliastic function, a signpost on the road to some cosmic overturning. For those attuned to a catastrophist vision of history, such symbols fuse powerful metaphors of birth and death in their insistence that one world must die before another can be born. The magnetism of such images lies in their capacity to link the terminal events of the individual life cycle with beliefs about universal generation and decay. Their danger, however, lies in their ability to induce self-fulfilling prophecies, for the millennial vision entails a struggle between normal desires for safety and routine and an anticipation of the climactic disasters to come. In a nuclear world, where human beings themselves possess the means for world destruction, fascination with the end time may introduce a potentially fatal passivity into precisely those areas of political life most in need of decisive control.

NOTES

INTRODUCTION

1. Alan R. Pred, *Urban Growth and the Circulation of Information*, pp. 48–49.
2. Charles G. Finney, *Memoirs*, p. 78. For a general discussion of the Burned-over District, see Whitney R. Cross, *The Burned-over District*.
3. Dolores Hayden, *Seven American Utopias*, pp. 199–202.
4. Whitney R. Cross, *The Burned-over District*, p. 173.
5. J. F. C. Harrison, *The Second Coming*, p. 231.
6. Arthur Bestor, *Backwoods Utopias*, pp. vii–viii.

CHAPTER 1—THE MILLENARIAN STREAM

1. Gershom Scholem, *The Messianic Idea in Judaism*, pp. 6–8.
2. Norman Cohn, *The Pursuit of the Millennium*, rev. ed., p. 24.
3. I have developed the themes in this and succeeding sections much more fully in an earlier work, *Disaster and the Millennium*.
4. Anthony F. C. Wallace, *The Death and Rebirth of the Seneca*. James Mooney, *The Ghost-Dance Religion and the Sioux Outbreak of 1890*.
5. On Brazilian movements, see for example, Maria De Queiroz, "On materials for a History of Studies of Crisis Cults." For a discussion of Inca concepts of history, see Freidhelm Hardy, "Despair and Hope of the Defeated." As De Queiroz demonstrates, there have also been numerous millenarian movements among Brazilian peasants. These, however, have Ibero-Catholic rather than Indian roots.
6. Michael Adas, *Prophets of Rebellion*. T. O. Ranger, "Connexions between 'Primary Resistance' Movements and Modern Mass Nationalism in East and Central Africa."
7. Guenther Lewy, *Religion and Revolution*, pp. 176–93.

161

8. Kitsiri Malalgoda, "Millennialism in Relation to Buddhism." Jean Chesneaux, *Secret Societies in China in the Nineteenth and Twentieth Centuries.* Jean Chesneaux, *Popular Movements and Secret Societies in China, 1840–1950.* Eugene P. Boardman, "Millenary Aspects of the Taiping Rebellion (1851–64)," in Sylvia Thrupp, *Millennial Dreams in Action,* pp. 70–79.

9. The most systematic survey of this vast literature is I. C. Jarvie, *The Revolution in Anthropology.* See also, Peter Worsley, *The Trumpet Shall Sound,* and D. Glynn Cochrane, *Big Men and Cargo Cults.*

10. James Billington, *Fire in the Minds of Men.*

11. The conference papers were published as Thrupp, *Millennial Dreams of Action.*

12. The literature has grown at a pace that has outrun bibliographies. The best review remains, despite the passage of time, Weston La Barre, "Materials for the History and Studies of Crisis Cults."

13. Norman Cohn, "Medieval Millenarism," in Thrupp, *Millennial Dreams in Action,* p. 31. Cohn, *The Pursuit of the Millennium,* rev. ed., p. 15.

14. This material appears in the 1961 edition of Cohn's *The Pursuit of the Millennium,* pp. xiii–xvi, 307–15, but not in his revised edition.

15. Cohn, *The Pursuit of the Millennium,* rev. ed., pp. 59, 60.

16. E. J. Hobsbawm, *Primitive Rebels.*

17. Anthony F. C. Wallace, "Revitalization Movements."

18. The stigmatization of "enthusiasm" is discussed in Michael Heyd, "The Reaction to Enthusiasm in the Seventeenth Century"; George Rosen, "Enthusiasm"; and Susie Tucker, *Enthusiasm.*

19. Harrison, *The Second Coming,* p. 13.

20. Alan Heimert, *Religion and the American Mind,* pp. 84–85.

21. Nathan O. Hatch, "The Origins of Civil Millennialism in America," p. 427.

22. Ibid., p. 409.

23. James W. Davidson, *The Logic of Millennial Thought,* p. 259.

24. James W. Davidson, "Searching for the Millennium," p. 258. In certain respects, although not in this one, Davidson takes different positions in *The Logic of Millennial Thought,* published five years after this article.

25. Heimert, *Religion and the American Mind,* p. 548.

26. William G. McLoughlin, "Revivalism," in Edwin S. Gaustad, *The Rise of Adventism,* p. 134. Roland Berthoff, *An Unsettled People,* p. 243.

27. Winthrop S. Hudson, "A Time of Religious Ferment," in *The Rise of Adventism,* p. 16.

28. John L. Hammond, *The Politics of Benevolence,* pp. 48–49.

29. Cross, *The Burned-over District,* pp. 5–6.

30. Finney, *Memoirs,* pp. 370–71.

31. Timothy L. Smith, "Righteousness and Hope," p. 39. James H. Moorehead, "The Erosion of Postmillenialism."

32. Smith, "Righteousness and Hope," p. 39.

33. Hammond, *The Politics of Benevolence,* p. 28.

34. Jean B. Quandt, "Religion and Social Thought," p. 396.

35. Moorehead, "The Erosion of Postmillennialism," pp. 76–77.

36. Ibid., p. 74.

37. Ernest L. Tuveson, *Redeemer Nation.*

38. Quandt, "Religion and Social Thought."

39. Will Herberg, *Protestant—Catholic—Jew.*

CHAPTER 2—THE RISE OF THE MILLERITES

1. Richard Carwardine, *Trans-Atlantic Revivalism*, pp. 49–53.

2. E.g., David Ludlum, *Social Ferment in Vermont*, pp. 238, 253.

3. Robert Bruce Flanders, "The Succession Crisis in Mormon History."

4. Ernest D. Sandeen, *The Roots of Fundamentalism*, p. 44.

5. William Miller, "Apology and Defence," p. 22.

6. Jonathan M. Butler, "Adventism and the American Experience," in the *Rise of Adventism*, p. 175. Cross, *The Burned-over District*, p. 287.

7. David Rowe, "The Millerites: A Shadow Portrait," in Ronald L. Numbers and Jonathan M. Butler, eds., *The Disappointed*.

8. *Historical Statistics of the United States*, p. 13.

9. Miller's genealogy appears in Francis D. Nichol, *The Midnight Cry*, p. 477.

10. Aleine Austin, *Matthew Lyon*, pp. 13, 81.

11. Miller, "Apology and Defence," p. 3. "The Second Advent. No. I," *The Liberator* 13 (February 10, 1843): 23.

12. Joshua V. Himes, "Memoir of William Miller," pp. 7–8.

13. Miller, "Apology and Defence," pp. 6, 11.

14. Louis Billington, "The Millerite Adventists in Great Britain, 1840–1850."

15. Clarke Garrett, *Respectable Folly*.

16. Ludlum, *Social Ferment in Vermont*, p. 15.

17. Miller, "Apology and Defence," pp. 20, 22.

18. Sylvester Bliss, *Memoirs of William Miller*, passim.

19. Cross, *The Burned-over District*, pp. 68, 289.

20. Miller, "Apology and Defence," p. 19. Nichol, *The Midnight Cry*, pp. 51, 57–58.

21. *The Liberator* 13 (February 10, 1843): 23.

22. Letter to Henry C. Wright, March 1, 1843, Walter M. Merrill, *The Letters of William Lloyd Garrison* III: 135.

23. Charles Johnson, *The Frontier Camp Meeting*, p. 79.

24. Nichol, *The Midnight Cry*, p. 100.

25. David Rowe, *Thunder and Trumpets* (1985), p. 36.

26. Nichol, *The Midnight Cry*, pp. 105–106, 121.

27. Miller, "Apology and Defence," pp. 24–25. Cross, *The Burned-over District*, p. 304.

28. Le Roy Edwin Froom, *The Prophetic Faith of Our Fathers* IV: 738–47. Ira V. Brown, "The Millerites and the Boston Press."

29. *The New York Daily Tribune*, March 2, 1843. Ira V. Brown, "The Millerites and the Boston Press." Jan Kobeski, "The Millerites: An Examination of Press Attitudes."

30. Charles Fitch, *"Come out of her, my people,"* pp. 17, 19.

31. Ibid.

32. Nichol, *The Midnight Cry*, p. 495.

33. "Millerism," *American Journal of Insanity* 1 (1845): 250.

34. Ronald Numbers and Janet Numbers, "Millerism and Madness," in Numbers and Butler, eds., *The Disappointed*.

35. Cross, *The Burned-over District*, p. 288.

36. David Rowe, "A New Perspective on the Burned-over District," p. 44. *Thunder and Trumpets* (1985), p. 47.

37. Rowe, in Numbers and Butler, eds., *The Disappointed*.

38. Cross, *The Burned-over District*, p. 303.

39. Barkun, *Disaster and the Millennium*, pp. 68–74.

40. David Rowe, "Thunder and Trumpets" (1974), pp. 285–355. Cross, *The Burned-over District*, p. 303.

41. Cross, *The Burned-over District*, pp. 4–6. Hammond, *The Politics of Benevolence*, p. 2.

42. Paul Johnson, *A Shopkeeper's Millennium*.

43. Rowe, in Numbers and Butler, *The Disappointed*.

44. Marvin Hill, "Quest for Refuge" and "The Rise of Mormonism in the Burned-over District."

45. Jonathan M. Butler, "Millerism to Seventh-Day Adventism," in Numbers and Butler, eds., *The Disappointed*.

46. Otohiko Okugawa, "Appendix A: Annotated List of Communal and Utopian Societies, 1787–1919," in Robert S. Fogarty, *Dictionary of Communal and Utopian History*, pp. 200–202.

47. William Hinds papers.

48. *Day Star of Zion*, July 1864, August 1864, Hinds papers.

49. Ibid., July 1864, December 1864.

50. Okugawa, "Appendix A: Annotated List of Communal and Utopian Societies," in Fogarty, *Dictionary*, p. 200. "The Germania Co. and Neighbors," Wisconsin Pioneer and Century Farms manuscripts, The State Historical Society of Wisconsin. I am grateful to Otohiko Okugawa for bringing these materials to my notice.

51. Herbert W. Schneider and George Lawton, *A Prophet and a Pilgrim*, pp. 13–14.

CHAPTER 3—THE IMAGERY OF APOCALYPSE

1. William Miller, *Evidence from Scripture and History of the Second Coming of Christ, about the year 1843: Exhibited in a Course of Lectures*. The few "modern" references may be found on pp. 218–21.

2. *Signs of the Times*, May 1, 1840, p. 22.

3. Ibid., March 1, 1841, p. 182.

4. Ibid., August 9, 1843, p. 184.

5. *The Midnight Cry*, February 8, 1844.

6. Stanford J. Shaw and Ezel Kural Shaw, *History of the Ottoman Empire and Modern Turkey* II: 56–58.

7. *Signs of the Times*, August 1, 1840, p. 70.

8. Ibid., November 1, 1840, p. 117 (emphasis in original)

9. Ibid.

10. Ibid., February 1, 1841, p. 162 (emphasis in original)

11. Eric Anderson, "Signs of the Times," in Numbers and Butler, eds., *The Disappointed*.

12. Ibid., July 26, 1843, p. 168.

13. *The Midnight Cry*, June 15, 1843.

14. Ibid., April 27, 1843.

15. Ibid., December 5, 1842.

16. *Signs of the Times*, October 11, 1843, p. 64.

17. *The Midnight Cry*, July 6, 1843.

18. *Signs of the Times*, October 15, 1841, p. 109.

19. Ibid., July 6, 1842, p. 110.

20. Ibid., August 17, 1842, p. 166.

21. *Signs of the Times*, February 15, 1841, p. 170.

22. Ibid., November 1, 1843, p. 90 (emphasis in original). November 22, 1843, p. 123.

23. *The Midnight Cry*, November 25, 1842; April 20, 1843. Ray Allen Billington, *The Protestant Crusade*, pp. 118–30.

24. David Rowe, "Comets and Eclipses," pp. 15–16.

25. Ibid., p. 18.

26. *Signs of the Times*, March 22, 1843, p. 19 (emphasis in original).

27. Ibid., October 12, 1842, p. 28; February 22, 1843, p. 178.

28. Quoted in Stephen Marini, *Radical Sects of Revolutionary New England*, p. 47; see also p. 183.

29. Ibid., p. 78.

30. *The Midnight Cry*, December 14, 1843.

31. Ibid., February 1, 1844.

32. *Signs of the Times*, June 15, 1842, p. 85.

33. *The Midnight Cry*, March 10, 1843.

34. Ibid., December 3, 1842.

35. *Signs of the Times*, October 11, 1843, p. 64.

36. Garrett, *Respectable Folly*, pp. 153–54.

37. *The Midnight Cry*, March 10, 1843.

38. *The Liberator*, February 17, 1843, p. 27 (emphasis in original)

39. Christopher Hill, *The World Turned Upside Down*, p. 13.

40. Leon Festinger, Henry W. Riecken, and Stanley Schachter, *When Prophecy Fails*, p. 23.

41. Ibid., p. 28.

CHAPTER 4—THE GROWTH OF UTOPIAN COMMUNITIES

1. Stow Persons, "Christian Communitarianism in America," in Donald Egbert and Stow Persons, *Socialism and American Life* I: 134–35, 140–41.

2. Lawrence Foster, *Religion and Sexuality*, p. 22.

3. Ibid., p. 28.

4. Ibid., p. 32.

5. *The Perfectionist and Theocratic Watchman*, March 22, 1845.

6. Robert Thomas, "The Development of a Utopian Mind," p. 110.

7. In the " 'The Wind Sweeping over the Country' " I discuss Noyes' convoluted millennialist theories at greater length, in Numbers and Butler, eds., *The Disappointed*.

8. *The Perfectionist*, August 31, 1835, p. 5.

9. Ibid., March 20, 1835, pp. 30–31 (emphasis in original).

10. John Humphrey Noyes to Alexander Wilder, October 31, 1840. George Wallingford Noyes papers, box 1. The GWF papers contain typescripts of correspondence and other materials subsequently lost or destroyed.

11. John Humphrey Noyes, *Confessions of John H. Noyes*, p. 39 (emphasis in original).

12. John Humphrey Noyes to his mother, May 1835. George Wallingford Noyes papers, box 1.

13. Joanna Noyes Hayes to her family, June 23, 1835. George Wallingford Noyes papers, box 1. This letter appears in George Wallingford Noyes, *The Religious Experience of John Humphrey Noyes*, pp. 226–27. However, the reference to vicarious suffering and immortality is omitted from the published version.

14. Noyes was given to the use of marine metaphors. Barkun, in Numbers and Butler, eds., *The Disappointed*.

15. Carl J. Guarneri, "Importing Fourierism to America."

16. Ibid., p. 582.

17. Quoted ibid., p. 586.

18. H. H. van Amringe, *Nature and Revelation*, pp. 115, 160–61.

19. Redelia Brisbane, *Albert Brisbane*, p. 208. This work was largely dictated by Brisbane to his wife. For an extended discussion of its credibility, see Arthur Bestor, "Albert Brisbane," pp. 154–58.

20. Albert Brisbane, *Social Destiny of Man*, pp. 239–40 (emphasis in original).

21. Ibid., pp. 457, 480.

22. *New York Daily Tribune*, March 15, 1843.

23. Arthur Bestor, "Patent Office Models of Society," in *Backwoods Utopias*, pp. 230–52.

24. Jeffrey B. Russell, *Dissent and Reform in the Early Middle Ages*, pp. 241–47. The same area is discussed at greater length in Cohn, *The Pursuit of the Millennium*.

25. Bestor, *Backwoods Utopias*, p. 23.

26. Ibid.

27. Ibid., pp. 277, 283–84.

28. Henri Desroche, *The American Shakers*, p. 56.

29. Foster, *Religion and Sexuality*, pp. 23–24, 267. Hillel Schwartz, *The French Prophets*, pp. 211–12.

30. Bernard J. Siegel, "Defensive Structuring and Environmental Stress."

31. The major exception is, of course, the Mormons. Their large numbers, compared to the utopian communities, and their active political participation deprived them of the protections granted to groups whose beliefs and practices represented comparable deviations from orthodoxy. For an insightful comparison of the politico-legal problems of Mormonism with those of the Shakers, Oneidans, and other utopians, see Carol Weisbrod, *The Boundaries of Utopia*, pp. 16–33.

32. Desroche, *The American Shakers*, p. 293. J. F. C. Harrison, *Quest for the New Moral World*, p. 219.

33. Ibid., pp. 56, 152–53.

34. Quoted in E. P. Thompson, *The Making of the English Working Class*, p. 788.

35. Harrison, *Quest for the New Moral World*, p. 68.

36. Robert Owen, *The Life of Robert Owen*, p. 212.

37. Ibid., pp. 212–13.

38. Harrison, *Quest for the New Moral World*, p. 99. Foster, *Religion and Sexuality*, p. 266.

39. Bestor, *Backwoods Utopias*, pp. 253–54.

40. Desroche, *The American Shakers*, p. 279. Harrison, *Quest for the New Moral World*, p. 107. Foster, *Religion and Sexuality*, p. 90.

41. Quoted in ibid., p. 81 (emphasis in original). Noyes's reckless candor occurred during a time of frustrated romantic attachment to Abigail Merwin, news of whose marriage to another Noyes received immediately before writing the letter. Robert Thomas, *The Man Who Would Be Perfect*, pp. 85ff.

42. George Wallingford Noyes, *John Humphrey Noyes*, p. 123.

43. Ibid., pp. 68–72, 116. Thomas, *The Man Who Would Be Perfect*, p. 105.

44. Ibid., pp. 109–10.

45. M. L. Carden, *Oneida*, pp. 40–41.

46. Foster, *Religion and Sexuality*, p. 94.

47. Ibid., p. 16. Beginning in 1868, Noyes introduced stirpiculture, an experiment in selective breeding in which reproductive pairs were approved on the basis of the participants' personal characters. Ibid., pp. 118–119. The tensions introduced by complex marriage and stirpiculture were substantially controlled by a process of regular semi-public criticism and confession, for which a manual (published anonymously but almost certainly written by Noyes) was eventually printed under the title *Mutual Criticism*.

48. *Favorite Hymns for Community-Singing*, p. 6.

49. Foster, *Religion and Sexuality*, pp. 237–38.

50. *The Perfectionist*, July 15, 1843, p. 42 (emphasis in original).

51. Ibid., July 13, 1844, p. 34.

52. Ibid., August 10, 1844, p. 44.

53. Ibid., April 20, 1844, p. 11.

54. Ibid., September 7, 1844, p. 51.

55. *The Spiritual Magazine*, May 15, 1846, p. 39.

56. Ibid., March 15, 1846, p. 5.

57. Ibid., p. 6 (emphasis in original).

58. Bestor, *Backwoods Utopias*, pp. 280–81. Okugawa, "Appendix A: Annotated List of Communal and Utopian Societies," in Fogarty, *Dictionary*.

59. Michael McCrary, "Albert Brisbane (1809–1890)," p. 13. This school composition, written by Brisbane's grandson, is annotated by his mother, Sarah Brisbane Mellen. Brisbane papers.

60. R. Brisbane, *Albert Brisbane*, p. 50.

61. Bestor, "Albert Brisbane," pp. 132–33.

62. Quoted in Daniel Bell, "Charles Fourier," p. 53.

63. Bestor, "Albert Brisbane," p. 146, reflecting the judgment of Frank Luther Mott.

64. Arthur Bestor, "American Phalanxes" I: 263.

65. Ibid., pp. 274–76.

66. R. Brisbane, *Albert Brisbane*, p. 246. On the preferred economic basis for phalanxes, see Hayden, *Seven American Utopias*, pp. 155–56.

67. Foster, *Religion and Sexuality*, pp. 22–23.

68. The Oneida Community experienced natural increase through both stirpiculture and accidental conceptions, but like some other long-lived communities, encountered rebelliousness among the second generation.

69. Foster, *Religion and Sexuality*, p. 22.

70. Marini, *Radical Sects*, p. 94. The 1823 figure is cited in William Sims Bainbridge, "Shaker Demographics 1840–1900," p. 353.

71. Andrews' estimate appears in Foster, *Religion and Sexuality*, p. 23.

72. Bainbridge, "Shaker Demographics."

73. Ibid., p. 355.

74. Otohiko Okugawa, "Defining a Population of the Communal Societies in 19th-Century America." Okugawa, "Appendix A," in Fogarty, *Dictionary*. Bestor, *Backwoods Utopias*, pp. 273–85. Although listings of communities have been undertaken ever since the unpublished research of A. J. Macdonald in the 1850s, the two most recent and complete tabulations have been those of Bestor (1970) and Okugawa (1980). The enumerations differ

slightly due to slightly different judgments about projected communities that may never have been fully established and the status to be accorded branches of communities. Nonetheless, the lists are strikingly similar.

75. The most extensive listing of post-World War I communities is Robert Fogarty's in his *Dictionary of Communal and Utopian History.* The subject will be treated more fully by him in a forthcoming work.

76. Michael Barkun, "Communal Societies as a Cyclical Phenomenon."

77. Okugawa, "Appendix A," in Fogarty, *Dictionary.* Bestor, *Backwoods Utopias,* p. 285. Interestingly, while there are clear concentrations of community foundings, there are no comparably clear waves of dissolutions. The appearance of such a bunching about the time of World War I can be explained largely by the migration of the pacifist Hutterites from the Upper Midwest to Canada.

78. Okugawa, "Appendix A."

79. Bestor, *Backwoods Utopias,* p. 235.

80. Ronald Abler, "The Geography of Nowhere."

81. Ibid.

82. Table 2 and see maps in Hayden, *Seven American Utopias,* pp. 8–13.

83. *The Phalanx,* December 5, 1843, p. 34.

84. Seymour Ronald Kesten, "Utopian Episodes."

85. Anne C. Rose, *Transcendentalism as a Social Movement,* pp. 132, 152–53.

86. Bestor, *Backwoods Utopias,* pp. 133–34. Hyman Mariampolski, "New Harmony as a Voluntary Community."

87. Weisbrod, *Boundaries of Utopia.*

88. Rosabeth Moss Kanter, *Commitment and Community,* chapt. 4, passim.

89. Edward Deming Andrews, *The People Called Shakers,* p. 108.

90. Foster, *Religion and Sexuality,* p. 49. Bainbridge, "Shaker Demographics," pp. 358–59. Andrews, *The American Shakers,* p. 328.

91. Foster, *Religion and Sexuality,* pp. 54, 56.

92. Bainbridge, "Shaker Demographics," p. 360.

93. Rose, *Transcendentalism as a Social Movement,* pp. 153, 239–40.

94. Hayden, *Seven American Utopias,* p. 157.

95. Cross, *The Burned-over District,* p. 332.

96. Bestor, "American Phalanxes," v. i, pp. 54, 217–218.

97. Robert S. Fogarty, "Oneida," p. 206.

98. Carden, *Oneida,* p. 25.

99. Fogarty, "Oneida," p. 206.

CHAPTER 5—MILLERISM AND THE UTOPIANS

1. Hayden, *Seven American Utopias,* pp. 42–43.

2. Bestor, *Backwoods Utopias,* p. 58.

3. For a discussion of an analogous contemporary phenomenon, see Kenneth Keniston, "Heads and Seekers."

4. Cross, *The Burned-over District,* pp. 56ff. Hill, "Quest for Refuge."

5. Pred, *Urban Growth,* p. 166.

6. Nathan Hatch, "Spreading the Millerite Message."

7. For an inventory of Owenite publications, see Harrison, *Quest for the New Moral World*, pp. 347–54.

8. G. W. Noyes, *John Humphrey Noyes*, p. 60. Thomas, *The Man Who Would Be Perfect*, p. 136.

9. Quoted in G. W. Noyes, *John Humphrey Noyes*, p. 60.

10. *The Perfectionist*, June 15, 1844, p. 26.

11. Bestor, "Albert Brisbane," pp. 149–50. For an inventory of American Fourierist publications, see Bestor, "American Phalanxes," II: passim. On the history of *Phalanx* and *The Harbinger*, see II: 17–22.

12. Desroche, *The American Shakers*, pp. 258–63.

13. Bestor, *Backwoods Utopias*, pp. 53–54.

14. *The Phalanx*, December 9, 1844, p. 297.

15. W. H. G. Armytage, "Owen and America," in Sidney Pollard and John Salt, *Robert Owen*, pp. 228–29. Harrison, *Quest for the New Moral World*, p. 245.

16. Hayden, *Seven American Utopias*, pp. 181, 191.

17. Bestor, *Backwoods Utopias*, pp. 53–54.

18. Hayden, *Seven American Utopias*, pp. 181, 191.

19. Rowe, *Thunder and Trumpets* (1985), p. 24.

20. Hayden, *Seven American Utopias*, p. 65. Desroche, *The American Shakers*, pp. 102–03.

21. Bestor, *Backwoods Utopias*, p. 55.

22. Otohiko Okugawa, "Intercommunal Relationships Among Nineteenth-Century Communal Societies."

23. Bestor, *Backwoods Utopias*, p. 55.

24. Desroche, *The American Shakers*, p. 271. Harrison, *Quest for the New Moral World*, p. 166.

25. Cross, *The Burned-over District*, p. 311. Andrews, *The People Called Shakers*, p. 223. Foster, *Religion and Sexuality*, p. 97.

26. Hayden, *Seven American Utopias*, p. 65. Andrews, *The People Called Shakers*, p. 223.

27. Lawrence Foster, "Had Prophecy Failed?" in Numbers and Butler, eds., *The Disappointed*.

28. "Henry B. Bear's Advent Experience." I am indebted to Lawrence Foster for bringing Bear's account to my attention.

29. Desroche, *The American Shakers*, p. 268.

30. G. W. Noyes, *John Humphrey Noyes*, p. 123. *The Witness*, Dec. 10, 1842, p. 184.

31. Letter to William Hinds. Hinds papers.

32. Quoted in Cross, *The Burned-over District*, p. 321.

33. *The Perfectionist*, May 1, 1843, p. 15.

34. *The Witness*, December 10, 1842, p. 184.

35. *The Communitist*, December 11, 1844, p. 54.

36. Letter to Elizabeth Pease, April 4, 1843, *The Letters of William Lloyd Garrison*, III: 150.

37. *The Liberator*, February 10, 1843, p. 23.

38. *The Witness* published one article on Millerism in 1840, 2 in 1841, 5 in 1842, and 2 in 1843. *The Perfectionist* published 3 in 1843, 4 in 1844, and 1 in 1845.

39. *The Witness*, June 6, 1840, p. 152 (emphasis in original).

40. Ibid., October 9, 1841, p. 47.

41. *The Communitist*, December 11, 1844, p. 54.

42. *The Perfectionist*, November 2, 1844, p. 64; November 16, 1844, p. 66.

43. *The Communitist*, December 11, 1844, p. 54.

44. *The New York Daily Tribune*, October 21, 1844.

45. Letter to Henry C. Wright, March 1, 1843, *The Letters of William Lloyd Garrison* III: 135.

46. *The Liberator*, February 10, 1843, p. 23.

47. Rowe, *Thunder and Trumpets* (1985), p. 92. Nichol, *The Midnight Cry*, p. 54.

48. Ronald Graybill, "The Abolitionist-Millerite Connection," in Numbers and Butler, eds., *The Disappointed*.

49. *The Perfectionist*, January 11, 1845, p. 84.

50. *The New York Daily Tribune*, September 27, 1842; September 30, 1842; October 4, 1842; February 10, 1843; February 14, 1843; March 31, 1843; April 5, 1843; and April 13, 1843.

51. *The Witness*, June 6, 1840, p. 152. *The Perfectionist*, May 1, 1843, p. 15.

52. *The Communitist*, December 11, 1844, p. 54.

53. *The Phalanx*, January 5, 1844, p. 55 (emphasis in original).

CHAPTER 6—NATURAL DISASTERS AND THE MILLENNIUM

1. Mary P. Ryan, *Cradle of the Middle Class*, pp. 24, 47.

2. Marini, *Radical Sects of Revolutionary New England*, pp. 29–30.

3. Roland Berthoff, *An Unsettled People*, p. 166.

4. Ruth L. Higgins, *Expansion in New York*, pp. 103–107.

5. Ibid., pp. 114, 148.

6. Lois Kimball Mathews, *The Expansion of New England*, p. 153.

7. Cross, *The Burned-over District*, p. 6. Lewis Stilwell, *Migration from Vermont*, p. 120.

8. D. W. Meinig, "Geography of Expansion," in John H. Thompson, ed., *Geography of New York State*, pp. 140–71.

9. Stilwell, *Migration from Vermont*, p. 120. Harold F. Wilson, "Population Trends in North-Western New England, 1790–1930."

10. Cross, *The Burned-over District*, pp. 9–10.

11. Wilson, "Population Trends in North-Western New England 1790–1930."

12. Stillwell, *Migration from Vermont*, pp. 118–20, 139–40.

13. Ludlum, *Social Ferment in Vermont*, pp. 8–14.

14. Marini, *Radical Sects of Revolutionary New England*, pp. 27–28.

15. Ibid., pp. 5, 38.

16. Nathan O. Hatch, *The Sacred Cause of Liberty*, p. 24. Robert D. Rossel, "The Great Awakening."

17. H. N. Miller, III, and John J. Duffy, "Jedidiah Burchard and Vermont's 'New Measure' Revivals," p. 5.

18. Stilwell, *Migration from Vermont*, pp. 95, 128–29. Ludlum, *Social Ferment in Vermont*, p. 49.

19. Miller and Duffy, "Jedidiah Burchard and Vermont's 'New Measure' Revivals," p. 6. Stilwell, *Migration from Vermont*, pp. 152–54.

20. John D. Post, *The Last Great Subsistence Crisis*, p. 1.

21. Charles E. Rosenberg, *The Cholera Years*, p. 1.

22. Henry and Elizabeth Stommel, *Volcano Weather*, pp. 25, 28–29. Although the scholarly usefulness of the Stommels' book is limited by the absence of citations, it remains the most thorough description and analysis of the climatic irregularities of 1816.

23. Ibid., pp. 69–70, 75.

24. Ibid., pp. 67, 84.

25. Ibid., p. 79.

26. Ibid., pp. 116, 118.

27. Ibid., p. 11.

28. Post, *The Last Great Subsistence Crisis*, pp. 4–6, 11–12, 24–25.

29. Marini, *Radical Sects of Revolutionary New England*, p. 30. Stommel and Stommel, *Volcano Weather*, pp. 153–54.

30. Post, *The Last Great Subsistence Crisis*.

31. Stilwell, *Migration from Vermont*, p. 130.

32. Ibid., pp. 134–35. Stommel and Stommel, *Volcano Weather*, p. 94. Wilson, "Population Trends . . . " Post, *The Last Great Subsistence Crisis*, pp. 105–07.

33. Stommel and Stommel, *Volcano Weather*, pp. 19–23. Joseph B. Hoyt, "The Cold Summer of 1816."

34. G. F. Pyle, "The Diffusion of Cholera." The perception of the epidemic by contemporary physicians may be found in the publication issued by doctors in New York City during the epidemic, *Cholera Bulletin*.

35. William H. McNeill, *Plagues and Peoples*, pp. 262–64. André Siegfried, *Routes of Contagion*, pp. 42–46. Rosenberg, *The Cholera Years*, pp. 2–3, 24.

36. Ibid., pp. 165–66.

37. *The Boston Medical and Surgical Journal* (1849): 354, 356.

38. Rosenberg, *The Cholera Years*, pp. 45, 47, 55.

39. Carwardine, *Trans-Atlantic Revivalism*, p. 64. For Charles Finney's brief but vivid description of the epidemic in New York City (he himself contracted the disease), see his *Memoirs*, p. 320.

40. Pred, *Urban Growth . . .* , pp. 245–46.

41. Wilson, "Population Trends . . . "

CHAPTER 7—SOCIOECONOMIC DISASTERS AND THE MILLENNIUM

1. James Roger Sharp, *The Jacksonians versus the Banks*, p. 27.

2. Percy Wells Bidwell and John I. Falconer, *History of Agriculture in the Northern United States 1620–1860*, p. 306.

3. Sharp, *The Jacksonians versus the Banks*, p. 27. Charles P. Kindleberger, *Manias, Panics, and Crashes*, p. 255. Reginald Charles McGrane, *The Panic of 1837*, passim.

4. Peter Temin, *The Jacksonian Economy*, pp. 141, 147.

5. McGrane, *The Panic of 1837*, pp. 41–42. Pred, *Urban Growth*, p. 247.

6. Ibid., pp. 248–52.

7. Temin, *The Jacksonian Economy*, p. 116.

8. Samuel Rezneck, "The Social History of an American Depression, 1837–1843," p. 665.

9. Temin, *The Jacksonian Economy*, pp. 148, 154, 156–60. For the parallel between the depression of 1839–43 and the 1930s, see also Milton Friedman and Anna Jacobson Schwartz, *A Monetary History of the United States 1867–1960*, p. 299.

10. Bidwell and Falconer, *History of Agriculture in the Northern United States 1620–1860*, pp. 247–48.

11. Ibid., p. 181. Sharp, *The Jacksonians versus the Banks*, p. 308.

12. Arthur Harrison Cole, *Wholesale Commodity Prices in the United States 1700–1861*, pp. 111–14.

13. Bidwell and Falconer, *History of Agriculture in the Northern United States*, pp. 312–15. Patricia E. McGee, "Issues and Factions," pp. 6–7.

14. The long-wave literature is large and in recent years has grown rapidly. For an introduction intended for non-economists, see the August 1981 issue of *Futures*, entirely devoted to the subject. In addition, an unusually full bibliography appears in Joshua S. Goldstein, "Kondratieff Waves as War Cycles."

15. N. D. Kondratieff, "The Long Waves in Economic Life."

16. G. Garvey, "Kondratieff's Theory of Long Cycles."

17. A. van der Zwan, "On the Assessment of the Kondratieff Cycles and Related Issues," in S. K. Kuipers and G. J. Lanjouw, *Prospects of Economic Growth*, pp. 183–222.

18. W. W. Rostow, *Why the Rich Get Richer*, pp. 86–97.

19. Attempts have been made to chart later cycles using data on industrial production in addition to prices. One example, which shows an upswing in the United States beginning in 1847, is J. J. van Duijn, "Comment on van der Zwan's Paper," in Kuipers and Lanjouw, *Prospects of Economic Growth*, pp. 223–33.

20. Robert H. Wiebe, *The Search for Order 1877–1920*, p. 97.

21. Thomas, *The Man Who Would be Perfect*, p. 121.

22. Ryan, *Cradle of the Middle Class*, pp. 56–57. Foster, *Religion and Sexuality*, pp. 12–13.

23. Ryan, *Cradle of the Middle Class*, p. 62.

24. Foster, *Religion and Sexuality*, pp. 12, 231.

25. Ryan, *Cradle of the Middle Class*, p. 76.

26. Ibid., pp. 79–81. For an extended discussion of religion as an outlet for women in a small industrial community, see Anthony F. C. Wallace, *Rockdale*.

27. Foster, *Religion and Sexuality*, p. 64. Desroche, *The American Shakers*, p. 104.

28. Carwardine, *Trans-Atlantic Revivalism*, pp. 49–53. Cross, *The Burned-over District*, p. 269. Although it has severe evidentiary weaknesses, one of the first attempts to link Millerism with the Panic of 1837 was Reuben E. E. Harkness' 1927 doctoral dissertation, "Social Origins of the Millerite Movement."

29. Foster, *Religion and Sexuality*, p. 39.

30. R. Brisbane, *Albert Brisbane*, pp. 198ff. Given the uneven reliability of the work, it is possible that this characterization of Brisbane's early views in fact constitutes a reading back into youth of the monetary theories he held in later life.

31. Irwin Unger, *The Greenback Era*, p. 110.

32. *The Perfectionist*, August 31, 1835.

33. John Humphrey Noyes, "A Sketch of the Remarks Made by J. H. Noyes . . . " Emphasis in original.

34. *The Phalanx*, Oct. 7, 1844.

35. R. Brisbane, *Albert Brisbane*, p. 206.

36. *The Communitist*, April 23, 1845.

37. *The Spiritual Magazine*, May 15, 1846 (emphasis in original).

38. A. Brisbane, *Social Destiny of Man*, p. viii.

39. *The Phalanx*, Oct. 7, 1844.

40. *The Perfectionist*, Sept. 7, 1844.

41. Quoted in Wendell Phillips Garrison and Francis Jackson Garrison, *William Lloyd Garrison 1805–1879* II: 145–48 (emphasis in original).

42. Foster, *Religion and Sexuality*, pp. 239–40.

CHAPTER 8—ORGANIZING FOR THE MILLENNIUM

1. Antinomianism among the Sabbatians is discussed in Scholem, *The Messianic Idea in Judaism*, particularly the essay "Redemption Through Sin," pp. 78–141. Sabbatian antinomianism was often associated with a breach of sexual taboos. Similar claims concerning the Brethren of the Free Spirit are made in Cohn, *The Pursuit of the Millennium*, p. 180, and in Jeffrey Burton Russell, *Witchcraft in the Middle Ages*, pp. 140–41. For a more skeptical view of Free Spirit practices, see Robert Lerner, *The Heresy of the Free Spirit in the Later Middle Ages*.

2. Barkun, *Disaster and the Millennium*, pp. 68–74.

3. Miller, "Apology and Defence," p. 28.

4. Ibid., p. 32.

5. Rowe, *Thunder and Trumpets* (1985), pp. 146–47.

6. Ernest R. Sandeen, "End Games," p. 9.

7. Herbert G. Guttman, *Work, Culture and Society*, p. 13. Pred, *Urban Growth*, p. 7.

8. Robert G. Leblanc, *Location of Manufacturing in New England in the 19th Century.*

9. George Rudé, *Paris and London in the Eighteenth Century*, p. 38. David Rothman, *The Discovery of the Asylum*, p. 13.

10. George Rogers Taylor, "American Urban Growth Preceding the Railway Age," pp. 316, 322.

11. Adna Weber, *The Growth of the City*, p. 22.

12. Ibid.

13. Ibid., p. 25.

14. Stephen Thernstrom and Peter R. Knights, "Men in Motion."

15. Pred, *Urban Growth*, p. 12.

16. Ibid., p. 16.

17. Bidwell and Falconer, *History of Agriculture in the Northern United States*, p. 307.

18. Bliss, *Memoirs of William Miller*, p. 106.

19. Cross, *The Burned-over District*, p. 63. Pred, *Urban Growth*, pp. 49, 166.

20. Ibid., p. 49.

21. Hatch, "Spreading the Millerite Message."

22. Carwardine, *Trans-Atlantic Revivalism*, p. 25.

23. Ibid., p. 20. Rochester, New York, appears to have been an exception. See Johnson, *A Shopkeeper's Millennium*. One of Charles Finney's greatest triumphs, the Rochester campaign, receives chapter-length treatment in his *Memoirs*.

24. Rowe, "Thunder and Trumpets" (1974), pp. 237–38.

25. Rowe, *Thunder and Trumpets* (1985), pp. 115–18.

26. Billington, *Fire in the Minds of Men.*

27. Abler, "The Geography of Nowhere."

28. Kanter, *Commitment and Community*, p. 245.

29. Ibid., pp. 72–125 passim.

30. Bestor, "American Phalanxes," v. i, pp. 221–23.

31. For Oneida the most detailed description of this process appears in *Mutual Criticism*.

32. Quoted in Bestor, "American Phalanxes," v. ii, p. 336. The entire text of the Union's constitutive document may be found on pp. 336–45. Kanter, *Commitment and Community*, p. 245.

33. Ibid., p. 83.

34. Abler, "The Geography of Nowhere."

35. Rothman, *The Discovery of the Asylum*. Raymond Mohl, "Poverty, Pauperism, and Social Order."

CHAPTER 9—THE MILLENARIAN PROCESS

1. Cohn, *The Pursuit of the Millennium*, pp. 53–60.

2. George Steiner, "The City Under Attack." Gustave Le Bon, *The Crowd* is the classic sociological statement of this position. For its cultural and intellectual context, see Leon Bramson, *The Political Context of Sociology*, pp. 47–72.

3. Barkun, *Disaster and the Millennium*, especially pp. 68–74.

4. Hobsbawm, *Primitive Rebels*. Rodney Hilton, *Bond Men Made Free*, pp. 98–99.

5. Michael Barkun, "Disaster in History."

6. Keith V. Thomas, *Religion and the Decline of Magic*, p. 661.

7. Richard D. Brown, "Modernization and the Modern Personality in Early America, 1600–1865," p. 222.

8. William I. Torry, "Anthropological Studies in Hazardous Environments," p. 528.

9. For a more extended presentation of this argument, see Barkun, "Disaster in History."

10. Samuel Z. Klausner, *Why Man Takes Chances*, p. v.

11. Allen H. Barton, *Communities in Disaster*, p. 38.

12. I have borrowed the phrase "theory of mistakes" from Ronald Dworkin, who, however, employs it in a context utterly different from the present one, since his concern is to sketch a theory of judicial decisionmaking. Ronald Dworkin, *Taking Rights Seriously*, p. 122.

13. Wallace, "Revitalization Movements."

14. Fred Somkin, *Unquiet Eagle*, p. 45.

15. Rothman, *The Discovery of the Asylum*.

16. Mohl, "Poverty, Pauperism, and Social Order."

17. Melvin J. Lerner, "The Desire for Justice and Reactions to Victims," in J. Macaulay and L. Berkowitz, *Altruism and Helping Behavior*, p. 207.

18. Thomas, *Religion and the Decline of Magic*, p. 107.

19. Ibid., p. 110.

20. James H. Moorehead, *American Apocalypse*.

21. Sandeen, *The Roots of Fundamentalism*, pp. 163–64. Timothy Weber, *Living in the Shadow of the Second Coming*, pp. 85–88. As both Sandeen and Weber demonstrate, premillennialists continued to write, argue, and organize in the century that followed the "Great Disappointment." In response to the Millerite episode, they also avoided date-setting as much as possible, opting instead for a "dispensationalist" model that pushed most prophetic fulfillment into the future. Despite the flexibility of premillennialists, however, they failed during this period to achieve the breakthrough that Millerism exemplified, when the millenarian

agenda briefly dominated the awareness of the country's elites. Not until the 1970s and 80s would religious millenarians be taken with comparable seriousness.

22. Richard Hofstadter, *The Age of Reform*, pp. 62, 70.

23. The interpretation of American Populism has been unusually contentious. A sampling of opposing views appears in the exchange between Norman Pollack, "Fear of Man," and Irwin Unger, "Critique."

24. Charles Albro Barker, *Henry George*. John L. Thomas, *Alternative America*.

25. The millenarian aspect of these figures is presented in David H. Bennett, *Demagogues in the Depression*. For an instrumentalist view, see Alan Brinkley, *Voices of Protest*.

26. Paul K. Conkin, *Tomorrow a New World*, pp. 332–37. Russell Lord and Paul H. Johnstone, *A Place on Earth*, p. 3.

27. Some of the private groups are listed in Ralph Albertson, "A Survey of Mutualistic Communities."

28. William Martin, "Waiting for the End."

29. William G. McLoughlin, *Revivals, Awakenings and Reform*.

30. Frederic C. Jaher, *Doubters and Dissenters*, p. 4.

31. Richard Hofstadter, *The Paranoid Style*.

32. Daniel Bell, *The End of Ideology*, p. 393.

33. Ibid., p. 398.

34. Irwin Unger, *The Movement*, pp. 205–26.

35. Kanter, *Commitment and Community*, p. 167.

36. Ibid., p. 66. Benjamin Zablocki, *Alienation and Charisma*, pp. 48–57.

37. Sandeen, *The Roots of Fundamentalism*, pp. 63–64. On dispensationalism generally, see Weber, *Living in the Shadow*.

38. *New York Times Book Review*, April 6, 1980, p. 27.

39. Michael Barkun, "Divided Apocalypse."

40. R. Laurence Moore, "Insiders and Outsiders."

41. Charles A. Heatwole, "The Bible Belt."

42. Stephen W. Tweedie, "Viewing the Bible Belt."

43. L. S. Stavrianos, *The Promise of the Coming Dark Age*, p. 196.

44. Alexander Solzhenitsyn, "A World Split Apart," in Ronald Berman, *Solzhenitsyn at Harvard*, p. 20.

45. Mihajlo Mesarovic and Eduard Pestel, *Mankind at the Turning Point*, p. 9.

46. Jonathan Schell, *The Fate of the Earth*, p. 174.

47. Robert Heilbroner, *An Inquiry into the Human Prospect*, p. 140.

BIBLIOGRAPHY

PRIMARY SOURCES

Books and Pamphlets

Henry B. Bear's Advent Experience. Harrison, Ohio: Whitewater [Shaker] Village, n.d.

Bliss, Sylvester. *Memoirs of William Miller, Generally Known as a Lecturer on the Prophecies and the Second Coming of Christ.* Boston: Joshua V. Himes, 1853.

Brisbane, Albert. *Social Destiny of Man: or, Association and Reorganization of Industry.* Philadelphia: C. F. Stollmeyer, 1840.

Favorite Hymns for Community-Singing. Sherrill, N.Y.: Oneida Community, 1855.

Fitch, Charles. *"Come out of her, my people."* Rochester, N.Y.: J. V. Himes, 1843.

Garrison, Wendell Phillips and Garrison, Francis Jackson. *William Lloyd Garrison 1805–1879. The Story of His Life Told by His Children.* London: Unwin, 1889; reprinted New York: Negro Universities Press, 1969.

Himes, Joshua V. *Views of the Prophecies and Prophetic Chronology, Selected from Manuscripts of William Miller with a Memoir of his Life.* Boston: Joshua V. Himes, 1842.

The Letters of William Lloyd Garrison, edited by Walter M. Merrill. Cambridge, Mass.: Belknap Press of Harvard University Press, 1973.

Miller, William, "Apology and Defense." Reprinted in *Advent Tracts,* v. ii. Boston: Joshua V. Himes, n.d.

––––––. *Evidence from Scripture and History of the Second Coming of Christ, about the year 1843: Exhibited in a Course of Lectures.* Troy, N.Y.: Kemble & Hooper, 1836.

Mutual Criticism. Oneida, N.Y.: Office of the American Socialist, 1876; reprinted Syracuse: Syracuse University Press, 1975.

Noyes, John Humphrey. *Confessions of John H. Noyes. Part I. Confessions of Religious Experience: Including a History of Modern Perfectionism*. Oneida Reserve: Leonard & Company, Printers, 1849.

————. *A Sketch of the Remarks Made by J. H. Noyes, at a Meeting Held in Putney, January 31, 1839*.

Owen, Robert. *The Life of Robert Owen*. London: G. Bell and Son, reprinted 1920.

van Amringe, H. H. *Nature and Revelation, Showing the Present Condition of the Churches, and the Change Now to Come Upon the World, By the Second Advent, in Spirit, of the Messiah, with Interpretations of Prophecies in Daniel, and the Book of Revelation*. New York: R. P. Bixby & Co., 1843.

Newspapers and Periodicals

American Journal of Insanity, 1845.
Boston Medical and Surgical Journal. Boston, Mass., 1849.
Cholera Bulletin, New York. Reprinted, New York: Arno Press, 1972.
The Communitist. Mottville, N.Y., 1844–45.
Day Star of Zion. Celesta, Sullivan County, Pa., 1864.
The Liberator. Boston, 1843.
The Midnight Cry. New York, 1842–45.
New York Daily Tribune, 1842–44.
The Perfectionist. New Haven, Ct., 1834–35.
The Perfectionist, Putney, Vt., 1843–45.
The Perfectionist and Theocratic Watchman. Putney, Vt., 1844–45.
The Phalanx. New York, 1843–45.
Signs of the Times. Boston, 1840–44.
The Spiritual Magazine. Putney, Vt., 1846.
The Witness, Putney, Vt., 1840–42.

Manuscripts

William Hinds papers and George Wallingford Noyes papers, Oneida Community collection, Syracuse University.
Albert Brisbane papers, Syracuse University.
Wisconsin Pioneer and Century Farms papers, The State Historical Society of Wisconsin.

SECONDARY SOURCES CHIEFLY CONCERNED WITH MILLENNIALISM,
UTOPIAN EXPERIMENTATION, AND PRE-CIVIL WAR SOCIETY

Books

Andrews, Edward Deming. *The People Called Shakers: A Search for the Perfect So-ciety.* New York: Dover, 1963.

Austin, Aleine. *Matthew Lyon: "New Man" of the Democratic Revolution, 1749–1822.* University Park, Pa.: Pennsylvania State University Press, 1981.

Berthoff, Roland. *An Unsettled People: Social Order and Disorder in American History.* New York: Harper & Row, 1971.

Bestor, Arthur. *Backwoods Utopias: The Sectarian Origins and the Owenite Phase of Communitarian Socialism in America: 1663–1829,* 2nd ed. Philadelphia: University of Pennsylvania Press, 1970.

Bidwell, Percy Wells, and John I. Falconer. *History of Agriculture in the Northern United States 1620–1860.* Washington, D.C.: Carnegie Institution, 1925.

Billington, James. *Fire in the Minds of Men: Origins of the Revolutionary Faith.* New York: Basic Books, 1980.

Billington, Ray Allen. *The Protestant Crusade 1800–1860: A Study of the Origins of American Nativism.* New York: Macmillan, 1938.

Carden, Maren Lockwood. *Oneida: Utopian Community to Modern Corporation.* New York: Harper & Row, 1971.

Carwardine, Richard. *Trans-Atlantic Revivalism: Popular Evangelicalism in Britain and America, 1790–1865.* Westport, Ct.: Greenwood Press, 1978.

Cole, Arthur Harrison. *Wholesale Commodity Prices in the United States 1700–1861.* Cambridge, Mass.: Harvard University Press, 1938.

Cross, Whitney R. *The Burned-over District: The Social and Intellectual History of Enthusiastic Religion in Western New York, 1800–1850.* New York: Harper Torchbooks, 1965.

Davidson, James West. *The Logic of Millennial Thought: Eighteenth Century New England.* New Haven, Ct.: Yale University Press, 1977.

Desroche, Henri. *The American Shakers: From Neo-Christianity to Presocialism.* Amherst, Mass.: University of Massachusetts Press, 1971.

Fogarty, Robert S. *Dictionary of Communal and Utopian History.* Westport, Ct.: Greenwood Press, 1980.

Foster, Lawrence. *Religion and Sexuality: The Shakers, the Mormons, and the Oneida Community.* Urbana, Ill.: University of Illinois Press, 1984.

Froom, Le Roy Edwin. *The Prophetic Faith of Our Fathers: The Historical Devel-opment of Prophetic Interpretation.* Washington, D.C.: Review and Herald, 1954.

Garrett, Clarke. *Respectable Folly: Millenarians and the French Revolution in France and England.* Baltimore, Md.: Johns Hopkins University Press, 1975.

Gaustad, Edwin D., ed. *The Rise of Adventism: Religion and Society in Mid-Nineteenth Century America.* New York: Harper & Row, 1974.

Hammond, John L. *The Politics of Benevolence: Revival Religion and Voting Behavior.* Norwood, N.J.: Ablex, 1979.

Harrison, J. F. C. *Quest for the New Moral World: Robert Owen and the Owenites in Britain and America.* New York: Scribner's, 1969.

———. *The Second Coming: Popular Millenarianism 1780–1850.* New Brunswick, N.J.: Rutgers University Press, 1979.

Hatch, Nathan O. *The Sacred Cause of Liberty: Republican Thought and the Millennium in Revolutionary New England.* New Haven, Ct.: Yale University Press, 1977.

Hayden, Dolores. *Seven American Utopias: The Architecture of Communitarian Socialism, 1790–1975.* Cambridge, Mass.: MIT Press, 1976.

Heimert, Alan. *Religion and the American Mind: From the Great Awakening to the Revolution.* Cambridge, Mass.: Harvard University Press, 1966.

Higgins, Ruth L. *Expansion in New York, with Especial Reference to the Eighteenth Century.* Columbus, Ohio: Ohio State University, 1931. Contributions in History and Political Science, no. 14.

Johnson, Charles A. *The Frontier Camp Meeting: Religion's Harvest Time.* Dallas, Tex.: Southern Methodist University Press, 1955.

Johnson, Paul E. *A Shopkeeper's Millennium: Society and Revivals in Rochester, New York, 1815–1837.* New York: Hill and Wang, 1978.

Kanter, Rosabeth Moss. *Commitment and Community: Communes and Utopias in Sociological Perspective.* Cambridge, Mass.: Harvard University Press, 1972.

Leblanc, Robert G. *Location of Manufacturing in New England in the 19th Century.* Hanover, N.H.: Dartmouth College, 1969.

Ludlum, David M. *Social Ferment in Vermont 1791–1850.* New York: Columbia University Press, 1939.

Marini, Stephen A. *Radical Sects of Revolutionary New England.* Cambridge, Mass.: Harvard University Press, 1982.

Matthews, Lois Kimball. *The Expansion of New England: The Spread of New England Settlement and Institutions to the Mississippi River 1620–1865.* Boston: Houghton Mifflin, 1909.

McGrane, Reginald Charles. *The Panic of 1837: Some Financial Problems of the Jacksonian Era.* New York: Russell and Russell, reprinted 1965.

Moorehead, James H. *American Apocalypse: Yankee Protestants and the Civil War, 1860–1869.* New Haven, Ct.: Yale University Press, 1978.

Nichol, Francis D. *The Midnight Cry.* Washington, Mass.: Review and Herald Publishing Association, 1944.

Noyes, George Wallingford, ed. *John Humphrey Noyes: The Putney Community.* Oneida, 1931.

———. *The Religious Experience of John Humphrey Noyes, Founder of the Oneida Community.* New York: Macmillan, 1923.

Numbers, Ronald L., and Jonathan M. Butler, eds. *The Disappointed: Millerism and Millenarianism in the Nineteenth Century.* Bloomington, Ind.: Indiana University Press, 1986.

Pollard, Sidney, and John Salt, eds. *Robert Owen: Prophet of the Poor.* Lewisburg, Pa.: Bucknell University Press, 1971.

Post, John D. *The Last Great Subsistence Crisis in the Western World.* Baltimore, Md.: Johns Hopkins University Press, 1977.

Pred, Allen R. *Urban Growth and the Circulation of Information: The United States System of Cities, 1790–1840.* Cambridge, Mass.: Harvard University Press, 1973.

Rose, Anne C. *Transcendentalism as a Social Movement, 1830–1850.* New Haven, Ct.: Yale University Press, 1981.

Rosenberg, Charles E. *The Cholera Years: The United States in 1832, 1849, and 1866.* Chicago: University of Chicago Press, 1962.

Rothman, David J. *The Discovery of the Asylum: Social Order and Disorder in the New Republic.* Boston: Little, Brown, 1962.

Rowe, David L. *Thunder and Trumpets: Millerites and Dissenting Religion in Upstate New York, 1800–1850.* Chico, Ca.: Scholars Press, 1985. AAR Studies in Religion 38.

Ryan, Mary P. *Cradle of the Middle Class: The Family in Oneida County, New York, 1790–1865.* Cambridge: Cambridge University Press, 1981.

Sandeen, Ernest R. *The Roots of Fundamentalism: British and American Millenarianism 1800–1930.* Chicago: University of Chicago Press, 1970.

Schneider, Herbert W., and George Lawton. *A Prophet and a Pilgrim; Being the Incredible History of Thomas Lake Harris and Lawrence Oliphant; Their Sexual Mysticisms and Utopian Communities Amply Documented to Confound the Skeptic.* New York: Columbia University Press, 1942.

Schwartz, Hillel. *The French Prophets: The History of a Millenarian Group in Eighteenth-Century England.* Berkeley, Ca.: University of California Press, 1979.

Sharp, James Roger. *The Jacksonians Versus the Bank: Politics in the States After the Panic of 1837.* New York: Columbia University Press, 1970.

Somkin, Fred. *Unquiet Eagle: Memory and Desire in the Idea of American Freedom, 1815–1860.* Ithaca, N.Y.: Cornell University Press, 1967.

Stilwell, Lewis D. *Migration from Vermont.* Montpelier, Vt.: Vermont Historical Society, 1948.

Stommel, Henry and Elizabeth. *Volcano Weather: The Story of 1816, the Year without a Summer.* Newport, R.I.: Seven Seas Press, 1983.

Temin, Peter. *The Jacksonian Economy.* New York: Norton, 1969.

Thomas, Robert David. *The Man Who Would Be Perfect: John Humphrey Noyes and the Utopian Impulse.* Philadelphia: University of Pennsylvania Press, 1977.

Thompson, E. P. *The Making of the English Working Class.* New York: Vintage, 1966.

Thompson, John H., ed. *Geography of New York State.* Syracuse, N.Y.: Syracuse University Press, 1966; 2nd ed., 1977.

Tuveson, Ernest Lee. *Redeemer Nation.* Chicago: University of Chicago Press, 1968.

Wallace, Anthony F. C. *Rockdale: The Growth of an American Village in the Early Industrial Revolution.* New York: Knopf, 1978.

Weber, Adna. *The Growth of the City in the Nineteenth Century.* Ithaca, N.Y.: Cornell University Press, 1963.

Weber, Timothy P. *Living in the Shadow of the Second Coming: American Premillennialism (1875–1982).* Grand Rapids, Mich.: Academic Books, 1983, enlarged edition.

Wiebe, Robert H. *The Search for Order 1877–1920.* New York: Hill and Wang, 1967.

Weisbrod, Carol. *The Boundaries of Utopia.* New York: Pantheon, 1980.

Articles

Bainbridge, William Sims. "Shaker Demographics 1840–1900: An Example of the Use of U.S. Census Enumeration Schedules." *Journal for the Scientific Study of Religion* 21 (1982):352–65.

Barkun, Michael. "Communal Societies as a Cyclical Phenomenon." *Communal Societies* 4 (1984):35–48.

Bell, Daniel. "Charles Fourier: Prophet of Eupsychia." *The American Scholar* 38 (1968–69):41–58.

Bestor, Arthur E., Jr. "Albert Brisbane—Propagandist for Socialism in the 1840s." *New York History* 28 (1947):128–58.

Billington, Louis. "The Millerite Adventists in Great Britain, 1840–1850." *Journal of American Studies* 1 (1967):191–212.

Brown, Ira V. "The Millerites and the Boston Press." *New England Quarterly* 16 (1943):592–614.

Brown, Richard D. "Modernization and the Modern Personality in Early America, 1600–1865: A Sketch of a Synthesis." *Journal of Interdisciplinary History* 2 (1972):201–28.

Davidson, James W. "Searching for the Millennium: Problems for the 1790s and the 1970s." *New England Quarterly* 45 (1972):241–61.

Fogarty, Robert S. "Oneida: A Utopian Search for Religious Security." *Labor History* 14 (1973):202–27.

Guarneri, Carl J. "Importing Fourierism to America." *Journal of the History of Ideas* 43 (1982):581–94.

Hammett, Theodore M. "Two Mobs of Jacksonian Boston: Ideology and Interest." *Journal of American History* 62 (1976):845–68.

Hatch, Nathan O. "The Origins of Civil Millennialism in America: New England Clergymen, War with France, and the Revolution." *William and Mary Quarterly* 31 (1974):406–30.

Hill, Marvin S. "Quest for Refuge: An Hypothesis as to the Social Origins and Nature of the Mormon Political Kingdom." *Journal of Mormon History* 2 (1975):3–20.

_____. "The Rise of Mormonism in the Burned-over District: Another View." *New York History* 61 (1980):411–30.

Hoyt, Joseph B. "The Cold Summer of 1816." *Annals of the Association of American Geographers* 48 (1958):118–31.

Mariampolski, Hyman. "New Harmony as a Voluntary Community: From Socialist to Scientific Utopia." *Journal of Voluntary Action Research* 6 (1977): 112–18.

Mohl, Raymond A. "Poverty, Pauperism, and Social Order in the Preindustrial American City, 1780–1840." *Social Science Quarterly* 52 (1972):934–48.

Moorehead, James H. "The Erosion of Postmillennialism in American Religious Thought, 1865–1925." *Church History* 58 (1984):61–77.

Muller, H. N., and John J. Duffy. "Jedidiah Burchard and Vermont's 'New Measure' Revivals: Social Adjustment and the Quest for Unity." *Vermont History* 46 (1978):5–20.

Okugawa, Otohiko. "Intercommunal Relationships Among Nineteenth-century Communal Societies in America." *Communal Societies* 3 (1983):68–82.

Pyle, G. F. "Diffusion of Cholera." *Geographical Analysis* 1 (1969):59–75.

Quandt, Jean B. "Religion and Social Thought: The Secularization of Postmillennialism." *American Quarterly* 25 (1973):390–409.

Rezneck, Samuel. "The Social History of an American Depression, 1837–1843." *American Historical Review* 40 (1935):662–87.

Rossel, Robert D. "The Great Awakening: An Historical Analysis." *American Journal of Sociology* 75 (1970):907–25.

Rowe, David L. "A New Perspective on the Burned-over District: The Millerites in Upstate New York." *Church History* 47 (1978): 408–20.

_____. "Comets and Eclipses: The Millerites, Nature, and the Apocalypse." *Adventist Heritage* (Winter 1976):10–19.

Smith, Timothy L. "Righteousness and Hope: Christian Holiness and the Millennial Vision in America, 1800–1900." *American Quarterly* 31 (1979):21–45.

Taylor, George Rogers. "American Urban Growth Preceding the Railway Age." *Journal of Economic History* 27 (1967):303–39.

Thernstrom, Stephan, and Peter R. Knights. "Men in Motion: Some Data and Speculations about Urban Population Mobility in Nineteenth-century America." *Journal of Interdisciplinary History* 1 (1970):7–35.

Wilson, Harold F. "Population Trends in North-Western New England 1790–1930." *New England Quarterly* 7 (1934):276–306.

Dissertations

Bestor, Arthur E., Jr. "American Phalanxes: A Study of Fourierist Socialism in the United States (with Special Reference to the Movement in Western New York)." Ph.D. dissertation, Yale University, 1938.

Harkness, Reuben E. E. "Social Origins of the Millerite Movement." Ph.D. dissertation, University of Chicago, 1927.

Kesten, Seymour Ronald. "Utopian Episodes: A Humanistic Study of Nineteenth-century American Experiments in Social Reorganization." Ph.D. dissertation, Syracuse University, 1983.
McGee, Patricia E. "Issues and Factions: New York State Politics from the Panic of 1837 to the Election of 1848." Ph.D. dissertation, St. John's University, 1970.
Rowe, David L. "Thunder and Trumpets: The Millerite Movement and Apocalyptic Thought in Upstate New York, 1800–1845." Ph.D. dissertation, University of Virginia, 1974.
Thomas, Robert D. "The Development of a Utopian Mind: A Psychoanalytic Study of John Humphrey Noyes." Ph.D. dissertation, State University of New York at Stony Brook, 1973.

Unpublished Papers

Abler, Ronald. "The Geography of Nowhere: The Location of Utopian Communities, 1660–1860."
Flanders, Robert Bruce. "The Succession Crisis in Mormon History: Dilemmas of a Radical Kingdom and a Realized Eschatology." Prepared for conference on "Popular Religious Movements: Failure or Transformation?" Oberlin College. Oberlin, Ohio, 1973.
Hatch, Nathan. "Spreading the Millerite Message." Conference on "Millerism and the Millenarian Mind in Nineteenth-century America," Killington, Vermont, 1984.
Kobeski, Jan. "The Millerites: An Examination of Press Attitudes Toward the Adventist Movement of the 1840s."
Okugawa, Otohiko. "Defining a Population of the Communal Societies in 19th-Century America." Prepared for Historical Communal Societies Conference, Hancock Shaker Village. Pittsfield, Mass., 1980.
Sandeen, Ernest R. "End Games: The 'Little Tradition' and the Form of Modern Millenarianism." Prepared for Annual Meeting of the International Society of Political Psychology. Boston, 1980.

OTHER SECONDARY WORKS CITED

Books

Adas, Michael. Prophets of Rebellion: Millenarian Protest Movements Against the European Colonial Order. Chapel Hill, N.C.: University of North Carolina Press, 1979.
Barker, Charles Albro. Henry George. New York: Oxford University Press, 1955.

Barkun, Michael. *Disaster and the Millennium*. New Haven, Ct.: Yale University Press, 1974.

Barton, Allen H. *Communities in Disaster: A Sociological Analysis of Collective Stress Situations*. Garden City, N.Y.: Doubleday, 1969.

Bell, Daniel. *The End of Ideology: On the Exhaustion of Political Ideas in the Fifties*. New York: Collier, 1961.

Bennett, David H. *Demogogues in the Depression: American Radicals and the Union Party, 1932–1936*. New Brunswick, N.J.: Rutgers University Press, 1969.

Berman, Ronald, ed. *Solzhenitsyn at Harvard*. Washington, D.C.: Ethics and Public Policy Center, 1980.

Bramson, Leon. *The Political Context of Sociology*. Princeton, N.J.: Princeton University Press, 1961.

Brinkley, Alan. *Voices of Protest: Huey Long, Father Coughlin, and the Great Depression*. New York: Knopf, 1982.

Chesneaux, Jean. *Secret Societies in China in the Nineteenth and Twentieth Centuries*. Ann Arbor, Mich.: University of Michigan Press, 1971.

———, ed. *Popular Movements and Secret Societies in China, 1840–1950*. Stanford, Cal.: Stanford University Press, 1972.

Cochrane, D. Glynn. *Big Men and Cargo Cults*. London: Oxford University Press, 1970.

Cohn, Norman. *The Pursuit of the Millennium: Revolutionary Messianism in Medieval and Reformation Europe and Its Bearing on Modern Totalitarian Movements*. New York: Harper Torchbooks, 1961.

———. *The Pursuit of the Millennium: Revolutionary Millenarians and Mystical Anarchists of the Middle Ages*. New York: Oxford University Press, 1970.

Conkin, Paul K. *Tomorrow a New World: The New Deal Community Program*. Ithaca, N.Y.: Cornell University Press, 1959.

Dworkin, Ronald. *Taking Rights Seriously*. Cambridge, Mass.: Harvard University Press, 1978.

Egbert, Donald, and Stow Persons, eds. *Socialism and American Life*. Princeton, N.J.: Princeton University Press, 1952.

Festinger, Leon, et al. *When Prophecy Fails: A Social and Psychological Study of a Modern Group that Predicted the Destruction of the World*. New York: Harper Torchbooks, 1964.

Friedman, Milton, and Anna Schwartz. *A Monetary History of the United States 1867–1960*. Princeton, N.J.: Princeton University Press, 1963.

Gutman, Herbert G. *Work, Culture, and Society in Industrializing America: Essays in American Working-class and Social History*. New York: Knopf, 1976.

Heilbroner, Robert L. *An Inquiry into the Human Prospect*. New York: Norton, 1974.

Herberg, Will. *Protestant-Catholic-Jew*. Garden City, N.Y.: Doubleday, 1955.

Hill, Christopher. *The World Turned Upside Down: Radical Ideas During the English Revolution*. New York: Viking, 1972.

Hilton, Rodney. *Bond Men Made Free: Medieval Peasant Movements and the English Rising of 1381*. New York: Viking, 1973.

Historical Statistics of the United States. Washington: United States Department of Commerce, 1960.

Hobsbawm, E. J. *Primitive Rebels: Studies in Archaic Forms of Social Movements in the 19th and 20th Centuries.* New York: Norton, 1965.

Hofstadter, Richard. *The Age of Reform: From Bryan to F. D. R.* New York: Knopf, 1955.

———. *The Paranoid Style in American Politics and Other Essays.* New York: Knopf, 1965.

Jaher, Frederic Cople. *Doubters and Dissenters: Cataclysmic Thought in America, 1885–1918.* New York: The Free Press of Glencoe, 1964.

Jarvie, I. C. *The Revolution in Anthropology.* Chicago: Regnery, 1969.

Kindleberger, Charles P. *Manias, Panics, and Crashes: A History of Financial Crises.* New York: Basic Books, 1978.

Klausner, Samuel Z., ed. *Why Man Takes Chances: Studies in Stress-Seeking.* Garden City, N.Y.: Doubleday Anchor, 1968.

Kuipers, S. K., and G. J. Lanjouw, eds. *Prospects of Economic Growth.* Amsterdam: North-Holland Publishing Co., 1980.

LeBon, Gustave. *The Crowd: A Study of the Popular Mind.* 1895; rpt. New York: Viking, 1960.

Lerner, Robert E. *The Heresy of the Free Spirit in the Later Middle Ages.* Berkeley, Ca.: University of California Press, 1972.

Lewy, Guenter. *Religion and Revolution.* New York: Oxford University Press, 1974.

Lord, Russell, and Paul H. Johnstone, eds. *A Place on Earth: A Critical Appraisal of Subsistence Homesteads.* Washington, D.C.: Bureau of Agricultural Economics, U.S. Department of Agriculture, 1942.

Macaulay, J., and L. Berkowitz, eds. *Altruism and Helping Behavior: Social Psychological Studies of Some Antecedents and Consequences.* New York: Academic Press, 1970.

McLoughlin, William G. *Revivals, Awakenings, and Reform: An Essay on Religion and Social Change in America, 1607–1977.* Chicago: University of Chicago Press, 1978.

McNeill, William H. *Plagues and Peoples.* Garden City, N.Y.: Anchor, 1976.

Mesarovic, Mihajlo, and Eduard Pestel. *Mankind at the Turning Point: The Second Report to the Club of Rome.* New York: Dutton, 1974.

Rostow, W. W. *Why the Poor Get Richer and the Rich Slow Down: Essays in the Marshallian Long Period.* Austin, Tex.: University of Texas Press, 1980.

Russell, Jeffrey Burton. *Witchcraft in the Middle Ages.* Ithaca, N.Y.: Cornell University Press, 1972.

Schell, Jonathan. *The Fate of the Earth.* New York: Knopf, 1982.

Scholem, Gershom. *The Messianic Idea in Judaism and Other Essays on Jewish Spirituality.* New York: Schocken, 1971.

Shaw, Stanford J., and Ezel Kural Shaw. *History of the Ottoman Empire and Modern Turkey.* New York: Cambridge University Press, 1977.

Siegfried, André. *Routes of Contagion.* New York: Harcourt, Brace & World, 1965.

Stavrianos, L. S. *The Promise of the Coming Dark Age*. San Francisco, Cal.: Freeman, 1976.

Thomas, John L. *Alternative America: Henry George, Edward Bellamy, Henry Demarest Lloyd and the Adversary Tradition*. Cambridge, Mass.: Harvard University Press, 1983.

Thomas, Keith V. *Religion and the Decline of Magic: Studies in Popular Beliefs in Sixteenth and Seventeenth Century England*. London: Weidenfeld and Nicolson, 1971.

Thrupp, Sylvia L., ed. *Millennial Dreams in Action: Essays in Comparative Study*. The Hague: Mouton, 1962.

Tucker, Susie I. *Enthusiasm: A Study in Semantic Change*. Cambridge: Cambridge University Press, 1972.

Unger, Irwin. *The Greenback Era: A Social and Political History of American Finance, 1865–1879*. Princeton, N.J.: Princeton University Press, 1964.

_____. *The Movement: A History of the American New Left 1959–1972*. New York: Dodd, Mead, 1974.

Wallace, Anthony F. C. *The Death and Rebirth of the Seneca*. New York: Knopf, 1970.

Worsley, Peter. *The Trumpet Shall Sound: A Study of "Cargo" Cults in Melanesia*, 2nd ed. New York: Schocken, 1968.

Zablocki, Benjamin. *Alienation and Charisma: A Study of Contemporary American Communes*. New York: The Free Press, 1980.

Articles

Albertson, Ralph. "A Survey of Mutualistic Communities in America." *Iowa Journal of History and Politics* 3 (1936):374–444.

Barkun, Michael. "Disaster in History." *Mass Emergencies* 2 (1977):219–32.

_____. "Divided Apocalypse: Thinking About the End in Contemporary America." *Soundings* 66 (1983):257–80.

De Queiroz, Maria Isaura Pereira. "On Materials for a History of Studies of Crisis Cults." *Current Anthropology* 12 (1971):387–90.

Futures 13 (August 1981). Special Issue on "Technical Innovation and Long Waves in World Economic Development."

Garvey, G. "Kondratieff's Theory of Long Cycles." *Review of Economic Statistics* 25 (1943):203–20.

Goldstein, Joshua S. "Kondratieff Waves as War Cycles." *International Studies Quarterly* 29 (1985), in press.

Hardy, Friedhelm. "Despair and Hope of the Defeated—Andean Messianism." *Religious Studies* 11 (1975):257–64.

Heatwole, Charles A. "The Bible Belt: A Problem in Regional Definition." *Journal of Geography* 77 (1978):50–55.

Heyd, Michael. "The Reaction to Enthusiasm in the Seventeenth Century: Towards an Integrative Approach." *Journal of Modern History* 53 (1981):258–80.

Keniston, Kenneth. "Heads and Seekers: Drugs on Campus, Counter-Cultures and American Society." *The American Scholar* 38 (1968–69):97–112.

Kondratieff, N. D. "The Long Waves in Economic Life." *The Review of Economic Statistics* 17 (1935):105–15.

La Barre, Weston. "Materials for a History of Studies of Crisis Cults: A Bibliographic Essay." *Current Anthropology* 12 (1971):3–44.

Malalgoda, Kitsiri. "Millennialism in Relation to Buddhism." *Comparative Studies in Society and History* 12 (1970):424–41.

Martin, William. "Waiting for the End." *The Atlantic* 249 (June 1982):31–37.

Moore, R. Laurence. "Insiders and Outsiders in American Historical Narrative and American History." *American Historical Review* 87 (1982):390–412.

New York Times Book Review. April 6, 1980.

Pollack, Norman. "Fear of Man: Populism, Authoritarianism, and the Historian." *Agricultural History* 39 (1965):59–67.

Ranger, T. O. "Connexions Between 'Primary Resistance' Movements and Modern Mass Nationalism in East and Central Africa." *Journal of African History* 9 (1968):437–53, 631–41.

Rosen, George. "Enthusiasm, 'a dark lanthorn of the spirit.' " *Bulletin of the History of Medicine* 42 (1968):393–421.

Siegel, Bernard J. "Defensive Structuring and Environmental Stress." *American Journal of Sociology* 76 (1970):11–32.

Steiner, George. "The City Under Attack." *Salmagundi* 24 (Fall 1973):3–18.

Torry, William I. "Anthropological Studies in Hazardous Environments: Past Trends and New Horizons." *Current Anthropology* 20 (1979):517–40.

Tweedie, Stephen W. "Viewing the Bible Belt." *Journal of Popular Culture* 11 (1978):865–76.

Unger, Irwin. "Critique of Norman Pollack's 'Fear of Man.' " *Agricultural History* 39 (1965):75–80.

Wallace, Anthony F. C. "Revitalization Movements." *American Anthropologist* 58 (1956):264–81.

INDEX

189

CRUCIBLE OF THE MILLENNIUM

was composed in 10-point Mergenthaler Linotron 202 Sabon and leaded 2 points
by Partners Composition;
with display type in Roman Compressed No. 3 and Thorne Shaded
by Rochester Mono/Headliners;
and ornaments provided by Job Litho Services;
printed sheet-fed offset on 50-pound, acid-free Warren's Olde Style,
Smyth sewn and bound over 80-point binder's boards in Holliston Roxite B,
also adhesive bound with paper covers
by Thomson-Shore, Inc.;
with dust jackets and paper covers printed in 2 colors
by Philips Offset Company, Inc.;
designed by Mary Peterson Moore;
and published by

SYRACUSE UNIVERSITY PRESS
SYRACUSE, NEW YORK 13244-5160

9 780815 623786